too close to the falls

CANADIAN CATALOGUING IN PUBLICATION DATA
Gildiner, Catherine Ann
Too close to the falls

ISBN 1-55022-396-8

1. Gildiner, Catherine Ann — Childhood and youth. 2. Lewiston (N.Y.) — Social
conditions. 3. Women psychologists — Ontario — Toronto — Biography. I. Title

BF109.G54A3 1999   150'.92   C99–931986–85

Cover and text design by Tania Craan
Edited for the press by Michael Holmes
Layout by Mary Bowness
Printed by AGMV

Distributed in Canada by General Distribution Services,
325 Humber Blvd., Etobicoke, Ontario M9W 7C3

Published by ECW PRESS
2120 Queen Street East, Suite 200,
Toronto, Ontario, M4E 1E2
ecwpress.com

Third edition. Fifth printing.

Photo credits: Cover: National Gallery of Canada; cover author photo: Karen Levy;
page 21: Museum of Radio and Television; page 41: Niagara Falls Public Library;
page 79: *Niagara Falls: A Pictorial Journey*, photo by Margaret Dunn, Buffalo and
Erie County Historical Society; page 155: *Marilyn Monroe and the Making of
Niagara*, photo by Dr. Thomas H. Morton, Courtesy of The Maid of the Mist
Steamboat Company; page 221: Loren Greene; page 235: Louis Armstrong House &
Archives, Queens College, New York; page 301: *Niagara Falls: A Pictorial Journey*,
Margaret Dunn.

The publication of *Too Close to the Falls* has been generously
supported by The Canada Council, the Ontario Arts Council,
and the Government of Canada through the Book Publishing
Industry Development Program. Canadä

too close to the falls

CATHERINE GILDINER

ECW PRESS

To Helen McLean

There is always one moment in childhood when the door opens and lets the future in.

— *Graham Greene,* The Power and the Glory

CHAPTER 1

r o y

Over half a century ago I grew up in Lewiston, a small town in western New York, a few miles north of Niagara Falls on the Canadian border. As the Falls can be seen from the Canadian and American sides from different perspectives, so can Lewiston. It is a sleepy town, protected from the rest of the world geographically, nestled at the bottom of the steep shale Niagara Escarpment on one side and the Niagara River on the other. The river's appearance, however, is deceptive. While it seems calm, rarely making waves, it has deadly whirlpools swirling on its surface which can suck anything into their vortices in seconds.

My father, a pharmacist, owned a drugstore in the nearby honeymoon capital of Niagara Falls. My mother, a math teacher by training rather than inclination, was an active participant in the historical society. Lewiston actually had a few historical claims to fame, which my mother eagerly hyped. The word *cocktail* was invented there, Charles Dickens stayed overnight at the Frontier House, the local inn, and Lafayette gave a speech from a balcony on the main street. Our home, which had thirteen trees in the yard that were planted when there were thirteen states, was used to billet soldiers in the War of 1812. It was called into action by history yet again for the Underground Railroad to smuggle slaves across the Niagara River to freedom in Canada.

My parents longed for a child for many years; however, when they were not blessed, they gracefully settled into an orderly life of community service. Then I unexpectedly arrived, the only child of suddenly bewildered older, conservative, devoutly Catholic parents.

I seem to have been "born eccentric" — a phrase my mother uttered frequently as a way of absolving herself of responsibility. By today's standards I would have been labelled with attention deficit disorder, a hyperactive child born with some adrenal problem that made her more prone to rough-and-tumble play than was normal for a girl. Fortunately I was born fifty years ago and simply called "busy" and "bossy," the possessor of an Irish temper.

I was at the hub of the town because I worked in my father's drugstore from the age of four. This was not exploitive child labour but rather what the town pediatrician prescribed. When my mother explained to him that I had gone over the top of the playground swings making a 360-degree loop and had been knocked unconscious twice, had to be removed from a cherry tree the previous summer by the fire department, done Ed Sullivan imitations for money at Helms's Dry Goods Store, all before I'd hit kindergarten, Dr. Laughton dutifully wrote down all this information, laid down his clipboard with certainty, and said that I had worms and needed Fletcher's Castoria. His fallback position (in case when I was dewormed no hyperactive worms crept from any orifice) was for me to burn off my energy by working at manual labour in my father's store. He explained that we all had metronomes inside our bodies and mine was simply ticking faster than most; I had to do more work than others to burn it off.

Being in the full-time workforce at four gave me a unique perspective on life, and I was exposed to situations I later realized were unusual for a child. For over ten years I never once had a meal at home, and that included Christmas. I worked and went to restaurants and delivered everything from band-aids to morphine in the Niagara Frontier. I had to tell people whether makeup looked good or bad, point out what cough medicines had sedatives, count and bottle pills. I also had to sound as though I knew what I was talking about in order to pull it off. I was surrounded by adults, and my peer group became my co-workers at the store.

My father worked behind a counter which had a glass separating it from the rest of the store. He and the other pharmacists wore starched white shirts which buttoned on the side with "McCLURE'S DRUGS" monogrammed in red above the pocket. The rest of us wore plastic ink guards in our breast pockets which had printed in script letters "McClure's has free delivery." (The word *delivery* had wheels and a forward slant.) I worked there full-time when I was four and five and I suspected that when I went to school the next year I would work a split shift from 6:00 to 9:00 a.m. and then again after school until closing time at 10:00 p.m. Of course I would always work full-time on Saturday and Sunday when my mother did her important work with the historical board. I restocked the candy and makeup counters, loaded the newspaper racks, and replenished the supplies of magazines and comics. I read the comics aloud in different voices, jumped out of the pay-phone booth as Superman and acted out Brenda Starr "in her ruthless search for truth," and every morning at 6:00 a.m. I equipped the outdoor newsstand of blue wood with its tiered layers with the *Niagara Falls Gazette.*

My parents were removed from the hurly-burly of my everyday existence. My father was my employer, and I called him "boss," which is what everyone else called him. My mother provided no rules nor did she ever make a meal, nor did I have brothers or sisters to offer me any normal childlike role models. While other four-year-olds spent their time behind fences at home with their moms and dads, stuck in their own backyards making pretend cakes in hot metal sandboxes or going to stagnant events like girls' birthday parties where you sat motionless as the birthday girl opened *her* presents and then you waited in line to stick a pin into a wall while blindfolded, hoping it would hit the rear end of a jackass, I was out doing really exciting work. I spent my time in the workforce delivering prescriptions with Roy, my co-worker.

One thing about a drugstore: it's a great leveller. Everyone from the rich to the poor needs prescriptions and it was my job to deliver them. Roy, the driver, and I, the assistant who read the road maps and prescription labels, were dogged as we plowed through snowstorms and ice jams to make our deliveries. The job took us into mansions on the Niagara Escarpment, to the home of Dupont, who invented nylon, to deliver hypodermic needles to a new doctor on the block, Dr. Jonas Salk, an upstart who thought he had a cure for polio, to Marilyn Monroe on the set of *Niagara*, to the poor Indians on the Tuscarora reservation, and to Warty, who lived in a refrigerator box in the town dump. The people we delivered to felt like my "family," and my soulmate in this experience was Roy.

He was different from my father, the other pharmacists, and Irene, the salmon-frocked cosmetician. He was always in a good mood and laughed at all the things I found funny and never told me to "calm down." He made chestnuts into jewels, bottle tops into art, music into part of our joy together, and he always saw the comedy in tragedy.

He never put off a good time, yet he always got his work done. To me that was amazing, a stunning high-wire act done without a net. He effortlessly jumped into the skin of whomever he was addressing. He made each life we entered, no matter where it was pinned on the social hierarchy, seem not only plausible, but inevitable, even enviable.

Every town has its elaborate social hierarchy and cast of characters. Maybe all children are fascinated by the idiosyncratic, those who have difficulty walking the tightrope of acceptable behaviour in a small town where the social stratification is so explicit and the rules feel so inviolable. Those who opt out of the social order are as terrifying as they are enviable. Maybe I identified with these people because I was trying, even at four, to work out how and why *I* was different. Whatever the reasons, my interest in whatever it took to be different, or to be the same, began early and has persisted. They say architects always played with Lego. Well, I'm a psychologist who was always interested in what the social psychologists refer to as "individual differences," or the statisticians refer to as "the extremes of the bell curve," or what we colloquially refer to as "the edge."

Roy and I made up complicated systems for working together efficiently. He threw magazines to me. I printed "Return" on them if they were past a certain date, threw them on the bright red upright dolly, and we whipped out to pile them on the return truck when it beeped. I always rode on top of the magazines and Roy pushed the dolly, tearing around corners of the store. (We set an egg timer and always tried to beat our last time.)

Roy loved to bet, and after I got the hang of it from him, I found it gave life just that bit of edge it needed. Our days were packed with exciting wagers. For example, we never just rolled the dolly back from the truck; instead we played a game called "dolly-trust." Roy would drop the dolly backwards with me standing upright on it and then he would grab it one tiny second before it hit the cement. I felt my stomach dropping and my knees would go weak but I *had* to trust him. If I twitched or stiffened one muscle, I lost the bet and had to line up all the new magazines and he got to be boss. If I never made a peep, I got to be boss and he had to do the job. The winner was merciless in extracting obeisance from the other. The magazines had to be arranged exactly as the "boss" suggested. If one was not equidistant from the next or, God forbid, hidden behind another, the "assistant" had to pile them up and start all over again.

At precisely 10:30 a.m. each Saturday all the employees had a break. We sat around the large red Coke cooler where the ice had melted and we fished out our Cokes. I had to stand on a wooden bottle crate to reach inside. Roy had a game, of course, to make it more interesting. Each twisted green Coke bottle had the name of a city on the bottom indicating which bottling plant it had come from. Roy would yell out a city and whoever had the bottle with the closest city had to pay for all seven of the Cokes. Roy knew every city and what cities were closest to it. Whenever anyone challenged him and we looked at the map of the U.S. in the toy section, he was right. Once I lost my whole salary when he yelled out "Tulsa" and I had Wichita and Irene had Oklahoma City.

When I was in grade one Sister Timothy, my teacher, told my mother that she had never met a child who knew more about geography than I did and that one of the advantages of having an only child is you can give her so much in terms of travel. My mother was perplexed since I had never been more than thirty miles from Lewiston. Roy said people learn best when the stakes are high.

I liked looking at things Roy-style. When my mother's best friend's son finally died after being in an iron lung for years, my mother said it was so unfair to die at the age of six. When I told Roy that Roland had died, he seemed happy and said, "I'll bet he was glad to get out of that iron caterpillar and move around."

He also knew things that were interesting to *me*. My father dabbled in chemistry as a hobby and my mother was devoted to history, neither of which interested me. One smelled and the other had already happened. Roy had been all over the United States. He had driven semis and been a cowpoke. When we loaded Borden's Milk Chocolate with the cow on the package, he would tell me about his sojourn out west when he branded cattle and birthed calves. If some of the calves had "hard times gettin' out" (I wasn't exactly sure *where* they came out) they had to have their little legs handcuffed together and then the cowboys pulled them out with all of their strength. The poor critters who lost oxygen at birth were so dumb they couldn't learn to stay away from the electric fence and had to be tied up.

At exactly 12:30 p.m. each Saturday, Roy and I headed out for an afternoon of prescription deliveries. My mother taught me to read when I was four but Roy's mother had never taught him to read because, as Roy said, she had so many children she didn't know what to do. Roy had to quit school and go out and work from the age of eight. I told him to stop "bellyaching" (a word I got from him) since I was only *four* at the time. Roy said he could top me in two ways: he had brothers and sisters in fourteen states of the Union and he had what I longed for — a driver's licence. It was a match made in heaven. I read the address aloud, and Roy drove to it.

Music was not a part of my life. My father listened to the news and my mother sang in the church choir and my mother's friend Mrs. Aungier taught piano. I was going to start piano lessons when I was six. I had no idea that there were ways to make music other than through the piano or the church organ, until I met Roy.

He always blasted a radio listening to Bessie Smith, Louis Armstrong, and Jelly Roll Morton. Roy and I would perform duets and I would be Ella Fitzgerald and he would be Louis Armstrong. I remember the seasons by the songs we sang. We drove our green Rambler into the sun with burnt-orange maple leaves gracefully floating over the gorge in the cool air and we sang "Ain't Misbehavin'." Sometimes we'd forage along the gorge for the best specimens of acorns and chestnuts for jewellery-making and Roy would make glittering necklaces which I wore till they shrivelled in the winter. For the employee Christmas party we sang a duet of "Mean to Me" in Loretta's Italian-American Restaurant and even Loretta's husband came out of the kitchen to clap.

Sometimes we would have deliveries that were far away. My father specialized in rare medicine that only a few people needed so he had customers in other cities and on Indian reservations and even in Canada. Roy and I would have lunch on the road. My parents would never let me play the jukebox, saying it was a waste of money — "Five plays and you could have bought the record" was my father's take on leased fun. Roy always plied me with nickels and we played everything right from the machine in our booth. As usual we shared our mania for time management and we would bet how many songs we could hear before our hamburgers arrived and how many while we were eating. He was right the first few times and won money off me, but I began to catch on and learned to eat with great speed or to languish over my pie.

I was amazed that everyone from Batavia to Fort Erie knew Roy. There wasn't one truck stop where people didn't wave and call out his name, especially the waitresses. I guess Roy stood out, with Tootsie Roll fingers that looked bleached on the palm side, and a funny accent that I figured was Western. He also had a laugh which shook his whole body and filled any room we were in — even our church with its vaulted ceilings.

One day I said that I'd seen Annette Funicello on *Spin and Marty* wearing a tee-shirt with decorations on it. "No problem," he said, "leave me a tee-shirt and I'll make somethin' you've never seen or ever will see." Within a week he presented me with a tee-shirt that was covered in bottle caps that made a clinking sound when I walked. He had taken the cork out of the inside of the bottle caps and squeezed the material in between holding the cap in place. I had 144 bottle caps on my shirt and a photographer took my picture and it appeared in the *Niagara Falls Gazette*. I never went anywhere that kids wouldn't ask if they could read all the caps. I loved that shirt that clinked when I walked and wore it till it fell apart. The best part was it could never be washed. Roy said, "Just pitch it out like a Kleenex." My mother had trouble with this disposable concept.

The most exciting event of my childhood occurred on a winter's day in January of 1953. I was going to go to a birthday party at the Cataract Theatre in Niagara Falls to see *Cinderella*. My mother had a big day at the historical board so I went to work with my dad in my red organza party dress, ankle socks with lace trim, and black patent leather Mary Janes. My blond braids were forgone and I wore my hair down my back with a red taffeta ribbon in the front. I also carried a strawberry-shaped purse which zipped open under the green felt stem. When I arrived at work I made a grand entrance and Roy screamed in a high-pitched voice and got out his sunglasses, saying he couldn't take so much dazzle so early in the morning. I told him my mother's warning which was I couldn't get dirty with newsprint and he had to drive me to the theatre at exactly 2:00 p.m.

It had been snowing all day and we had trouble driving the few blocks to the cinema. As I looked out of the delivery car window I saw all the girls huddled under the marquee in their matching hats, coats, and muffs. The party had been organized by Mr. Reno (Roy called him Mr. Richo), the Cadillac salesman whose dealership was next to my father's store. I really didn't know the stuck-up daughter, Eleanor (Roy called her El Dorado), that well. Now that I saw her with her friends I realized she was older and I was out of my league. Those girls went to school together and I was going to be the baby who didn't go to school. Who would I sit with? What would I say when they asked whose class I was in? Another girl arrived and I watched as all the girls ran up to her and crowded around her. I knew it was time to get out of the car. I could hear my mother's voice beating in my head, "You've accepted the invitation, now it would be rude not to attend," or my father who would say, "Just go over and introduce yourself."

I told Roy I was a little worried about how he would find the addresses for the deliveries without me and that maybe I should skip the party. He looked through the window, nodded, and said, "Those are *some* alley cats!" I remember feeling relief that he also found them scary and I wasn't being a total baby. I suddenly felt like crying and I got mad, "carrying on," as my mother would say, claiming I didn't want to go to the party because the girls were huge and looked like monsters, and I hated my dress and I tore the ribbon out of my hair. Roy leaned back, put the car in park, and said, "It's your call." I continued sitting. Finally Roy said, "I got a bet for ya. . . ." When I didn't bite he continued. "I bet when we walk up there together all those young ladies will run up to you wantin' one of them fruit pocketbooks. If they don't I'll owe you a Coke and a magazine-rack boss." I jumped out of the car knowing he didn't like losing a bet. I held his hand tightly as we headed under the marquee and I leaned on him a bit. The girls ran over and admired my strawberry-replica purse and chatted and I dropped Roy's hand and he waved goodbye.

After the party the snow was worse. It was hard to see across the street. The windshield wipers couldn't keep up with the downfall and the plows were nowhere to be seen. Roy turned off the radio, which was a first, and said, "We have to get all the way out to LaSalle to drop off this insulin. Read the map and give me new directions because we'll have to stick to the main streets." (I knew they were the red lines.) "We just doin' the emergencies — leave the rest till tomorrow. This the worst squall I see'd since panning up Alaska way."

I looked around. We were the only car on Niagara Falls' busiest street. It got windy on the way to LaSalle and we had whiteouts on the road that felt as though we were sewn into a moving cloud so thick we couldn't fight our way out. Suddenly there was no more road so we pulled over to a spot we hoped was the shoulder and heard the wind whistle through the window tops and sway the car. We watched the wet snow freeze on the windshield faster than the wipers could snap it away, and the trees glistened exactly as they had in *Cinderella*. I recounted the whole plot to Roy and he asked all kinds of questions about the glass slipper and how they got all around the town. He said they needed our delivery services instead of a pumpkin. We were laughing about the ugly stepsisters, saying the king was betting two-to-one the shoe wouldn't fit *their* feet. We really killed ourselves laughing about my pre-party temper tantrum and he imitated me pulling off my ribbon and hurling it on the dash.

Finally the car couldn't move at all and I had to drive out and Roy had to push. That was the most fun. We howled with laughter as I sat on our coats, moved the seat all the way forward, grabbed the knob on the steering wheel, looked out the slit of the windshield I could see if I stretched my neck over the leather-tied steering wheel, and floored it while Roy pushed. Finally we pulled out of the drift and gave each other the high five and jumped up and down. After that episode we decided to keep going and not stop at all, so we drove slowly through red lights. Mr. Heinrich was shaking when we got there because he needed his insulin and was really worried. He seemed truly amazed we made it at all, saying it was "a tribute to our pioneer spirit." Roy tried to call my father from Mr. Heinrich's home but ice had pulled down the phone lines.

It was dark when we got to the top of the steep Lewiston hill with its narrow road carved into the Niagara Escarpment. The beginning of the descent was blocked by a police cruiser with a red pulsing light making the snow look like red dream dust from *Cinderella*. He shone a flashlight into the car as he stopped us. I noticed that Roy was not his usual cheery self and Mr. Lombardy, who was sometimes a policeman in emergencies, usually parades, said, "No one is goin' down that sheet of ice. Even the sanding truck couldn't make it with chains on its caterpillar wheels."

"I got Jim McClure's girl in the car here and I got to get her home."

"Where were you three hours ago, Roy?"

Roy didn't answer. I didn't think Mr. Lombardy was being as polite as he usually was. I leaned over and told Mr. Lombardy that Roy had to wait for me during the birthday party and then we had to get out to LaSalle to drop off some emergency medication before coming home.

"Not to worry, little lady. I'll call on my radio and let your dad know you're staying up in the Falls and we'll have 'er cleared in the morning." Someone yelled for Mr. Lombardy from across the road and he ran over to a big tow truck.

"I don't like the smell of this," Roy said while rubbing his chin. I noticed he did this when he got nervous. "I guess I shoulda gone into that movie and got ya out. I didn't want to embarrass ya in front of all them big gals. But none of 'em had to get down the Lewiston hill. They all live in the heights."

I'd never seen Roy show concern for things that had happened already. What was the big deal here! Why was Mr. Lombardy grouchy and why did Roy care? I was happy that I had the chance to be nice to Roy because he was always nice to me. "Don't worry, you did your best. I'll stay overnight at your house and tomorrow I'll go home."

I'd never thought of Roy as having a life outside of my father's store. He never mentioned a mom or a wife or children. As we inched along I asked him if he lived with his mom and dad. He told me his mamma lived in Alabama. I figured that's why he often guessed Mobile in the Coke game. Maybe he missed her. When I asked if he had a wife he said, "No *way!*" I knew then that he wouldn't have children. As far as I could see God only gave children to people who were married. He was a little late with my parents but He did finally make me. I wondered aloud who made

Roy's dinner but he said he ate "round town," mostly just across the street where we were to dine this very evening. I was surprised to find that Roy lived alone. He was so much fun I pictured him being part of a big happy family like the Canavans, who went to family picnics at Brock's monument. I'd never met anyone who lived alone. Even Father Flanagan had priests from the missions boarding there so he wouldn't be lonely.

We began travelling in a part of the city that I'd never seen before. As we turned into a parking lot I could see he lived in a long ranch-style house with lots of doors and a pink light that flashed his address: *Rainbow Inn — 24 rooms — vacancy*. He had more than one driveway. He had arranged for guest parking with white lines demarking all the extra parking spots. In fact, there was one in front of each of his doors. I had no idea why Roy was worried about having me over, because his house was big. He even had a hot plate in his bedroom — I guessed it was there so when he was tired he wouldn't have to go to the kitchen. Typical of Roy, when he opened his closet a bed fell out! I couldn't wait to see the rest of the place. We made hot chocolate with milk he took in from between the storm windows. He was always efficient. Roy went in to the bathroom and got dressed up in a starched shirt and pinstriped trousers. When I asked him if this was a fancy restaurant like a country club he said that he *had* to dress up to go out on the town with a girl in red taffeta.

We crossed a big slippery street which was deserted and lined with huge piles of snow on each side. When we climbed one mound we came upon orange flashing lights and I sounded out the name of the restaurant in my usual loud voice — Hot and Sassy's.

"That's where we goin' for one *big* meal," Roy said, and we agreed we had never been so hungry and that we deserved a good meal for the overtime we'd put in as "pioneers" in the storm.

As we entered I was flabbergasted to see a sea of faces that looked a lot like Roy's. I had never seen anyone who looked like Roy before, had his hair style or his accent. I was amazed on two counts: first, that he had such a large extended family, even the waiters and waitresses looked related, and, second, I was shocked that I had lived near this city for my entire life yet I had never run into any of his relatives before. I would have known in a second that they were related to Roy. I asked if this was a family reunion and Roy only laughed, later saying it was the first time he had ever seen me speechless.

When I got over the shock of seeing his huge family I realized they lived in the rest of his house across the street. I was so glad because I didn't want to think of him as being lonely. It was an odd restaurant with no small tables but only one long high table with stools for his big family and Hots was the waiter for everyone. It must have still been cocktail hour because he was busy serving drinks and people stood up three deep at the long table. "Well, well, look what Roy brought out of the storm, mmm-*mmmm*," Hots said, shaking his head. Lots of Roy's friends came over and Roy lifted me up and put me on a stool and I remember exactly what he said to the crowd that had assembled. "This is my date for tonight. Her name is Dale Evans and we been out beatin' the trails today at work and we're mighty thirsty for a Shirley Temple and a Johnny Walker, so clear the way for Hots to move." Hots yelled for Sass — his wife, I think — to come out of the kitchen. Sass was a fat woman who didn't buy into my mother's theory that overweight women should wear dull colours. It was amazing to me that someone would be named "Sassy" since it was such a bad thing to be; but when I thought about names, it was not as bad as my father's aunt Fanny.

I was marooned outside of my life for a night and it was great. While swivelling on my stool, I had lots of pink Shirley Temples in cocktail glasses, with maraschino cherries and pineapple speared on tiny swords. I took the swords home for my dollhouse. Between Shirleys, Roy and I had a great dinner, a crispy chicken I'd never eaten before which Roy called "Sassy-fried." I was amazed at how friendly everyone was and how much fun people seemed to be having. They were laughing really hard at things my parents failed to find even a little amusing. One guy was killing himself describing how his car slid on the ice and was wrapped around a pole like a donut. Things that had always seemed like big disasters were only funny events that were no longer threatening. It was a "we're-all-alive-so-what's-the-problem" attitude. I shared our disaster and how I'd driven out of the snowbank sitting on Roy's coat so I could see out the window and how Roy got covered in snow when I spun the wheels. We cried, we were laughing so hard.

Roy asked me to dance and I giggled, telling him I was too little, but he picked me up and we flew all over the dance floor, and I also danced with the bartender and his fat wife, who taught me some dance steps. I was relieved I was wearing my Mary Janes for the dance and because everyone else seemed to be dressed up in bright clothes so I was appropriately dressed in my red taffeta. I'd always liked bright colours and I never bought into my mother's concept of dressing up, which was changing from black-watch navy plaid to solid navy.

Finally it was time to go home and Roy and I trudged across

the street and waved to the snow plow as it passed. Roy pulled down the closet bed for me and when I asked him for extra pyjamas he said I was going to sleep in my clothes. He put me to bed in my party dress and Mary Janes. When I suggested I take off my shoes, he said we were going to leave everything "as is." I woke up in the night with foot cramps and had to jump up and down to get them to stop. I saw Roy asleep in a chair with his party clothes still on.

The next day was sunny to beat the band and we got up and Roy told me to brush my teeth with my finger, a new manoeuvre which worked surprisingly well. I tried to use his comb for my tangled hair but it was shaped like a tiny pitchfork and didn't catch any snarls. It worked for his hair and his relatives'. I wondered how he'd found a comb that worked so well for his family and their unique hair. I was sure we didn't have them in the drugstore.

We grabbed a donut at Freddies' (a donut shop owned by two brothers *both* named Freddy: my father said they must've been from the Ozarks, not to be able to come up with another name) and ate as we buzzed along. Roy had little bumps on his face where he hadn't shaved and the whites of his eyes looked yellow as his cigarette dangled from his upper lip. The plows had sanded the escarpment hill and it was hard to believe that yesterday had been treacherous enough to knock me right out of my regular life.

As we turned onto my street we saw Mr. Lombardy's cruiser parked in our driveway. I opened the large oak door and the first thing I saw was something I'd never witnessed before; my mother was sitting on the couch crying, clutching a wad of scrunched-up Kleenexes. My father looked mad and worried at the same time. I'd never seen either of them even mildly upset before. I was speechless. My father crouched down to my eye level and said through cigar breath, "We were very worried about you, young lady." Then there was a big mess where everyone started talking at once and Mr. Lombardy said he had been going to get me and bring me down or put me in the police station for the night and had only moved away from our car for a minute to talk to someone when Roy had driven away. Roy said he had no choice but to take me to where he lived and there was no working phone. I had no idea why my mother was crying. What was the problem? I suddenly wished they'd lighten up and told them there was *no* problem. My father snapped to and actually agreed, saying emotions were running high at the moment and it was best to call it a day. He thanked Roy for his trouble and escorted him to the door, saying he was sorry for the misunderstanding. Mr. Lombardy tried to go on a bit more but my mother's crying drowned him out. Finally he and Roy left.

As I told my mother about my adventure, she cried at every new detail. As I got to dancing at Hot and Sassy's she was sobbing. My father said as long as I was safe it was best to save the details for another time when my mother was "not so under the weather." She was weepy for two days and sat with me on her lap, something she never did, even before I was working! At last she was "in the pink" again and ready to return to her important work at the historical society.

The following week when Sam Noyes, the wrinkled, pipe-smoking editor of the local paper, heard that Roy and I had made it all the way to LaSalle in that gale, he wrote an editorial about it. He marvelled that despite the storm (in which two hundred people died), the school closings, and what he referred to as "the infestation of the National Guard," McClure's Drugs still managed same-day delivery, even in LaSalle. He wrote that he wished he could count on getting to heaven with as much certainty as he counted on our "intrepid" delivery service. I cut this out, taped it to our dashboard, and Roy and I laughed every time we read it. I referred to him as "intrepid" (a word I liked because they used it on *The Lone Ranger* to introduce the intrepid Tonto during the *William Tell Overture*) and he referred to me as "intrepidette."

—

Roy was my best friend for a number of years. We went through rough times on the Tuscarora reservation, dined with millionaires when they visited the Falls, had lunch with Joseph Cotten, witnessed birth and death together, and helped each other out of scrapes — although now I realize he helped me out of more. Finally one day in grade six I went to work and Roy didn't show up. No one ever saw him again. Irene said that a few men had been in looking for him the day before. She said they didn't seem any too pleasant and she was sure gambling was involved. My father suggested to Irene that it was uncharitable to gossip about Roy's departure and told me if Roy could have said goodbye he would have. It was not like him to be rude and he must have had a good reason. When Irene "started up on him" — as Roy used to refer to her bossiness — my father said we would only remember Roy at his best. To me Roy was always at his best.

I went to Roy's office in the storage room. It was really a cove, separated by orange crates. He had a bulletin board with delivery dates on a clipboard and a picture from *Ebony* of Louis Armstrong smiling and waving from a white Cadillac. I carefully untacked it, knowing that it was Roy's goodbye note to me.

CHAPTER 2

RCA victor

My father was a true lover of gadgets. He bought every new thing

that came along, from hot-water birdbaths heated by the barbe-

cue to nail polish that came in plastic sheets with nail-size

perforations that you trimmed to fit your nail. At my grand-

mother's suggestion he invested lots of money in a newfangled sort of handkerchief that people could throw away. He called them "disposable handy hankies." Everyone in his Rotary told him that no one would be willing to blow money every time they blew their nose. My father said he'd read a book which prophesied that everything in America was headed toward efficiency. He also assumed that as the drug business goes, so goes the nation. For the Upjohn Drug Company, where he worked before he bought the store, efficiency meant disposability. My father bought into the disposable era because he was sick of the hassle and expense of using the autoclave every time he needed to sterilize something. He invested in a weirdly named product that would never catch on; even he agreed the name would have to be changed from the awkward "Kleenex." He made lots of money on Kleenex and then he got another efficiency inspiration. He took all the money he made on Kleenex and more and invested in a company ingeniously titled Paper Pants. After all, who wanted to wash dirty underwear any more than used handkerchiefs? The runaway success of Kleenex proved we had a strong desire to be protected from our active orifices. My mother and I wore the paper pants for months, getting paper cuts if we crossed our legs too quickly, until the company went bankrupt. When my mother said my father was simply ahead of his time for disposables, Dolores, our cleaning lady, said she thought his ideas were disposable.

My father's love affair with the future of technology did not end there. Naturally Mother and I felt some trepidation when Dad announced that he had ordered the ultimate gadget, a box that talked. Our concern was somewhat assuaged when he guaranteed us we would never have to wear it. He had ordered the talking box in 1948, the year of my birth. Every night for years he would come home from work, jump out of the delivery car, and ask if the talking box had arrived yet. He was assured by letter that he was on the list but they were back-ordered. However, by 1952 even *his* enthusiasm waned and finally he gave up. I'd been waiting for the talking box since birth and didn't know life without waiting for *it* to arrive.

One cold but sunny day in 1953, my mother was standing at the window watering her bearded cactus collection, and I was singing along to a Tex Ritter 78: "There are two little magic words that can open any door with ease, one little word is thanks and the other little word is please." I heard the eager revving of a truck on the gravel driveway. I ran to the window, where Mom and I saw a huge transport, with a picture on the side of a dog looking askance at an old-fashioned Victrola. Two men in grey one-piece jumpsuits, bearing the same dog insignia on their pockets, unloaded a large wooden crate. The men lumbered under the obviously heavy object, and carried it, sidestepping like skittering crabs, up our front steps. My mother and I exchanged bewildered looks as the doorbell rang.

I opened the door and one sweaty man announced with flair, "RCA Victor with your television!" as though he were Michael Anthony bearing John Beresford Typton's million dollars.

Mom said, "How do you do, Mr. Victor, I'm Mrs. McClure."

He laughed, saying, "No, I'm Bob. This," he said, pointing to the television, "is RCA Victor." I had no idea what a "television" was, but at least now I knew its name.

I watched, as puzzled as the quizzical dog, as they crowbarred open the box, which had a greenish opaque empty picture frame on the front and thousands of multicoloured wires in the back.

Mother and I looked blank, if not downright dubious, having suffered a number of my father's great ideas, while Bob tried to drum up some enthusiasm. "Well, this is the first tel-*e*-vision I've delivered anywhere in Niagara County. We had to travel for six hours to get here today." While he was describing his odyssey, I again noticed a tiny picture of the strange dog with the neck cramp in the lower right-hand corner of RCA Victor's wooden frame. I told Mother that the picture window had something to do with a dog with a stiff neck. I thought maybe it was a doghouse that plugged in for warmth. She looked alarmed, and then I had another brainwave. I quickly explained to her my new hypothesis, that really you could tell from the name *tell-a-vision* it was like my stereoscopic Viewmaster that I held up to the light, placing round discs in a slot and advancing each picture by pushing a lever. My favourite was Hansel and Gretel; the gingerbread house sparkled when I held the Viewmaster close to my father's desk light.

After unfolding their tool kits, which gracefully parted into cascading trays, they fiddled with the box for hours, one man behind the set with tools and one in front yelling odd phrases like "more horizontal!" They finally packed up and left, and there I was alone in a dark room looking at an Indian in full war head-dress in the centre of concentric circles. The Indian obviously felt uncomfortable in my house. He never faced forward but always remained in profile, facing the door, clearly longing to leave. I watched him for a very long time, yet the Indian never moved, nor did he ever turn to look at me. I wanted to leave the room but felt rude abandoning him in *my* house and not entertaining him in any way. Finally, reluctantly, I began speaking to him. Although he didn't answer directly he listened, much as I imagined a brother or sister might have, if we could have played together.

——

As the weeks went by and I had already spent hours on my own with the Indian, I began to understand that RCA Victor was indeed something that had altered my life. Clearly I was not alone in finding RCA Victor a mesmerizing phenomenon, for everyone who approached the house, including the milk, dry-cleaning, and grocery deliverymen, made excuses to come in and catch a live moment of the spectacle before them. My favourite visitor was Alexander Hamilton, who drove the bakery truck. (Of course, much was made of his historical lineage, particularly in the Lewiston Centennial Parade when all the men from the town grew beards and wore bowler hats; our own baker, Alexander, dressed in period costume, led the parade in an open Packard convertible next to a woman from Lewiston whose real name was Martha Washington.) Alex arrived every day during *The Guiding Light* and, needing an excuse to sit down, would suggest that I try his sticky buns to make sure they weren't stale as we were the last stop on his route. He even brought a Milkbone for Willie, our dog. Friends of my parents from the village of Lewiston, as well as mere acquaintances who ran farms way out the Ridge Road, came pouring into our living room to pay homage to the talking heads on RCA Victor.

Some evenings we had guests who arrived moments before the Indian left and John Cameron Swayzee came on. John was far different from the Indian in that he actually talked to me and shared his love of favourite products with me. I began to know him quite well, and much to the amazement of my parents' friends, I was able to predict what he would say and when he would hold up the Camel cigarettes. He often chatted to me about what was going on in the world. He, like my father, was an Eisenhower fan, and showed me lots of pictures of the president and his wife, Mamie. Whenever he showed the Eisenhower snapshots, I held up my "I-like-Ike" button and my mother's white gloves that had the same slogan stamped all over them in tiny red, white, and blue letters.

I was aware that my mother called John's chats "news," while other people who talked to me on RCA Victor, such as Milton Berle, Ed Sullivan, and Roy Rogers, were called "programs." I didn't get the distinction. It was all news to me. Mother was completely uninvolved with RCA Victor, and clearly confused because she said things like "Do you believe that Lucy and Desi are married in *real* life?"

My favourites were cowboy programs of any variety. I always wore my cowboy suit for any show like *Roy Rogers* or *The Cisco Kid*. Now that I had the RCA Victor window on the world I began to realize that Indians were really dangerous, and that the Tuscaroras, whose reservation was near Lewiston, must have secret meetings and scalp people in the dead of night, because you never heard about their chief, Black Cloud (it said "Elton Greene" on his prescriptions), the way you heard about Cochise. I assumed the reason Cochise from out west was so visible was because he attacked in the daytime when it was too hard to hide on open plains. The Tuscaroras, on the other hand, could walk through the woods near Devil's Hole and probably through the entire town without making a sound. In fact, I never heard the Indians my father said were outside of cigar shops in every city. I felt sorry for the westerners in covered wagons who wore those long skirts and bonnets; they always sent scouts ahead to look for Indian war parties. If only they had RCA Victor, they would know that whenever they travelled over the plains they had to look *up* for Indians who waited to ambush them in those craggy mountain rocks. If you lived on a cattle ranch like the Schmidts' cousins you must be very brave and stand watch and make sure you're not surrounded, and a flaming arrow is not thrown into your ranch house by a war party.

Now that I saw what went on the world, I began to understand why my mother didn't want me to go to Shim-Shacks tavern with Roy on the edge of the Tuscarora reservation when we were on delivery. While I'd previously found her trepidation inexplicable, I now realized that the Indians could kidnap me and raise me as one of them and then twenty years later someone would find me and know from my blond hair that I'd been abducted. By the time I was found on the reservation it would be too late to return home because I would have adopted Indian ways.

Not only were there scenes of wagon trains being ambushed, but the *Senator Joe McCarthy Show* was on our RCA Victor. My mother said she didn't like cowboy programs or RCA Victor in general, but she really liked the Joe McCarthy program. Senator McCarthy told me, and a roomful of other people, that nearly everywhere there were communists amongst us; they were people who looked like you and me; they were in local government right up to Washington. His lawyer, Roy Cohn, yelled at communist sympathizers and said things like "I bet" or "This is your *last* chance to tell the truth" when he interrogated traitors. My mother said that Roy Cohn was rude and that McCarthy needed more information. My father, who usually agreed with her, said that this was "no tea party" and that by the time they got hard evidence it might be too late. The communists had taken over Russia and China and now they were giving the Koreans weapons. They might let off the atomic bomb while we were looking for evidence. Who would have thought to look in a pumpkin for Alger Hiss's spy information? If communists had infiltrated the army and the government, as McCarthy said, then we couldn't be soft on them or we'd all be living on collective farms getting our prescriptions from the state and not allowed to go to mass.

This really terrified me. I remembered Sister Timothy, my kindergarten teacher telling us at nap time, as we lay curled up on our rugs, that the reason the Chinese used chopsticks was so the communists could perforate the ear drums of little Catholic children if they ever heard them pray. I'd never seen a Chinese person, but I pictured them with blood dripping from their earlobes. My friend Donna Ormsby's father was stationed in Formosa with the U.S. Army, and she went to visit him for Christmas. I told her to wear earmuffs. She, like the rest of Lewiston, didn't have RCA Victor to tell her what was really happening.

I began to worry about communists. If my father was right, they were infiltrating everywhere. Mr. Helms, the butcher, once told me that the miracle at Fatima was "bunk" and I'd seen him leaving church for a cigarette right after communion and not waiting for the closing prayers. All of this seemed very suspicious to me and my worst fears were confirmed one day when I overheard a snippet of conversation at Schoonmaker's Restaurant. While my mother waited for our order in the dining room, I had wandered into the bar to play the bowling game. I also enjoyed lying on my stomach and twirling on the bar stools. While I was swivelling at the long wooden bar, Bill Helms strolled in for a nightcap, and bold as brass asked for a "white Russian." He hadn't seen me as my head wasn't above bar level; I was lying flat with only my stomach on the stool in a Superman flying position. I sat up and shot him a glance that indicated I didn't need a pumpkin patch to recognize a spy. Clearly he'd been schooled in the art of nonchalance at his spy academy. Pretending nothing was wrong, he went so far as to challenge me to a bowling game with Mr. Schoonmaker. I decided never to be alone with him again. His wife, Betty Helms, was the town reeve and she could be infiltrating the government. I warned my mother that I might have smoked out some communists. She suggested that I never say anything about anyone unless I had absolute proof about them, but my father assured me it didn't hurt to be on our toes. When Father and I went to The Horseshoe for breakfast on the way to work, all the men at the counter talked about the McCarthy show. All the suited Rotarians who were perched in a row on their stools agreed with Loretta's husband, Giuseppe, known to the patrons as "Lorry," when he poked his head out through the order window and said, as he smashed down the breakfast specials (I always ordered a Cock-a-doodle-doo #3) that it was high time *someone* cleaned up this country before the American flag was no more than a tablecloth.

Although people crowded into our house to watch the McCarthy show, there were far more people over to watch Ed Sullivan. He visited on Sunday at 8:00 p.m. I never understood why people enjoyed his show. He had idiots like Topo Gigio, an

Italian mouse who said about three lines, one of the most inane being "Hey, Eddie, kiss-a-me-goodnight." I had two questions about that. First, who wanted to be kissed good night by *Ed Sullivan*? Second, why was it funny? Then there was his idiot rival, Pedro, who said, "S'all right? S'all right." I watched my parents' friends laugh at these antics and I didn't get it.

I never really enjoyed RCA Victor when others were present. It lost its intimacy. In a way it was like praying. When we said the rosary aloud at school it was boring, but when I talked to God on my own in my good-night prayers, after my mother left the room, I felt His presence. What I cherished was my personal interaction with John Cameron Swayzee and, as time went on, I became more and more fond of the Indian who never spoke but with whom I had formed a friendship. While almost everyone else had brothers and sisters to play with early in the morning while parents slept, I had the Indian. No matter what I played I kept him informed with a running monologue.

As the months went on I began to realize that the Indian who came to my house on RCA Victor was like the other Indians at Shim-Shacks on the reservation. Although I knew Indians were terrifying as a *group*, since they were trying to kill us for some reason I didn't understand or RCA Victor never made clear, I had a great affinity for them *individually*. The RCA Victor Indian was like the Bear Clan or the Turtle Clan when we played the bowling game or when I gave away the rifle to Black Cloud. I *knew* how they felt, even if they never showed it.

It made me nervous when people made some kind of brouhaha about their feelings, especially affection. I'd certainly rather be yelled at than kissed. Displays of that sort gave me the jitters, and my heart would pound as though someone had scared me on Halloween. I hated it when Desi kissed Lucy or when Ralph Cramden became all mushy on *The Honeymooners*. I always left the room before Alice threw her arms around Ralph, forgiving him for his weekly indiscretion, like bowling with Norton on her birthday. Whenever I hadn't seen someone in a long time, like my grandmother or some visiting priest who was a relative, I was expected to kiss them, or say I'd missed them, or express some sentiment that I really dreaded. The Indians who I knew dealt with affection the way I did. They left things understood.

There was something comforting in the RCA Victor Indian's stoicism, and I became close to him, realizing that although he didn't gush with approval he never criticized, nor could I hurt his feelings. Because he was just *there* as a kind of emotional witness, for some reason I began telling him how I felt about things. He never reacted to anything I said, which gave me a strange sense of freedom. At first I looked for a reaction so I could gauge what to say next, and when it wasn't there I pushed on, telling secrets I didn't know I had.

Sometimes I told him all the things that worried me. I felt I wasn't like other people, which was in itself terrifying, since I had no idea why or what happened to people who were "different" when they grew up. Would I be a weird adult like Warty who ran the dump? I knew it was a fact that people who were bad burned in hell. I got yelled at for being bad more than almost anyone at school, certainly more than any other girl. What if I perpetually burned in hell and every day cursed my wretched soul for not being good on earth, which was such a tiny testing patch compared to eternity? I told the Indian that every day I turned over a "new leaf" (a phrase often suggested by my mother) resolving to be a good girl, which I knew meant being a quiet one. Mary Alice Cary, the girl who wore a large bow squarely on the top of her head, was always quiet, even in the washroom lineup as she offered up "ejaculations" — the rhythmic repeating of religious phrases which become trancelike, such as "Jesus, Mary, and Joseph" said hundreds of times. I became determined to perpetually ejaculate or "offer up" my silence to God. ("Ejaculations" was a word that Dr. Small, the psychiatrist I was sent to see after stabbing Anthony McDougall, found interesting and he encouraged me to describe its meaning on repeated occasions.)

These "new leaves" never lasted more than ten minutes. They withered when the first chill of my normal personality blew in by 9:15 the next morning. I was either asking "doubting Thomas" questions (as Mother Agnese called my religious inquiries), or talking to my neighbour in the O through P aisle, or getting out of my seat. I would rather have been beaten or punished than be made to sit in my seat for four hours at a stretch. By twelve o'clock I felt as though I were in an iron lung. In fact I liked punishments, such as cleaning the lunch room or peeling gum off desks, far more than sitting there. I assumed that everyone wanted to talk and move around as much as I did, but all of the other girls and many of the boys were made of stronger stuff. They succeeded in "offering up their desires to the Holy Ghost," as Sister Immaculata suggested. The devil started me fidgeting by 9:15 and by 9:30 I was up and moving. After I explained all this to the Indian I felt better and sensed his approval. I figured he wasn't bothered by any of this, since he still came back, and therefore, I must be OK.

It was definitely a give-and-take relationship. I also took great pains to entertain the Indian as an audience. I felt that although he never actually beamed, he was internally warmed by my antics. His smile was like the Mona Lisa's. You had to look for a long time before you could detect it. Sometimes I staged acts from the *Ted Mack Amateur Hour* for him and let him be the applause-o-metre. Although his movements were infinitesimal and could be missed if you didn't know him well, I could tell his top choice was my rendition of Kate Smith singing "God Bless America." His favourite part was when I belted out "Stand beside her and guide her." I was sure that the Indian had been a guide before agreeing to come to my home on the RCA Victor.

We of the RCA Victor coterie observed one another's privacy. John Cameron Swayzee never yelled at me and was always polite, even if it took me a few extra seconds to find a product; in fact he covered for me by pretending not to notice. The Indian never looked at me straight on. He always remained in profile, as though he were saying to me, "It's enough we share space, let's not crowd each other with dew-eyed expectant stares and fawning approval." I too tried to give them their space. I was careful never to look behind the RCA Victor as I felt it was not part of viewing protocol any more than it would be acceptable to enter the projection booth when I went to see *Rear Window* with my grandmother, nor would I wander backstage when Gramma took me to see *The Nutcracker* at Christmas. I felt it was rude for Dolores to go behind the RCA Victor to vacuum and I became agitated when she refused to follow simple audience etiquette.

Within a year there was other "news" and other "programs" or "shows," but I was mostly attached to John. (We were on a first-name basis within a few months.) That's when what my mother called my "strange behaviour" began. I was the only one in Lewiston that John was addressing. He was always extremely friendly, had all kinds of news, and visited at the same time daily. He shared a number of products with me and actually asked me directly what I thought of his favourites. I knew that since I saw him, he must therefore see me. I had no intention of ignoring him as my mother so often suggested. After all, I felt I should break the news to her that he hadn't come to see *her*. When he asked if we had Spic & Span or when the cigarette girl bellowed "John Phillip Mo*rris*" or when John held up Camel cigarettes, I tore to a cupboard where I had all my RCA Victor products stored, and presented the correct one to John. Once he saw me display my product, he returned to the news. It got to the point that I couldn't leave the house for fear John would ask *me* if I had Camels and I would have to run and get the product and hold it in front of the RCA Victor where he smiled back approvingly.

I was living proof that television was not a passive form of entertainment. I was jumping around all the time, lining up my products, and answering all questions asked. John asked me if I could stand the sight of built-up wax, if I wanted to know about the weather, and several other adult questions. Actually, I was quite flattered when he addressed me as "the lady of the house."

As advertising caught on, my RCA Victor products began to fill the living room. After I had a fit of rage one day when Dolores moved my 20 Mule Team Borax, my mother finally consulted the "the media guru of Lewiston" — Dr. Laughton, the pediatrician who had already placed me into forced labour. Dr. Laughton asked me incredibly stupid questions, such as, did I think Cinderella was talking to me in the Walt Disney movie. Why would I think Cinderella was talking to *me* when I'd seen it in a theatre where there were hundreds of people in the audience? *Strange.* He asked why I thought that John Cameron Swayzee wanted to see *my* products. As if I'd have any idea why John Cameron Swayzee had chosen me. Why had the Virgin Mother appeared at Lourdes instead of Niagara Falls? How would I know?

I was sick of Dr. Laughton wasting my time, but since I was the one sitting on the examining table in my underwear and he wore the stethoscope, I felt some pressure to comply. I tried to explain the obvious, that John was in *my* living room and that he, unlike Cinderella, asked *me* questions about household products. Cinderella never spoke to me directly; she expressed her longings for a better life with the prince and we, the audience, listened in. The doctor then asked me if John Cameron Swayzee ever called me by name. I informed him that no, he hadn't, and then I caught him at his own game. I said, "Dr. Laughton, did you say to me, 'Do you think Cinderella is talking to *you*?' or did you say to me, 'Do you think Cinderella is talking to *Cathy*?'" I think that little linguistic dilly let him know that although he might be a good doctor, he was in the bush leagues as far as the media was concerned.

Dr. Laughton, realizing he was out on a limb, quickly scampered to safer ground. Changing topics, he asked me if I ever heard other things talking to me. Did he mean when the trees talked in *Snow White*? Suddenly I got it. Dr. Laughton was trying to see if I was crazy. I guess he wondered if I would stab people like Elder Mad Bear did and then never move again, or sit in front of the post office like ol' Jim and yell out swear words to no one in particular.

Dr. Laughton's technique was a little more obvious than Dr. Small's, the psychiatrist I visited after I stabbed Anthony

McDougall. Dr. Small had little cards with a dog named Blacky who did really disgusting things. At least Dr. Small asked me my opinion about Blacky's shenanigans. Dr. Laughton never asked my opinion on anything. I realized I had to get out of there, so I slid off the examining table, licked my Tootsie Roll Pop that I got for being cooperative, took another one for the road, and said I had to get back to work. As I hightailed it out of there, next door to my father's store, I was relieved on several fronts: first, I was thankful my mother wasn't with me so I wouldn't have to explain anything to her or see her upset, bewildered face; second, I gave myself a little credit for keeping the lid on my relationship with the Indian. What no one knew about, no one could attack. But just when I thought I was out of the woods, thinking Dr. Laughton was accepting defeat like a man, he pulled out the big enchilada. He referred me to the priest. Dr. Laughton was one of the first media gurus who realized that addiction to television was a moral and not a medical problem.

Why a doctor and a priest presumed to be authorities on RCA Victor I had no idea, but I wasn't falling for it. When you think about it, I took the theory of germs on faith from Dr. Laughton, and God on faith from Father Flanagan. Neither of them was willing to acknowledge that I was the authority and knew a tad more than they did about John, nor were they willing to take anything about his motives on faith from me.

Of course neither of these "experts" had an RCA Victor. No one could deny the existence of John Cameron Swayzee or the fact that he was in my living room and in no one else's. Both these men shared the misconception that you were supposed to sit in a chair, not move one muscle, and silently *watch* RCA Victor. I couldn't imagine *anyone* who would want to do that. I really felt that same kind of agitation I felt in the presence of the nuns at school. As usual, what was purely virtuous was silence and sitting still — for me two unattainable "virtues."

Father Flanagan and I lit a candle and knelt together at the communion rail, saying five Hail Marys to our blessed Virgin to deliver me from John's clutches. The good thing about Father Flanagan, and most priests, from what I could see, was that he left most of the work to God. After finishing our prayers, no more was said about the RCA debacle, and he and I strolled over to Helms's Dry Goods Store for a Three Musketeers and talked about who would win the World Series. When I told him I was a Dodgers fan, Father Flanagan seemed far more appalled than he was about the RCA Victor case, passionately stating that although he was born in Ireland, County Cork, the good Lord shone his favour upon him and carried him on the blessed wings of St. Patrick to the United States to be a Yankees fan.

The one person who brutally disrupted my black-and-white relationships was Dolores. She accomplished what Dr. Laughton and Father Flanagan had failed to do. She reduced what I once called "joining the RCA Victor" to the common phrase "watching television," something I did very little of after her successful deprogramming. Her method was ruthless, nearly soul-destroying, but it did force me to realize that John was no more than electrons firing away, and the correlation between John's smiles of relaxed satisfaction and my interactive participation with his commercials was, in fact, random.

The day of Dolores's exorcism began with a tirade on how fed up she was with my messy bedroom and dishevelled playroom.

Pointing to my collection of jars of caterpillars that would have turned into monarch butterflies if she'd only let them alone, and to my Coke bottles from every state in the Union, she accused me of making her job impossible. She ranted that my collections had spread from room to room and were now infecting the living room with my RCA Victor–untouchable products which I had encircling the set. I pointed my .45 at Dolores, calling her a "dirty rotten double-crosser," a phrase I'd picked up from *The Cisco Kid*. She warned me that I'd pay for my snippiness, repeating her usual refrain about how I thought I ran this house, but that I was heading for a comeuppance.

I'd heard this vitriolic monologue before, so after firing one more bullet at her from under my bed, I dashed down to the RCA Victor to catch Mr. Manners, a tiny man in a finely tailored suit. He often spoke to me from under a table, politely inquiring if I purchased napkins that had the embarrassing habit of slipping off my lap. Since he lived under tables he had a bird's-eye view of those who bought clinging napkins and those who did not. In an effort to be prepared for his next visit, I'd scoured Helms's aisles until I found the familiar face of the tiny yet authoritative British Mr. Manners on the box cover and quickly charged it. My mother thought it was an odd purchase since we never ate at home, so errant crumbs, or for that matter crumbs of any kind, were never a problem in our home. However, anything that smacked of "manners" was in my mother's mind a turn in the right direction.

Sure enough at 12:13 p.m. Mr. Manners appeared and addressed me from his unique vantage point under a dining table, where he was surrounded by a picket fence of thick stumpy legs. He asked if I wanted to be caught out with a slippery napkin that slid to the floor exposing my bare lap. Being ready for him, I reached for my napkin box, and to my horror I noticed that all of my products were gone. I felt as though I were in a performance and the stage director had walked off with all the props, while the audience waited, watching me flounder as the seconds ticked by.

As I tore around fuming and flinging things from the pantry, my mother called to Dolores from the front parlour, where she was working on her "emerging African nations" research, that it was not a good idea to "relocate" my products. Dolores retorted that I was "one spoiled brat." She grabbed my hand and began pulling me behind the RCA Victor. I resisted and tried to put on the brakes with my feet, but my slipper socks burned across the rug and I lost the tug-of-war. I was furious at her for messing up my products and now for forcing me into this disrespectful behaviour of going behind the RCA Victor.

"I've a job to do, and I can't be held up by every ninny who thinks they're the belle of the ball," she said, unplugging the RCA Victor. Suddenly John disappeared and Mr. Manners was ominously silent. She plugged them in again and they came to life. She said she could be in charge of all the products on RCA Victor. She then pulled out the plug and plugged the vacuum into the same outlet and made the Hoover hose roar in my face, blowing dust on my hair ribbons, and demanded, "Who is talking to you now?" Confused, I shrugged my shoulders. She continued, "It's the same energy, only now it's the vacuum. Is this vacuum talking to you? It's electricity lined up different ways to do different things." As I blinked away a cyclone of dust, she moved on to her second line of offence. "John Cameron Swayzee is also on a television in a display window in a store in New York City and he asks everyone outside on the street the same questions he asks you. I saw it in *Life* magazine. Do you want me to bring it in?" I shook my head in defeat as the dust cleared. "He doesn't care what you answer. John Cameron Swayzee just says it, waits a second, and goes on. He gets paid by Procter and Gamble. He doesn't care what soap you use as long as someone buys it. He doesn't even know you exist."

I was dumbfounded. I thought John waited to go onstage when I turned the knob. Suddenly I realized what a television was and how impersonal its messages were. Then I had the dawning realization that I'd been duped, *betrayed.*

Clearly Dolores felt it was her job to enlighten me regarding my truly insignificant status in the universe, which I guess had to happen, as that seems to be a stop on the road of growing up. However, I never truly forgave her for depriving me of my first intimate relationship. The Indian was like the priest in confession, the big brother, the always present Dad. Finally, he was someone who never criticized. As he faded from the screen that day and was replaced in my mind as a mere test pattern, I lost one of the few people who really knew me.

CHAPTER 3

mad bear

In our escapades across the Niagara Frontier, Roy and I usually had

some deliveries in the Tuscarora Indian reservation. I had seen

what the Creek Indians did on the "Davy Crockett, Indian Fighter"

show on *Disneyland*. I knew that Davy had to kill them with Betsy,

his Winchester, before they attacked and pulled the ol' Indian torture trick of tying the settlers to trees, covering them with honey, and letting them be eaten alive by red ants. It was a slow death. Sometimes it took two weeks before their bones were picked clean. I, like Davy, had my own beloved coon-skin hat, fringed jacket, and plastic rifle which my mother suggested be kept in a box with my Mouseketeer ears labelled "for inside use only."

I considered Roy and myself courageous for heading under the viaduct into the reservation where I suspected we were surrounded on all sides. When I looked up at the jagged Niagara Escarpment, my heart pounded as I was sure Cochise was hiding on every shale ledge. Roy, not as knowledgeable in "Indian ways" as I, wanted to play his radio; I, however, nixed that idea, telling him that Indians could sneak up on us and scalp us at any time if we weren't ready for them. As we tooted along we played a game called Pony Express — the Nash Rambler delivery car metamorphosed into a stagecoach where Roy drove the team and I was the scout. I drove ahead on reconnaissance missions and reported back on any known war parties.

If we were feeling particularly jovial after our deliveries and I was sure we were making it out of Creek territory with our shirts on, we played Cisco and Pancho, two Mexican scouts in my favourite TV program, *The Cisco Kid*. My favourite part was the concluding scene, their signature piece, repeated weekly, where Cisco and Pancho came back on after their adventure of killing Indians and the occasional extraneous gringo. Filling the screen with leering grins and rakishly tilted wide sombreros with dancing tassels, they were perched high on their twitchy palominos. Then they held their horses still long enough to give forth with great belly laughs and Pancho would say, "Hey, Cisco" and

Cisco, doubled over in great guffaws, responded with "Hey, Pancho." At this point they slapped their horses and sped away. Roy and I loved that scene, which we reenacted. Although we had no idea what their inside joke was, we agreed we enjoyed their display of convivial camaraderie.

Every week after we managed to deliver our prescriptions without having our wagon surrounded, we celebrated by going to Shim-Shacks, a tavern on the edge of the reservation which had great beef-on-wecks. (This is a western New York delicacy consisting of shavings of beef with burning horseradish sand-wiched in a hard roll covered with rock salt and caraway seeds.) Shim-Shacks had its own protocol that was understood and followed to the letter by all of its patrons. Indians, always male, sat at the bar and never ate but drank, and whites sat at the tables and ate and drank. (Roy sat at the table for whites; I had no idea he was black, but I knew neither of us was Indian.) The same dozen or so Indians frequented the bar and had reserved seating on particular stools. If a regular came in and another patron had taken his seat, the newer patron moved, giving the regular his stool. They were usually men from the Bear or Turtle Clan, one of whom was Black Cloud, whom I knew from delivering insulin to many of his clan members. I also had to deliver hypodermic needles for him to administer the insulin, and since he'd had to sign the narcotics book for them with me as a witness — my father referred to this procedure as "giving us your John Hancock" — we'd developed a tenuous but begrudgingly friendly relation-ship over the years.

There was one neutral landmark in the tavern and that was the electronic bowling machine. Whatever "watering hole" Roy and I found ourselves in, we always availed ourselves of all games, from pinball to darts. At Shim-Shacks we always played the electronic bowling game, not once, but at least a dozen times for a nickel a game. Over the years I had become quite good at rolling that steel puck with the red-dot centre through the sawdust. Most of the men had too heavy a hand. I had even learned how to bounce it off the sides to clear a split. Roy and I were a team and we often stood Black Cloud and his clan members a game or two. Whenever anyone asked Roy if he wanted to place a little wager on the game he would ask, "Does a bear shit in the woods?" (Once I said that to my mother when she asked me if I wanted a frozen custard and she was speechless — too shocked even for punish-ment.) Within fifteen minutes others would bring their beer and sandwiches over to the game and eat standing up watching the proceedings. I noticed Indians were not like white people when it came to games. They never said, "good shot," or laughed at your gutter balls. Instead they simply nodded and stepped up for their turn. I, however, kept up the banter that Roy and I had developed over the years, but they never acknowledged that I was saying anything. This silence wasn't hostile and I found it reassuring in that I always knew their reaction — nothing. Also I never minded giving a "one-woman show," as Roy called it.

This year Buzz, the owner of Shim-Shacks who also drove the school bus in the daytime wearing a long white bloody apron, ran a contest for Christmas. Anyone with over 1,500 points in the bowling game could reach into a huge jar and pick a number. If it was the lucky ticket you won the expensive rifle displayed on the wall which had a sign attached: *Donated by Gold's Sporting and Hunting Shop for Christmas of 1953, retail value $88.98.* I was the only one to get that score and I reached in the bottle. I had been this far before and lost but this time Roy said he felt a rustling in his bones and sure enough I won the double-barrelled rifle with the mahogany handle. Everyone crowded around and I could hardly lift it when Buzz took it down off its wall hooks. As I stood next to the gun everyone laughed because it was as tall as I was; Buzz caught the moment with his Brownie Starflash and my toothless grin was forever immortalized as the "1953 winner" on the wall between the men's room and the bowling game. The best part of it all was that everyone seemed to be having such a good time.

I didn't need a ballistics test to know that I couldn't arrive home with a rifle I'd won by playing a bowling game at a tavern on the Tuscarora Indian reservation. First of all, I had no desire to alert my mother to my secret life as the Annie Oakley of the electronic bowling set. Surely she'd keep closer tabs on my delivery schedule, curtailing the best part of my life. Secondly, she'd suggest I give the gun away to someone who hunts and that would be to Dr. Carroll, my parents' friend, the local veterinarian. It seemed weird to me to save animals during the week and kill them on the weekend. I figured I won the gun and I could give it to the person of *my* choice. I had seen Black Cloud admiring it and looking through its sight several times since it went on display in the fall. I went over to Black Cloud and laid it on the bar, knowing he didn't like fusses. He put his hand on the barrel and that was the only time I saw Black Cloud smile so you could actually see his teeth.

Aside from the seating arrangement and the neutral turf bowling game, there was one other rule at Shim-Shacks. No one talked while the television was on. It would have been as rude as talking in the theatre during a movie. Most people still didn't have a television and they were captivated by whatever was presented. There were only a few shows on a day and usually we silently watched the TV test pattern — that same Indian in profile in a full war party headdress amidst concentric circles — until the screen sprang into animation at 6:00 p.m. with the *Howdy Doody Show*. We at Shim-Shacks sat in rapt attention with those in the peanut gallery, listening to Buffalo Bob, laughing at Chief Thunderthud, Princess Summerfall Winterspring, Clarabell, and Mr. Flubadub. This dinner theatre was taken totally seriously with all serving, eating, and game-playing done before *Howdy Doody's* commencement.

One cold winter day before Christmas Eve, Roy and I were dreadfully behind schedule. We had far more prescriptions than usual to deliver and as the day wore on several people had invited us in for some Christmas cheer. Usually we hit the reservation before anyone was up and left the medication between the doors, but it was too cold for that this day and we were hours late in getting there. Instead of lunch we had dinner at Shim-Shacks, and as we got back in the stage coach I noticed one bag had fallen on the floor. I picked it up and read aloud the prescription stapled to the front of its white bag: *"Mad Bear Power. Tuscarora reservation. Phenobarbital 120 mg. Sedative. Taken three times a day/or as needed. Emergency — deliver immediately."*

"Uh-oh, kimosabe, we should've been out there first thing," Roy said, slamming the car into gear as he quickly drove out to the far edge of the reservation. As we approached the Mad Bears' mailbox by the side of the road, I always held my breath when I saw the carved wooden figure perched on top — an angry bear rearing and baring its teeth. Mad Bear's family needed a lot of medicine and I'd been there before, usually in early morning when everyone was asleep and we tiptoed away, not wanting to stir the Mad Bears.

Today was the first time we were there when the family was stirring. Mad Bear was sometimes seen in town at a bar, but his wife was never off the reservation. (At least, I'd never seen any of the family before.) Mad Bear was known to "tie one on," as my father termed it, and when he took to kicking fire hydrants and yelling, Constable Lombardy stuffed him in a cruiser and drove him home. Roy told me it took the whole Lewiston force of three, plus volunteers, to get him in the car.

Roy went to the door and I stayed outside to explore their yard. It was a museum of rust, littered with the intestines of old machines, which I found interesting. I liked to put stones in the old cement mixer and twirl them. I also found the old cars and parts on the lawn a remarkable ancient element of the landscape, especially since some had weeds growing out of them. I knew that Mad Bear had a lot of kids and I hoped that one was a girl my age who would see me out of the window and come running out to play Fox and Geese with me.

Roy had remained inside a long time. Getting bored and feeling lonely, I went around to the side of the house and saw a deer hanging up with parts of its body cut out. It looked as though someone had just been hungry and ripped off the occasional limb. Most of the windows were broken in the back of the house and were stuffed with oily rags to keep out the cold.

Mad Bear had the kind of house that never quite gets finished. It was covered in large squares of black paper which were bound to the house with giant silver staples and each sheet said "Bethlehem Steel" in silver lettering. I thought how perfect the name was for the holiday season.

Roy called me to the front door. Mad Bear seemed to have burned out before building a front porch so I stretched my Santa-mitten-tipped arms up and Roy had to hoist me into the house through the windowless storm door. As I was still in his arms, he looked into my eyes and said in a tone of quiet nonchalance that he needed me to be a big girl and do just what he said. I had never heard him pull rank before so I knew his insouciant tone was an act.

Inside their home, which had curling linoleum set on top of unfinished wooden planks, I saw an exhausted Mad Bear sitting in a kitchen chair breathing heavily with his spent arms dangling at his side. As I blinked the snowflakes from my lids, I noticed he had a deep gash on his arm. It was so lacerated you could see a shiny twisted white muscle that was still trying to hold things together, but a large slice of the red tissue was coming out like a crinkled Christmas ribbon. I thought a human arm had only a bone and blood, and was simultaneously fascinated and repulsed to see all of the different tissues — I realized the human arm looked no different from a flank cut of meat at Helms's grocery.

Mad Bear's teenage son, also named Mad Bear, was standing at the entrance of the bedroom door with his arms outstretched on each side of the door frame. One hand held a bloody knife. He was not yet as tall as his dad but he was already wider, sturdier. His father's eyes were set far apart and looked like a black cat's-eye marble, and his own were the same except the size of aggies. He hung his head and his thick ducktailed hair hung forward, covering one side of his scratched face. He had stretched brown skin over broad cheekbones and a high forehead. His dusky thick lips looked like they were outlined in grey velvet. In my mind he looked more like an Indian than his father, who was no longer taut and had even lost his facial definition. They both looked as though they'd been fighting, but the elder Mad Bear looked defeated.

The room was hot with the heavy breath of the two men. The teenager pounded the door sill with his swollen fingers, saying to no one in particular, "That's the last time, the last time."

I was sure the teenage boy had been very bad and fought with his father, and Roy was going to have to straighten him out. Fighting with your father in this beastly way, right before Christmas, was going to ruin the holiday for everyone, and I looked at Roy to let into him. However, Roy put his hand on the boy's arm and said, "He got drinkin', inside too long, hadn't renewed his medication, then he started up. You did what you had to do." The teenager with the ducktail and slit eyes never looked up. Roy continued in a soothing voice. "There's no phone so I'll have to take your father into Forest Lawn. He's lost some stuffing. They can probably sew him up there and knock him out for a week or two."

I blinked. Forest Lawn was the *loony* bin. No one went there unless they talked to themselves, or were like my friend Gretchen's aunt who thought one of the Marx Brothers was swearing at her.

"Cathy, I'm going to stay here between the Bears and I want you to get four pills for Mad Bear and take them to him in the kitchen." Elder Mad Bear provided no resistance when I plunked down the plastic jelly glass with Pluto on the side and told him to take his pills and drink up. Then Roy said very softly to me, "Mad Bear is dangerous, so I'm going to leave you here and come back for you after I drop him." Leave me *here*? I was shocked. But I remembered that Roy said I had to be a big girl and it was time to forget the Davy Crockett games and do what I was told. I could tell he was counting on me. I nodded and he leaned down and I felt his Brillo-pad hair brush against my face as he whispered in my ear and squeezed my shoulder. "This is a time when a woman needs another woman."

I was bewildered by his remark on a number of levels. I had no idea I was a "woman," and I had absolutely no idea what a woman did for another woman, or that females were somehow paired in the universe at certain mysterious times. Finally, I didn't see any woman there other than myself, the new-found woman. Roy led Mad Bear out the door, and as it closed behind him, I looked into the bottomless eyes of the teenager holding the knife, who frankly looked far more dangerous to me than the elder. I then sat on the only kitchen chair, which was still warm from Mad Bear. We said nothing to each other and it seemed as though hours passed. The young Mad Bear never moved from the bedroom doorway, as though he was resigned to always standing guard. I began to hear muffled cries from the bedroom and searched the younger Mad Bear's face for signs of recognition, but he remained impervious. The muffled cries turned into whimpers and then sobs. As I sat on the vinyl I began to itch from prickly heat. It was no wonder as I was still wearing my red plaid boiled wool coat with the velvet collar and my red beret. I wanted to punch some of the rags out of the windows to let in some cool air, but I was afraid to make any move at all for fear of setting him off.

Finally I couldn't stand it any more and decided to answer the smothered cries of pain that pulled at my heart. Besides I couldn't sit any longer. However, to reach the bedroom I'd have to walk right under the arm of the young Mad Bear, who still held the knife. As I scurried beneath his arm in a scary game of London Bridge, I held my breath and closed my eyes and walked as fast as I could without looking alarmed. I kept repeating to myself what Roy had said about being a big girl.

When I opened my eyes I saw rivulets of red blood that had coagulated while running along the cracks in the linoleum. The walls were smeared with dried brown blood and the bedsheet was saturated with purple blood which still splashed down on the floor. The room smelled of urine and terror. Crouched up on the bed was Mad Bear's fat wife, lying on her back, and a boy about my age was huddled against her — the child I'd hoped would come out to play Fox and Geese. There was some sort of creature that looked like a gingerbread man not quite ready to come out of the oven yet, lying in a pool of blood, and there was a cord and a lot of pulpy flesh attached to it. Mad Bear's wife was bleeding from somewhere below her stomach and had cuts on her face where she had been hit. The little boy started crying again and she leaned over and covered the pulpy thing with the edge of the sheet. She looked at me through her terrified puffy black eyes and I knew we were both somehow in the same boat. She whispered to me, "He said he wasn't havin' no more babies."

"He's gone now," was all I could think to say.

"He'll be back," she said, turned, and faced the wall.

There was no phone and Roy and I had to do the best we

could. As we silently departed, I noticed the temperature had dropped since we'd gone in and, shuddering, I got into the passenger seat. Roy went straight to the trunk, emptied a box of Upjohn unicap multivitamins and carried the empty casket into the house, leaving it just inside the door. Roy stomped back on the frozen ground and we rode silently back to the store. It was pitch-black but I was too tired to look for war parties on the cliffs.

We managed to get back to the store before it closed at 9 p.m. and Roy and I shared the unspoken knowledge that we would never tell what we'd seen. I didn't want my parents to know that things like this happened. I knew I was alone with my own feelings of responsibility and shame. If only we hadn't been fooling around, eating Christmas fruitcake and drinking Christmas cheer, going to Shim-Shacks and getting so carried away with Cisco and Pancho, we would have gotten there earlier and given Mad Bear his medicine so it wouldn't have happened.

mother

My mother was sent by central casting to play the role of the fifties

housewife. She could just as easily have been given the role of a

spy exploiting her remarkable talent for *fitting* in while not *buying*

in. The only giveaway was that her public persona, the typical

woman of the Eisenhower era, was a bit too pat. She was like a foreign agent whose English was too perfect for her to have been a native speaker. While she was "the spy who came in from the Buffalo cold," my father and I made her American-small-town-stay-at-home-1950s-wife-mother caricature possible by providing the camouflage and picking up the pieces that made her impersonation believable.

She had no tradition to lean on, so she simply refused to participate in what was expected. She did just enough to drift into the Betty Crocker landscape; however, in terms of her behaviour at home, she was more radical than anyone who ever joined the Bader-Meinhoff gang. The strength of her passive resistance put Gandhi and Martin Luther King to shame.

Mother was tall and thin and pretty. She adhered strictly to all the fashion rules. In the cold weather it was tweed Pendleton wool suits with matching sweater sets or three-piece Butte knits for the meetings that filled her calendar. In the summer she had a collection of cotton flowered shirt-waist dresses. Shorts were for gardening in the backyard only. Straw hats were *de rigueur* for her garden club, with white eyelet gloves and white shoes which she touched up nightly with cakey Esquire liquid applied with a tiny pom-pom applicator. On Labour Day, a holiday my father referred to as a "communist's day off," all white garments and accessories were packed away and fall clothes came out of the cedar chest, where each item was wrapped individually in tissue paper. From Easter to May 31, you could wear pastels, and then the whites came out again June first.

On Labour Day weekend Mother took me on what seemed like an arduous trip from Lewiston to Buffalo, where I picked up my monogrammed pencils for the upcoming school year. Then we went to Hengerer's Department Store to buy back-to-school clothes and Mother's winter outfits. On this occasion we dined in Hengerer's tea room, where I ordered "the-cow-jumps-over-the-moon" from the children's menu. This translated into a grilled cheese sandwich cut into eight parts, potato chips, and a tiny white pleated paper cup of cole slaw. The beverage was chocolate milk, which I assumed was the "over-the-moon" part of the meal.

After lunch while our food was settling (digestion was a big issue in my family) we needed to do sedentary shopping, so we trekked up one flight to the shoe department. "Our" salesman was Mr. McTeer, and if perchance he was at lunch we patiently waited for him, relieved when he dashed off the escalator in his clan tie and rushed to our sides saying, "It wouldn't be Labour Day weekend without the McClures, now, would it?" First we were x-rayed by standing erect and putting our feet under a large grey box that whirred and we could see our foot bones glow in green. (Mr. Wolfson, our scientist neighbour, said that he thought x-ray machines in shoe stores were bad for people and were actually giving us a bit of Hiroshima in every x-ray exposure; my father said that Mr. Wolfson didn't even cut or weed his lawn and voted for Adlai Stevenson so he was hardly an authority.) Then our exoskeletons were measured with a black metal foot which marked length, and width was measured by a piece that extended out of the side of the metal foot like a slide rule fanning A, B, C, or, God forbid, D. Our arch height was never neglected and we placed our feet on a dark purple foot pad which gave a carbon imprint of our foot, leaving a white spot indicating our arch location and height. Armed with an exact size and arch angle, Mr. McTeer went straight to work. I assumed that behind his curtained stockroom

Hengerer's had thousands if not millions of shoes in every size, width, and sundry arch angle and only Mr. McTeer could summarize this information and choose the right pair.

For me we always bought Stride-Rite shoes, saddle shoes for school and Mary Janes for parties, and my mother bought pumps and clutch bags to match her new outfits. Mr. McTeer carefully held her new tweed under the light and then found the perfect matching shoe. Mother said it was crucial to get shoes to fit because she never returned an item to a store. She said doing so was a "shifty practice."

Mother had her hair done once a week with a "standing appointment" and then preserved the hairdo throughout the week with a stretchy band that expanded around her ears and tied with a grosgrain ribbon above her forehead, like the one Lucille Ball wore in I Love Lucy when she was cleaning the apartment. When she went out she protected her 'do with a see-through plastic rain hat that folded into a comb-size case that went into a small compartment in her purse lining designed for just this purpose. When our robin's-egg-blue Chevy Impala convertible top was down she wore a matching blue net hood that tied under the chin. She refused to take part in other activities that could ruffle her hair. By the time her next appointment rolled around, Mother's hair would be flat on the sides and coming to a sprayed point on the top of her head. I never once saw Mother wash her own hair or attempt to manage it in any way. If she had an important meeting inconveniently placed between appointments, she called Mary, the hairdresser, for an emergency "comb-through."

She wore seamed stockings, which she donned by sitting on the bed and kicking her leg in the air like a Rockette so she could see in the mirror opposite whether her seam was straight. She never graced the outside world without being bound in a girdle and a "long-line bra" which reached from breast to waist and was held together by what seemed to be hundreds of hooks and eyes. For dances she had a strapless version of the same foundation, which I had to help her into through a three-part process of folding her skin, having her take a deep breath, and then hooking her in Scarlett O'Hara–style.

Her outfits were invariably accompanied by high-heeled shoes, and she even had high-heeled rubber boots to fit over them in bad weather. When my father suggested she wear flats at home because her spike heels were digging into the linoleum, she said she couldn't wear them. Her calves hurt when she wore flats; since she'd been wearing high heels from the age of thirteen, the tendons in her calves had shrunk over time. Each pair of shoes had a matching bag — alligator, spectators, patent leather, suede — and most of these had a matching pillbox hat. I always thought "pillbox" was a perfect hat for a pharmacist's wife. On Sundays she wore feathered hats to church in what she referred to as "fall transitional colours," with black diamond meshed veils descending over her eyes, making her look as remote as the priest behind his grid in the confessional. In winter she wore white fur hats and carried a white fur muff with red satin lining.

She was ready an hour early for every occasion. While waiting to leave for church in the summer she sat with arms outstretched in a wing chair, with a Kleenex tucked into each armhole of her sleeveless dress and her feet stretched out, resting on top of a floor fan. Often we left so early for Sunday mass that the previous mass wouldn't have let out yet, and we'd have to circle the parking lot for a half-hour. Strict punctuality and silence in church were her only rules. The first was easy for her to follow because she rarely went anywhere and when she did she never attempted to undertake more than one activity, such as going to the bank, in a single day. When anyone questioned her about why we had to be early for anything, she said, "Then no one could say we were late."

I could whisper before mass began but I had to be silent the second the priest walked up to the altar. *Once* she spoke when we were filing out of mass. She put her hand on my shoulder, bent her veiled face close, and whispered for my ears only that she'd heard a rumour that Susan B. Anthony was going to be canonized. When I asked why it was a secret, she said I should keep a lid on it so she and I could start praying to her before everyone else got on to it.

She was a member of the garden club, Altar and Rosary Society, and a member of a bridge club where she excelled at the game and was designated "a master bridge player." However, she dropped out of bridge saying it was full of "eggheads" and she was sick of taking it *so* seriously. She'd say, "Who needs it?" She was also a member of the historical society, which she took seriously, and she sometimes discovered new documents in people's basements or through previously unnoticed published material. I firmly believed that Lewiston was more important than ancient Rome in its store of hidden treasure.

She was in a study club with other women who met weekly to give papers or progress notes on their research. Each one of these reports was of momentous importance in our household. She read them aloud to my father and me every night for weeks before her presentations. We always clapped at the end and my father whispered to me beforehand that I should ask a question to show

I was following — which I wasn't. She was interested in Africa and the different tribes and their habits. I remember the tiny but fierce pygmies in her paper "Emerging African Nations." She was also interested in ancient history and in the history of medicine. She used my father's old prescription drawers in the basement for keeping thousands of notes in case we ever needed to access the information quickly. Once when I came across the word *alchemy* in a Nancy Drew mystery story, she had the history of the word on one of her file cards. I was amazed and simultaneously comforted to have this information in my own home in the event we had an etymological emergency.

While she engaged in all these outside tasks, she committed herself to none of the everyday duties of the fifties housewife. In my entire childhood I never recall her making a meal. We ate all of our dinners in restaurants. My father worked most evenings, and Mother and I went to Schoonmaker's Restaurant almost every night for twelve years where we had a dinner of beef-on-wecks. Since we were regulars there I would often wander into the kitchen, perch on a high stool, and talk to Marge Vavershack, the waitress, as she sped around. I watched the world of the kitchen with fascination, wondering how they kept everything straight and how all the food came out cooked at the same time. I wondered where they got the food to start with and how they knew what people might want to order. I was amazed to see that hamburger didn't come in patties. I was at least six when I first saw a raw egg broken on the grill and I was astonished that it changed form. It never occurred to me that people accomplished these same feats in their homes. Our fridge contained only allergy serum, Coke, and maraschino cherries. Our oven was only turned on to dry wet mittens on the door and the only cooking smell I remember from my youth was that of burning wool.

On the occasions when my father came home at dinnertime the tradition changed only slightly. He pulled into the driveway and beeped the horn and Mother and I ran out to the car and we all headed to the restaurant. It was always a Friday when my father was with us and we sat in the barroom of Schoonmaker's, which was overflowing with Catholics performing their weekly fast. (When my mother and I dined alone we had to eat in the dining room that adjoined the barroom because only women who "risked their reputations" would be seen in a barroom without a man.) The paper place mats described "the edible fish of the world" and showed a giant fisherman in thigh-high boots catching something that looked like a swordfish with a snout. We always had a halibut fish fry caught fresh from Lake Erie by Mr. Schoonmaker. It was many years later that I learned halibut didn't live in the Great Lakes.

Since everyone knew everyone else we often pushed the tables together and on the Fourth of July we sang "God Bless America." On St. Patrick's Day we all sang "Danny Boy" and "When Irish Eyes Are Smiling." Every St. Patrick's Day my father wore a green bow tie with shamrocks on it which had plastic tubing attached connected to a rubber ball. He hid the tubing inside his shirt and when he squeezed the ball, snakes jumped out from behind the tie and wiggled wildly to commemorate St. Patrick driving the snakes out of Ireland with his blessed staff. This tie was one of the highlights of my year until I was about ten. My mother, however, never appeared to tire of the tie or any other part of my father's humorous repertoire.

On Sunday mornings we ate bacon and eggs in Schneider's Restaurant. I regularly ordered peameal Canadian bacon, thinking it quite sophisticated to order "foreign food." We always took home a few hard rolls from brunch, put orange marmalade on them, and called it supper, dining on TV tables as we watched Ed Sullivan, featuring the infinitely unfunny Topo Gigio. When I told Mother I didn't find Topo at all funny, she said maybe people in the Midwest liked him because Ed wouldn't continue to have such an idiot on TV if everyone thought he as stupid as we did.

After the age of seven or so, I ate dinner at a friend's house once in a while. I was shocked that they ate at a table, together, at home, and that the mothers did the cooking. When I asked why the Canavans ate at home my mother said, "Because they have food at home."

When I played with my friend Susan I could see that her mother seemed to be run ragged. She was always taking care of a baby or cooking or ironing. I asked why Mrs. Canavan did all that work and my mother said she had always wondered the same thing. As far as babies were concerned, Mother said it was a mystery to her why, after people had one baby, they went ahead and had another. She thought the odd part was that women considered themselves holy or virtuous when they announced they had houses bursting with six children. My mother reminded me that the Holy Family only had only one child, as our family did. I was a bit confused by this entire discussion because I assumed *God* decided how many children a woman had, but Mother was implying that she and other women played some role in the decision. I finally realized the link; the mother prays to God to give her a certain number of children. Depending on how pleased God is with her behaviour on earth, He heeds her request. I began to pray fervently that I did not have a baby like Sara Welch did at the age of fifteen. Sara got pregnant from reading filthy magazines at the bus station and had to go to a home for unwed mothers in Lancaster.

Mother was convinced that it was important "never to learn to cook or type or you'd be requested to do both against your will forever." When I told her that Mrs. Canavan had a big ironing machine on a giant roller and even ironed *bed* linen, she replied that Mrs. Canavan would someday be a saint. My mother said — and this conversation was "not to be taken outside of our home" — she thought I should throw out any irons I might receive someday as wedding gifts, because there might be too much of a temptation to use them. She said for every seam you iron there will be fifty you wish you hadn't bothered doing. She said her rule of thumb was, if it wasn't important enough to go to the cleaners it wasn't worth ironing.

I first realized my family life was not like everyone else's when the public health nurse was giving a lecture at our school. She carried a lot of clout because she was not a nun, not even Catholic, and therefore somewhat exotic. She wore a starched white uniform, was middle-aged, unmarried, and accepted being referred to as *Miss* Stayner on the street, but she insisted on *Head Nurse* Stayner when performing her public role as health educator. Mother Agnese, our principal, said we had to set a good example for Head Nurse Stayner so she could see how orderly Catholic children could be. She reminded us that it was not just the job of missionaries to convert the heathen, but our personal job every day to convert those in our midst to Catholicism through our holy example.

When Head Nurse Stayner lectured us on nutrition and advised against the heinous crime of eating between meals — clandestine munching would "spoil our dinners" — she called upon me to name three snack foods from my icebox (my mother told me to inform her *we* had a Frigidaire) which could ruin a meal. I looked blank, having no idea what a "snack food" was. She rephrased the question, asking me what food we had for snacks. I was totally relieved to finally understand the question. "Oh, we don't have any food, so we don't have anything between meals." I sat down, relieved at having answered the question correctly. I heard sniggers from the back of the class and then everyone was laughing. I had no idea why our culinary habits should cause such mirth. Before I had a chance to understand what was going on around me, Head Nurse Stayner said something which seared my brain: "If you have a mother then you *sometimes* have dinner at home." Knowing I did have a mother, but knowing I didn't eat at home, I was momentarily thrown into panic. However, I recovered my equilibrium, assuming she was mistaken as only Protestants can be, and I quickly rose to the occasion rather haughtily, assured that I had truth on my side, telling her I knew I'd never had dinner at home, nor had I ever had a snack other than a Coke at my father's store, and I assumed liquids didn't count. I then sat down, feeling I had outfoxed her.

Suddenly there was muffled giggling which turned into outright guffaws all around me. All the grade twos and threes who were older than me were laughing, and Head Nurse Stayner said, and I quote because I remember it verbatim, "Miss McClure, I don't know who you think you are. Obviously you fancy yourself a comedienne; however, I advise you to remember that people are laughing *at* you and not *with* you." I was devastated by that phrase, which was forever branded with a white-hot poker into my tender memory. Were people laughing *at* me? I pictured people hiding behind telephone poles or the altar at church, laughing *at* me. I pictured myself running through the forest like Snow White with the trees coming to life for the sole purpose of cackling *at* me. All these seven years I'd thought I was genuinely amusing, entertaining people at home and at school and the store, and now I find out that actually people were laughing *at* me? I was horrified — I never wanted to speak again. I decided when I grew up I'd join a Carmelite order like my cousin Sister Polly Rose, who had taken the vow of silence and was only allowed to talk to visitors once a year through a three-by-five-inch window covered with wrought-iron grating.

Needless to say I was very quiet for the next few days and finally my mother asked if I was on a private retreat. I told her what happened, and she said Miss Stayner was jealous of our "carefree lifestyle." Since I never saw our life as having any particular style at all, I looked a bit dubious. Picking up on my scepticism she asked me if I'd rather be a frowzy old woman washing out my white stockings at night, making a dinner from a greasy fry pan, going to a church where they didn't even have an altar; or would I like to be a young girl dining out from a full-page menu. As for the "comedienne" part, my mother said it was not uncommon for Protestants to lack a funnybone and if Head Nurse could appreciate humour she wouldn't be a Unitarian who wore her uniform on the weekend. My mother said we were all God's children; however, some come into the world more able to appreciate life's beauty than others. She assured me I had more humour in my big toe than Nurse Stayner had in her whole ramrod body. She convinced me Head Nurse Stayner needed more than our prayers. She explained that some people don't appreciate art, to them it's just paint, some think history is only facts, and some think humour is only words. My mother concluded by saying that if we listened to the Head Nurse Stayners of this world no one would do anything more important or fun than eat a balanced diet. The most consoling part of my mother's speech was that we both agreed that she was the type who probably found Topo Gigio funny, especially when he kissed Ed Sullivan good night.

In those days, in Lewiston, at any rate, people didn't seem to make formal arrangements to visit one another; they simply dropped in unannounced. My mother had a system for such spontaneous occurrences. Whenever headlights hit the curtains of the picture window, we all had to drop to the floor in hopes that they hadn't already seen our shadows. When the company rang the doorbell, the dog would bark furiously, growling and biting the throw rug in the hall, shaking it mercilessly as though to warn the visitor what might happen to him. When Mother yelled, "Hit the floor!" we'd all lie prostrate until the caller gave up and left. Sometimes the more tenacious visitors would go around to the back door and we'd hear them say in a bewildered tone, "All the lights are on," or "The car's in the driveway." When they left, my mother would say, "Thank God," and my father and I shared her relief.

A number of years later, the day after he died of a brain tumour, some robbers read about my father in the obituary section of the paper and broke into the house to steal things. The police who came to our house explained that this is a common scam because valuables are unattended and everyone is supposed to be at the funeral home at the times announced in the paper. My mother, who had returned home for her headache pills minutes before the robbers arrived, was, of course, well-hidden behind the couch by the time the robbers got in and she was never detected. She wrote down what each of them said, got their car licence number through a slit in the curtain, and was later able to identify all of them. The police were amazed she could have hidden so quickly and that she was so self-possessed. Little did they know she found them no more frightening than anyone else who may have dropped in.

Once in a while on the way home after Sunday mass and brunch, my father, the gregarious type, would suggest dropping in on some acquaintance, since we were already dressed in our Sunday best, but Mother would remind him that if we dropped in on them, then they would drop in on us, and it would be never-ending, and we'd have no one to blame but ourselves. She explained that one had to have refreshments for people when they dropped in, and we couldn't provide any. Seeing the wisdom of this, we drove home to pursue our individual interests. When my father, on rare occasions, suggested calling people and then going over to visit them, Mother said she'd like to go except that Willie, our dog, always chewed my father's electric blanket if we left him for more than an hour.

My mother and father invariably treated each other with politeness. They never contradicted each other and their mutual agreement never seemed strained or an uneasy compromise. (When my friends' parents disagreed mildly about when they should leave for their cottage, I was sure they were headed for a divorce.) I had never met anyone who was divorced; nuclear-family meltdown was still two decades away. The only people who got a divorce in the 1950s that I had even heard of were Debbie Reynolds and Eddie Fisher. Even that wasn't a real divorce; it was Hollywood filtered through *Silver Screen*. Liz Taylor stole Eddie while she was crazy with grief because her own husband, Mike Todd, died tragically in a plane crash. Poor Debbie was left to climb the walls with Donald O'Connor.

Father called Mother at three-thirty to see if she was enjoying her day and if I had gotten home from school safely. She routinely put on lipstick and changed her dress before my father came home and insisted that I put on a clean T-shirt. Every time he walked in the door she acted relieved, as though he had returned from a dangerous journey.

My mother would spend a great deal of time planning trips. They were more than daydreams but less than reality. She would go to the automobile association and get "Trip Tiks" to all over the country and even to places in Europe. She wrote to hundreds of Chambers of Commerce and got all kinds of brochures. She would figure out the projected daily mileage and what historical spots we could see along the way. She even planned a quick trip to Susan B. Anthony's shrine in Rochester and then to her home in Massachusetts before it got too crowded. Although my father always acted interested in her travel plans, he made it clear that it was far more sensible to read *National Geographic* from the comfort of our own home and without the hassle of eating foreign food. He told us about all the prescriptions for killing parasites he had to fill for people who travelled even out-of-state. Mother agreed, showing no disappointment, and said the most fun was in the planning anyway. She continued planning expeditions, yet we never travelled more than sixty miles from home.

When I was eight years old, mother-daughter matching dresses were the rage and one Easter I suggested we make some. Mother said that would be wonderful but she had no idea how to sew. I bought the Simplicity patterns and fixed up the old treadle machine left by my grandmother and made the dresses, carefully following the instructions. (I had always had a compulsive streak, which is essential for any successful seamstress.) Mother said that seeing the dresses in parts made her too nervous to watch, so I stayed down in my playroom until they were completed. When they were finished she raved about her yellow linen shift and we both wore our matching dresses to church as I'd planned. I was bursting with pride when my father said we looked like two buttercups going to communion. Mrs. Bradshaw, the luncheonette owner who always had her hair in pincurls (believing they might conduct lightning, she took them out for rain and thunder), had us both walk the full length of her place when we arrived for brunch. She took our pictures as we posed in front of a chafing dish of scrambled eggs that matched our dresses.

My mother and I had one daily ritual that we shared while sitting together on the couch in our blue-and-white-striped seer-sucker outfits. She wore clam-diggers and a matching blouse and I wore an accordion-pleated skort and shell. We watched a TV show called *Queen for a Day*. I could imitate Jeanne Cagney, the hostess with the throaty voice who always chattered to Jack, the maniacally empathetic and appallingly cheerful MC, about the beautiful fashions donated by Lanvin. Jack asked each of four contestants to describe the horrors of their lives. The audience then clapped for the most unfortunate person, and the one with the worst life was crowned Queen for a Day and walked down the aisle sobbing in a trailing robe. Jeanne then reappeared and the Queen got the one thing she needed to make her life perfect (for a day), such as a washer, dryer, or wheelchair. During the commercials I used to pretend I was the fifth unfortunate on the show and I would make my situation so impossible even Jack wouldn't be able to help me. I'd play all the parts — Jeanne, Jack, and the contestant. I would sob and say I was living in an abandoned school bus and all I wanted was a heater for the bus because I had lost fingers to frostbite. Jack would agree, the audience would clap, and then I would say, "Oh, Jack, I forgot, I'm in a wheelchair and can't get in and out of the bus." Jack would be his accommodating old self and give me a wheelchair, and then I would say that the bus was at the top of a hill and I couldn't roll the wheelchair up because of my lost fingers. As this went on, Jack would become enraged and scream and finally throw me off the show. My mother, a great lover of black comedy, would at this point be curled up on the couch laughing hysterically and telling me I had to go on Jack Paar with my Queen for a Day act.

If I made comedy out of tragedy for her, she made historical intrigue out of everyday life for me. Once when we were having lemonade on the wraparound porch of the two-hundred-year-old Frontier House Inn, Mother told me how the word *cocktail* was invented, right in the spot where we were sitting. During the War of Independence the waitress of the inn worked undercover for the American Revolutionaries and she was assigned the task of rooting out the Loyalist infiltrators who had crossed the border from their haven in Canada only a few miles across the river. As

was true with most old inns, there were chickens and cocks strut-
ting around on the dirt floor, future dinners for the guests. The
waitress, Betsy Flanagan, a Revolutionary sympathizer, placed a
feather from the rooster's tail in each of the Loyalists' drinks,
assuring them it was a drink she'd invented called a "cocktail."
These cocktails told the Revolutionaries exactly who were their
enemies and they acted accordingly, ambushing the Loyalists en
route to their headquarters in Fort Erie. The story spread and
cocktails were served there for the next hundred years at the
Frontier House as the ultimate in patriotic drinks.

James Fenimore Cooper, then a midshipman, was staying for
an extended period at the Frontier House and most probably
witnessed Betsy's patriotic cocktail concoctions. While boarding
there he wrote *The Spy*, in which one of the characters is actually
named Betsy Flanagan. His appreciation for the allegiant heart
under Betsy's rough exterior obviously made an impression on
him for she appears again in *The Pioneer*. Washington Irving and
Henry Clay also stayed for extended visits.

The local library was a place where Lafayette made a speech,
and Charles Dickens stayed in town at the Frontier House on his
stagecoach tour of the U.S. He even wrote sections of *Our Mutual
Friend* in one of the guest rooms upstairs. Mother took me to the
room marked "the Dickens" and read the sections that he had
supposedly composed while looking out the window there. I
assumed that he was moved to write because Lewiston was so
marvellously inspiring in its frontier spirit and revolutionary
history. I was surprised when he wrote about London, which as
far as I could gather was simply a place overrun with Peter Rabbit
and his boring, camomile-tea-drinking family. I was equally

shocked when the opening scene was not set in Niagara Falls, one of the seven wonders of the world, but on a river, the Thames! We did notice that the story opened with an inn on a river much like the Frontier House on the Niagara River. We marvelled at the coincidence, and as we sleuthed around town we tried to think of local spots which may have inspired him.

The Hooker family of Lewiston was famous for a number of reasons. First of all they were rich and technically our neighbours in that they lived on our street. However, they lived in a mansion compared to our simple home. It was along the Niagara River on top of a hill we used for sledding in the winter. The grounds were surrounded by an eight-foot wrought-iron fence with spears on top to impale the curious climber. The front of the white clapboard house with its six Greek columns and dozens of windows sat majestically on "Hooker's Hill" while the house itself backed on the dramatic shale cliffs of the Niagara River. Hooker fame later spilled over into infamy as the family business, Hooker Chemical, was ultimately responsible for dumping an unprecedented volume of chemicals in the Niagara River and also burying chemicals under what would eventually be known as the notorious Love Canal.

On Halloween I put black chalk on my face and masqueraded as a minstrel. My mother took me to the Hookers' house and, after getting my treat, we moved on to "Tryon's Folly." In 1818 Amos Tryon built a home for his wife-to-be without consulting her and she refused to live in it or to ever even lay eyes on it, so it lay empty for years and acquired its name. In the 1820s, Amos's brother, Reverend Josiah Tryon, the local agent for the Underground Railroad, put the house to use by helping escaped slaves across the Niagara River to Queenston, Ontario, and freedom. Mother asked the owner to show me the three basements that were part of the Underground Railroad. There was one basement and a trap door which led to another basement and then a trap door which led to a third watery hole that had a tiny door about big enough for one of the seven dwarves which opened to the shore and led to a rickety dock. Sometimes the slaves had to hide for days in the third sub-basement until they were ferried to freedom in Canada. Some died in the last basement, too tired for the final leg of their journey, and were thrown into a watery grave. Apparently the Tryons' house was searched many times by the authorities but the sub-basements where the slaves were hiding were never found.

All this lore was intermixed into my everyday life. It was rare for me to pass a new spot in town without my mother telling me how it played a vital role in history. When we walked together hand-in-hand on our way to Schoonmaker's Restaurant we eschewed this century. We left Toni Perms, the Driftwoods, and the newly fashionable crinolines to those locals grounded only in the present.

Mother and I took imaginary travels back to the time when the Indians ruled the cataract and threw a virgin over the Falls every year to appease the fierce god who roared at the bottom of the foam. The legend suggested the spray from the Falls was the tears of weeping Indian virgins who were dubbed the "maids of the mist." At that time I thought "virgin" meant a woman who gave birth to a child who was the son of God. Mother said anyone who gives birth to a son usually *thinks* he's the son of God, anyway.

Sometimes we moved on to 1812 when our own historic home

was used to billet soldiers who lined the shores fighting for Commodore Perry against the British. We had lots of time for history, never cluttering our lives with cooking, company, or having relatives for unwanted holiday stays. In fact, my mother said of Thanksgiving, "Can you imagine putting your hand in either end of some dead fowl, pulling out its innards, then restuffing it with your own concoction and boiling up the gizzard? Sounds like 'Hansel and Gretel.'"

One thing I admired about my mother was she never stepped out of character. She died as she lived. When she found out she had leukaemia, she said that at least now she would have an excuse for sleeping in and people would say she was brave for getting up at all. One of the perks of a fatal disease is no one pushes you to host the bridge club.

When I told her that I believed Hooker Chemical had poisoned my family with carcinogens more toxic than Love Canal, citing evidence that my father died young from a brain tumour and our dog died the same year — also young — from the same brain tumour, she said, "Relax, everyone has to die of something." When I suggested that everyone in our immediate and extended family had died young of cancer she said that at least now no one would have to go to old-age homes, which was fortunate because she'd spent all of her retirement income on restaurants.

After her diagnosis, one of her major worries was what season she would die in. Would she be buried in spring, summer, fall, or winter colours? She kept one complete outfit plus full accessories for each season in four plastic bags. After she explained the full seasonal fashion agenda to the funeral director, he said, "I guess you're worried about leaving your daughter alone." My mother looked puzzled and said, "She's taken care of me since the age of four. I'm not *worried* about leaving her, but I'll miss her."

—

What's a mother supposed to do anyway? I guess most mothers cook and clean and have household rules. It's true I never learned to be a housewife, but I also never heard a harsh word from my mother. When I stabbed Anthony McDougall and had to go to a psychiatrist, she simply said, "Oh, for heaven's sake." When I was described by the school as unmanageable after I spiked Father Flanagan's holy water, she said I was perfectly fine at home, but if they felt they could no longer contain me then she understood perfectly and perhaps it was time to move on from "the confines" of the Catholic school. She never defended me but let me take my own rap for things, never feeling my behaviour had the least thing to do with her.

Although she was a stickler for the minutiae of fashion rules and other bourgeois affectations, she never placed any confines on my behaviour, and what other people in the town referred to as "strange" she referred to as "novel." I realize now that she needed the conventional cover-up to carry on what was quite an eccentric life in the 1950s. She never made me anxious about doing anything or trying something different outside of the parameters of the town.

When I took the plane alone to New York City for the state high-jumping meet, where I was to be billeted in Harlem, her only speech of preparation for a ten-year-old girl who had never been away and was now going for a week to *Harlem* was delivered casually as she waved her white lace monogrammed handkerchief from behind the fence on the airport runway: "Have fun! I know you'll love New York, and don't forget to give the box of choco-lates in your suitcase to your hostess. Bye-bye."

She never punished me — she let the rest of the world do that. When our neighbour, Trent McMaster, crashed through the ice of the Niagara River, descending into the swirling whirlpool, and lost his fingers to frostbite after taking me and the Schmidt broth-ers up on our suicidal sledding dare, his parents told me I should never have let him do it, but my mother said that although the incident was unfortunate, ultimately Trent had to take care of himself. Because she never criticized me, I often took on the job myself, saying I should never have let Trent go down on the sled knowing he wasn't emotionally equipped to handle the gathering speed and actually be level-headed enough to make the ninety-degree turns he needed to slow down. I should have known he would freeze both physically and emotionally. My mother just listened to my lament as she read the word-power quiz in the latest *Reader's Digest*, finally saying she knew how I must feel. She reminded me I was just a little girl and I wasn't responsible for the Schmidt boys' dares or for Trent McMaster's suicidal missions. She added as an afterthought, "After all, if someone told *you* to go over Niagara Falls in a barrel, would you *do* it?"

Once when I told my mother about a neighbour who said that the Donnellys were wrong to send their severely retarded boy to a "home," my mother answered me with the story of a tribe in Tierra del Fuego who believed that if the wife was unfaithful to her spouse, the husband had an obligation to kill her for the good of the tribe. One man moved away without killing his wife but wasted away from guilt and shame for having committed such an immoral act as shirking his duty to his tribe. While we in North

America are appalled by the act of murder, the Fuegian was ashamed he hadn't done it.

My father never criticized my mother's somewhat murky anthropological parables of cultural relativism, although I could tell he preferred something more grounded. Once in a while he would offer a John Wayne–style homespun "never-judge-a-man-till-you've-walked-a-mile-in-his-boots" version of moral justice with a biblical chaser such as "No one who hasn't done it knows what it's like to parent a severely retarded child for twenty-four hours a day. Never judge another lest you be judged." Although far more plebian, it was a message I could, at least, understand. I think my father understood that I, as a six-year-old, needed more grounding in how people *should* behave in Lewiston, New York, in 1955. However neither he nor I ran the house. Since I wasn't offered a clear game plan at home, I was a sponge absorbing human behaviour wherever I went. That's why the people of the town were so important to me — I studied them for clues.

I think one of the reasons Mother never cared too much what I did was because she never saw herself as totally of this world, particularly of Lewiston. In some unimportant ways she toed the line, but in others she was emotionally absent from the here and now. Each night when we walked to Schoonmaker's Restaurant we talked about the stars and pretended we were explorers from another country, or else we envisioned ourselves as two ancients on camels trying to read the stars to find our way to the diner. To this day I can always recognize each constellation on a starry night. We never passed the local landmarks, the red-brick school, Dr. Alderman's home office, the park bench and gazebo, without her talking about the Mau-Mau movement in Kenya or some tribe she was reading about in *National Geographic*. As we passed the school she'd tell me about life before schools and home tutoring. As we passed the doctor's office she'd tell me about theories of illness before the germ theory and how people had to be ostracized instead of their germs. If we saw boys fighting in the park she would tell me how Indian boys fought to the death at the age of thirteen; the one left was considered "the bravest" and then deserved the title of man, which translated to "brave." When we passed the octagonal gazebo she would tell me how the pioneers had to make their homes waterproof and snowproof. She would ask me if I was an Eskimo how I would build an igloo and how I would trap cold air yet have ventilation.

Lewiston was just her home base. She was really all over the map and she took me with her on all of her time travels. She never told me how anybody in history figured out the next step without asking me what I would have done or how I would have fixed it. When I gave my explanation, she always acted amazed at my perspicacity and then told me how it was in fact discovered or done; however, she always included at least a kernel of my idea somewhere in the explanation and found *some* way to implicate me in the history of ideas.

People used to ask us how we could walk all the way to the restaurant without freezing, but I never noticed the cold when I was with my mother on these walks. The snow seemed magical, transforming the town into a sparkling backdrop for our time together, which was always warm. These moments of my life were the only times I've ever felt perfectly happy and an integral part of the universe.

CHAPTER 5

ice

We were trapped, enveloped in a cocoon of ice. The dawn was

trying to light up the opaque frozen window, but we couldn't see

out, nor could we even see our own reflections. The phone was

dead. The doors were iced shut. My father had chiselled for an

hour to get out the back door and finally made it to the garage by

5:00 a.m. but he couldn't manage to open the garage door. Having been through this before, he knew he'd be high on the emergency list, so he decided to wait for the fire department to come with a blowtorch. Besides, my mother kept opening the milk-box door and telling him he'd have a heart attack if he didn't stop.

This, of course, meant we couldn't go to work and it also meant we couldn't have breakfast at The Horseshoe restaurant. My hunger finally spurred my mother to find a sample of shredded wheat dropped through the door *last* Christmas. As we sat gnawing on our dry wheat pellets by candlelight, we listened to the school closings on the battery-operated radio. I waited with bated breath until the announcer said, "Hennepin Hall!" All my life people have been telling me what the greatest feeling in life is, or should be, but the best I ever remember is when they announced my school was closed due to bad weather. It was as though the angel Gabriel had alighted upon my shoulder and handed me twenty-four glorious hours on a silver platter.

I immediately got on all my winter gear, except for the baby straps on my mittens, which I cut with scissors, and headed out for the day. My mother tried telling me that it was only 6:10 and most people would just be waking up, but I wanted to get a good start. Besides, I couldn't see waiting around for another dried cube of shredded wheat for lunch.

It was cold, really cold. Whenever I took a breath I got a stabbing headache like the one I got when I ate ice cream too fast. The snow was deep, and preserved with a thick layer of ice on top of it, like paraffin on jam. Having no traction, I glided over the ice in whatever direction the wind decided to take me, which was great since I really wasn't in a hurry. I kept tumbling down, feeling like an umbrella that had been turned inside-out in the wind, and I had trouble righting myself. Walking on top of the snow made me feel like Christ walking on water. I began blessing trees to my right and left like Jesus on Palm Sunday. I took a run and slid ten, maybe twenty feet. I fell, laughing my head off, and lay on the ground gazing above me at all the trees that looked heavy, burdened with diamonds. The sun reflected off the swollen branches. Some were so overloaded they'd snapped right off their trunks. The wind made the ice-dipped trees tinkle like the Chinese glass mobile we had at the beach.

I slid on my rear end across the Bakers' yard and into the Schmidts' when I saw something dark under me. I looked down, and gaping at me was a squirrel, frozen as an ice sculpture two inches below the surface. Through the layer of ice I could see his frenzied look as he'd tried to make it to safety before he was shot by the storm's icy stun gun. His paws were lifted, frozen in position, and his eyes looked desperate, pleading for a way out. I knew the Schmidt brothers would want to see this specimen. I tried to put a stick in to mark the spot, but the ice was like concrete and I couldn't make a dent.

I had to go up the Schmidts' steps on all fours and crawl onto their milk box to reach the bell. The Schmidts were Lutheran. We learned in school that Martin Luther was a man who broke away from the Catholic church to "abuse himself," whatever that meant. Worried, I had asked Mother Agnese if the Schmidt brothers could get to heaven if they weren't Catholic, and she said they could have "baptism by desire" if they were ever in a terrible accident and still go to heaven. My father told me not to bring it up — so I didn't. Besides, Franky Schmidt was so old, it seemed to me he'd figured out most things, so he had probably already figured out how to get to heaven.

I stood waiting for the doorbell to be answered while their yappy dog, Skippy, barked incessantly. Mrs. Schmidt was amazed that I'd made it across the street, although she said as soon as she heard the bell she knew no one else would be out this early. Her hair was in pincurls, as it was most of the time. She even wore them to Helms's grocery store with a stretchy scarf that went around the bobby pins on the back of her head and tied on her crown with a grosgrain ribbon. I think she actually believed that scarf hid the pincurls. I guess she thought no one noticed the bumps, or else they simply assumed she had a lumpy head. I couldn't figure out when she actually took the pincurls out. Maybe after I'd gone to bed or when I was at school.

She was always concerned about things like where the boys were going, and what they ate and when they would be eating next. This fussing seemed odd to me. Wasn't that their business? She told me not to touch any wires, as some live ones were down, and not to go near the streets, and to be sure not to go near any hills because we would be out of control, and on it went.

Franky was three years older than I was, and Dicky, his brother, was my age. They both nodded their hellos to me while Mrs. Schmidt told them, as they pulled on their leggings and boots, that they were to be very careful and not to go anywhere near the escarpment and not to go sledding because of the dangerous conditions.

Franky said dismissively, "Ma, don't worry." (I tried calling my mother "Ma" once I'd heard Franky use the term, but she said, "To whom are you speaking?" so I stopped.)

Mrs. Schmidt got all in a state saying, "I *mean* it, you boys. There is wind on top of cold and you know what that means."

Dicky kept clicking his bootstraps, making no eye contact, and Franky answered, "It means wind chill factor, Ma, I *know*."

She acted as though they were heading off to war or something. My mother never asked me where I was going. I don't know where Mrs. Schmidt got off with all this prying. "Franky, *where* are you going?"

With his hand on the doorknob, he said, "Out. I'm going *out*. That's why I put on my coat."

She folded her arms across her full-length apron. "That's it, Mr. Smartypants, *that's it*." She stomped over to the foot of the stairs and yelled up, "Frank, *Frank, Frank Senior!*"

Mr. Schmidt came thundering down in steel-toed workboots, wearing navy overalls with *Niagara Mohawk* written on the front pocket. The printing was arched over a yellow streak of lightning. He was carrying giant orange gloves with huge suede gauntlets. He grabbed Franky's collar as Dicky kept working on his boots and shouted, "Tell your mother where you're goin' to be at, *mister*."

Mrs. Schmidt, sounding terribly fretful, said, "Frank, tell them not to do anything dangerous!"

Mr. Schmidt shouted, "*Nothing dangerous!* Now do you hear me?"

Who wouldn't hear him? They heard him in Canada, for Pete's sake. I marvelled at this ritual kerfuffle they always had before Franky or Dicky went anywhere. With all this repeated interrogation, neither boy ever told his parents the truth about where we went, in all the years I knew them.

We started out the day on an impressive note by sliding right down the porch stairs and seeing who could slide the farthest. Even Franky, who rarely expressed admiration, acknowledged that the buried squirrel was impressive. After we'd climbed on the tree branches that had fallen, Dicky said, "The coast is clear. Ma turned off the kitchen light and has gone to the basement to get the laundry off the line." At that moment they went into the garage and got their sleds and I went home and got mine and we headed up the middle of the empty street.

We knew how fast it was going to be when the sleds kept hitting the back of our booted legs. Suddenly Franky announced in a staccato blast, *"Blood Symbol!"* We all immediately reached in our pockets and pulled out our red Pez dispensers. We each popped a Pez into our mouths. The great thing about Pez is you could accomplish the whole procedure with your mittens on. The Blood Club always wore something red, and we always carried our red Pez. We challenged others and "went for Blood"; that's how we got our name. To get into the Bloods you always had to be brave and never be afraid of the Thunder Roads — they were a gang headed by the Canavan brothers, who all lived on Fourth Street. There was a truly elaborate initiation procedure in order to be received into the Blood Brotherhood. In fact, since our membership had to be renewed seasonally, initiation comprised the greatest part of our activities.

It began with "vining" in the spring when the river flowed like a torrent. You had to swing on a long vine over the Niagara Gorge just a few miles below the Falls and at the moment when you were fully suspended over the water and could hear whirlpools gurgling like Gerber's babies under your feet, you had to yell "Blood Brothers," swing back, and hook onto the cliff rocks.

Trent McMaster, a mealy-mouthed neighbour, always tried to get into the Bloods just because he lived on our street. Franky and Dicky called him Trent Masturbator, which I believed was a Lutheran term for McMaster. Whenever Franky, Dicky, or I left the edge of the gorge to perform stunts on our bikes, Trent always came screaming after us, "Guys, I was just vining — I swear — but you missed it!" *Sure*, Trent. Whenever we climbed up to our tree clubhouse, his mother said someone had to hold the swing rope. Trent told her we shook it when he was halfway up, and she gave us a big lecture on how he had asthma, and how mean we were. Trent's mother told my mother that it would be an act of Christian charity to allow Trent to enter the Blood Brotherhood. I told my mother that if Trent's mother thought we were having someone in the Bloods who still had training wheels on his bike, then she must have been from the Twilight Zone. My mother agreed that it was my club and my life.

Trent's mother and mine were friends and in the same study club. As a dry run for their club presentation on emerging African nations, they made Trent and me assume the role of the trial audience. Trent clapped at the end. Trent's father was a researcher at Carborundum and he worked late like my dad. Both Trent and I were only children. A lot of people made a big deal about us being only children, but I didn't really get why. So often, much too often for my taste, the four of us went out to dinner together. As Trent's mother was fond of saying, "What's the point in cooking for one measly person?" I even had to go to the Ice Follies with him and to some plays put on by Stella Niagara, like *Saint Bernadette and the Burning Bush*. He liked it so much he wanted to go *again*. As if this wasn't bad enough he was also in my class at school, and on

Sundays we went for brunch after mass with his family. The only silver lining in this deal was it was dead easy to win money off him, particularly at the bowling game, even though his mother frowned on his betting. My mother said it was sometimes best to turn a blind eye to some things in life. I only hoped he wouldn't show up that cold morning and start his annoying routines.

As the three of us trudged along in the snow, I felt we were a family — the Blood Family. I wanted to remember that moment because I was perfectly happy. Could I freeze-frame that second of glittering ice, in the paradise of belonging? I wondered how big people remembered particular things or moments of time from long ago. It's interesting that people have figured out how to pickle, freeze, dry, and cure foods, how to preserve history in a book, events on television, but how do you preserve a moment in your memory?

Everything we did together was exciting. Our Blood clubhouse even had a fold-down table where we made battle plans. In the summer we went to the dump, hid behind abandoned fridges and stoves, and then popped out with our guns, firing a long red smoky row of caps. We went behind Schoonmaker's Restaurant and made forts out of empty beer cases, complete with lookout towers. We took my moronic dog Willie with us and shouted, "Yo, ho, Rinnie" when the Thunder Roads attacked us; however, all Willie ever did was look confused, walk in bewildered circles, and eventually go to sleep in a beer case.

As we approached the corner I said to the other Bloods, "Let's go to Hooker's Hill."

We marched along silently, the snow crunching under Franky's big boots. Finally he said in a deadly quiet tone, while looking straight through me, "Hooker's Hill is for girls. We're going to the escarpment."

Girls! I knew how dangerous it was when "girls" were mentioned. I didn't want to skate on *that* thin ice. Flashbacks crept into my mind like a dirty fog. The mere thought of my previous existence, which I had fortunately shed like a snake's skin, made my chest feel like it was bound in my grandmother's peach-coloured corset, the one with the long white bones in it. I could only take short shallow breaths when I thought of the time I'd spent with Susie and Judy Baker working on the Lennon Sisters paper dolls. Cutting them out took days on end of sitting still and clipping on a straight line, which I never managed correctly. Then Susie, three years older, ran the show like a drill sergeant. "OK, get on those prom dresses." We marched the doll of the day under the skirted chairs of the living room to dress her in her strapless gown with cummerbund and matching shoes and elbow-length gloves. As soon as we got there, Judy would say, "Time for the Miss America Pageant! Get out the swimsuits and cover-ups," and on it went. If I was really lucky even *they* would get sick of paper dolls and we would haul out our Betty Crocker bake sets, work all morning making a tiny cake the circumference of a coffee cup, and then have to do all the dishes, which were not nearly so tiny.

Now that I was in the Bloods, I knew where I belonged. My mother was upset about my new life. She said I was filthy every day and I could get polio from the dump. My father said, "She has the rest of her life to be a girl." Did he think I was going to play paper dolls later in life? I knew I couldn't flinch from whatever feats were demanded of me by the Bloods.

As we stood on the lip of the gorge, Franky said, "This is the last winter to sled here; they're building a power project, because next to the Falls, this spot has the greatest drop-off."

We looked over the edge. Dicky threw a stone, and it took a long, long time to land. Perched on a jetty, at the bottom of the gorge on the river side of a one-lane winding road, was the Riverside Inn, with its pathetic pink martini flickering in neon, and an arrow pointing to its two-car parking lot. It was built on a rock, and part of its dilapidated winterized porch was cantilevered over the river. It was two hundred years old and had once been used as a depot for the Underground Railroad. It had two basements cut into the rock, one with a trap door. Sometimes we slithered along the ground pretending we were slaves who had just escaped from Georgia.

Trent's mother said Marge Welsh had no right running a tavern. Even Father Flanagan said that men who left mass before the collection to go to the Riverside Inn were taking their chances with a God who sees all things. My mother said Mrs. Welsh's husband had taken ill and, with six children to feed, she had no choice but to run the tavern. Once, when I was hanging up coats at my mother's bridge club, Mrs. Aungier said that Mrs. Welsh's daughter got "in trouble" at the Riverside Inn. No one spoke, but they shook their heads in horror. When my mother told my father at breakfast the next morning, he said, "Girls who go to the Riverside Inn get into trouble — poor Mrs. Welsh. She's really had her cross to bear."

My mother shook her head and said, "I know I couldn't have sustained all her privations. Fortunately God gives the heaviest cross to those who can shoulder the load."

We stood at the lip of the gorge watching the pink neon flash in the distance, silently plotting our route down between the trees and rocks. I had a sick feeling in my stomach as I realized we were facing a straight drop that was solid ice. All that lay between me and the rapids was guts. I knew there was no turning back. I just forced my mind to narrow like a cattle chute and figure how I would get down. The trickiest part was making the last sharp turn on the ice before hitting the frozen river. The brown ice spots on the river had whirlpools under them. The river froze on the edges, but ran too fast to freeze over the whirlpools.

I knew the power of whirlpools. In the summer Dicky, Franky, and I, along with the other kids who lived along the river, used to throw cans into the whirlpools and watch them pop and collapse as the opposing currents crushed them; we marvelled at nature's power as she sucked them under. We assumed that our world was somehow all connected with foreign worlds piled one upon another, so we figured the cans eventually emerged in China, specifically Shanghai. We imagined the surprised face of a Chinese farmer who pulled a can of Campbell's tomato soup out of a rice paddy. Once, when we were fishing, Franky dropped his father's fishing rod into the water. Knowing both his family and mine would be furious because we were not allowed near the river bank, we desperately prayed to China for its return. We enacted our version of an Asian Shinto rite which consisted of Dicky and me taking tiny steps along the shore and bowing before Bobby while he screamed bizarre samurai grunts we had learned from comic books.

As we stood at the top of the escarpment capping what seemed like an iceberg, silently planning our runs, we heard a sled scrape behind us. Out of the corner of my eye, I saw a blight on the landscape which turned out to be none other than Trent McMaster. I didn't even tell Franky and Dicky what had happened the other night when I was at Trent's with my parents, after the Friday fish fry at Schoonmaker's Restaurant. It was too strange to even be a funny story, and believe me, I could make most stories funny in the retelling.

Trent had suggested we go to his room because he had wanted to "share the biggest secret in the world." Well, that really was a showstopper. I was quite surprised when I walked into Trent's room and saw a picture of hell painted by some nut named Salvador Dali, probably a relative of Loretta's. The people in the picture were burning in flames, their tormented faces upturned, pleading for help from the Virgin Mother who stood suspended in mid-air above the flames with her palms outstretched. The bottom halves of the unfortunate souls who were perpetually trapped in the flames of hell had already turned to charcoal. Mary's expression was one of sadness, sorrow, as if she wanted to say that going to hell was so unnecessary, yet that is precisely where we would wind up if we didn't repent. I'd seen that look on her face before. On *my* bedroom wall I had sets of painted woodblock cut-outs of Disney characters from different films. My favourite set was Peter Pan with Wendy, Tinker Bell, and Captain Hook. The hungry alligator swam below the big sailing ship as Hook walked the plank. What kind of kid *chose* mankind's descent into hell for their wall?

Trent closed his bedroom door. His usual hesitation had

vanished. As he got wound up he sounded almost like a Father Flanagan in full gospel tilt. He began by telling me there was something I needed to know about him. I figured for this I'd better sit down in his swivel desk chair. He told me he was a member of the "Blue Army." I lifted one eyebrow indicating that I had no idea what the Blue Army was, and furthermore I had no desire to know what it was. I also wanted to get out of his room. As I had a chance to look around, I spotted all sorts of weird, literally hellish pictures, icons, statues, and altars on nearly every surface. I had told my mother that Trent was totally off his rocker, but she only said Trent was the type who didn't fit in as a child but would make an interesting adult. (My mother was, as usual, right. Trent turned out to be a distinguished Sanskrit professor who owns a world-class collection of Hindu puppets.) I really didn't want to hang around waiting for Trent to grow up.

As I began to rise from my chair, hoping to make a graceful retreat, he began speaking in a booming voice I'd never heard from him before. The voice of authority, the imposing gentleman who only comes out in his bedroom, the commanding officer in the Blue Army. He spoke with an ominous hint in his voice: "Cathy, I *know* what you think of me. But you don't have any idea who I *am*. Allow me to backtrack." *Allow me to backtrack.* He was always trying to talk like an adult. "I fight for the immaculate heart of Mary — that's what we do in the Blue Army. I've been called upon to urge people to accept Her word. Our Lady of Fatima chose Lucinta, Francisco, and Jacinta, simple shepherd children, to share her three messages. We must pray the rosary and save souls from *that*," he said, pointing to the garish picture entitled "Vision of Hell" which hung on his wall. "The second message was to convert Russia and to establish devotion to Our Lady's immaculate heart and then there would be world peace. The third message is not going to be revealed until 1960, which is still four years away."

He began pacing up and down on his Raggedy Ann and Andy rug. I was definitely not going to get involved in this conversation. I looked around at Trent's room. He had Hopalong Cassidy wallpaper and curtains with horses on them. His mother had decorated his room as though he was just your average boy. I guess when you're a mom you have no idea what kid God will give you. It's what Roy would call a real crapshoot.

Sensing I was losing interest, Trent blared, "Cathy, I have some big concerns here . . . I *know* the third secret. It has been entrusted to me by Our Lady of Fatima. She appeared to me above the wild rhubarb patch in the empty lot. She is afraid the last secret will never be revealed. She wants me to hold on to it until 1960 so that at least some American will have the secret in case the Russians bomb Rome, where it is locked in the Vatican."

I couldn't resist asking with some of the derision I felt, "Why would Our Lady of Fatima travel all over the world, choose the USA, then New York, then Lewiston, then Third Street, then Trent McMaster?"

He raised his arms in the air and let them flap lifeless to his sides. "I don't know. I've asked myself the same question a thousand times. I *have* been interested in the miracle of Fatima for a few years and I have collected material on it whenever there is a Catholic book fair." He pointed to a shelf chockablock with Fatima pamphlets and books, most of which were covered with kneeling shepherd children wearing little scarves. "I had to share this burden with *someone*. Cathy, it's *hard* because I know that if this secret were to be revealed, it would help all of the world *today*, but I feel I have to keep it until 1960. The problem is there may be lost souls in between."

My advice was simple as I got up from my chair. "You're doing the right thing. Just keep it secret."

He seemed disappointed by my lack of debate on the topic. As I headed toward the door he said, "Well, Cathy, you can see how I can't be overly concerned with the Bloods and all the initiation rites. I've got a *lot* on my mind."

I nodded my understanding and then slipped out of his room to join my parents. I immediately began agitating to get them mobilized for departure. Knowing my dad liked *The Jackie Gleason Show*, I pointed out that we only had a few minutes to run home and warm up the set or we'd miss the June Taylor Dancers.

—

Now Trent McMaster was here again, loping along on the sheet of ice to join us and give us some silly idea or other. He's also the type that could tell his mother we were on the gorge and get us all in trouble. "Hi, guys," he squeaked. Thank God, he didn't have the nerve to wear something red. Franky and Dicky ignored him, and I nodded, but then looked the other way. I knew that my lack of enthusiasm made him feel crummy, because I was always nice to him when my mother and I went out to dinner with him and his mother. Of course, he didn't know that it was because my mom made me.

Franky said, "Listen, Masturbator, to be in the Bloods you have to sled to the bottom, and not turn till the Riverside Inn."

"That's only a foot or two from the water," Trent stammered, adding, "The weatherman said it's dangerous today."

"So play with the weatherman," Dicky piped in.

"I'll go first," Franky said. He got down on his sled and Dicky pushed him off. I never saw anyone go so fast. He leaned perfectly around all the stumps, but he was gaining too much speed. He had his hands on the front and we could see him trying as hard as he could to turn; he passed the pink Riverside Inn sign, turned ninety degrees, and stopped in the parking lot. He looked up triumphantly and signalled his success. We both raised our hands and gave the sign for the Bloods.

Trent was unusually quiet, although I heard his asthmatic rattle and saw thick disgusting yellow stuff frozen layer by layer under his nose.

Dicky went next. He didn't make as many turns as Franky and was going even faster. He looked squirmy; he began leaning one way then another. He tried dragging his feet, but nothing helped on the solid ice. Suddenly we heard a loud hollow thud and a snap as Dicky hit a tree. He lay there a long time. Trent said, "I think he's dead!" Finally Dicky stood up, staggered, and fell. He got up again and held up the thick curved cast-iron piece from the front of his sled, which had snapped off. He held it up as though he had participated in a joust and this was his crossbow, the way Robin Hood did with King Richard, in the Classic Comics. He turned all around to show it to Franky at the bottom and us at the top.

I was next. There was no point in talking about my terror. Trent pushed me off. As his hands touched my feet, I felt them shake through my fleece-lined red rubber boots. "Good luck," he yelped. I told myself to keep making tiny turns; that would be my only salvation. I wasn't strong enough to carve turns in the ice.

Leaning and unweighting was my only hope. It was fast, faster than I'd ever imagined. I couldn't see any of my former landmarks. I went so fast it was a blur; in fact I couldn't breathe. Where was the big stump? The tiny road? What if I missed them and I was in the middle of the river? My face was so close to where the sun hit the ice I was blinded. Oh God, I don't want to drown. What if I don't go to heaven? Then I saw it — the pink flash of the Riverside Inn sign. Now I had to lean hard, almost off the side of my sled — I couldn't afford to think of heaven or hell — just turn the crossbow and lean — I was past the sign — no more pink — that gave me three feet maximum — I gave it my all — I was slowing down coming out of the turn — I stopped. I looked up and pulled alongside Franky. We looked like parked cars in a lot. He smiled ever so slightly. We pulled out our Pez dispensers; my tongue was dry. In my terror and with the wind, I'd stopped making saliva. The Pez just sat there like dry ice until I put some snow in my mouth.

I stood up and heard the babbling of water under the ice in the river behind me. Dicky was staggering, trying to get down; however, his feet kept sliding out from under him and he persistently crashed on the ice. I looked up to the top of the gorge. There, a pathetic blue smudge on the cliff's ledge, stood Trent. I saw his mitten go to his face, undoubtedly his germy menthol nose stick. After making the trip, it was obvious to me, he couldn't do it, now or ever. Why didn't I tell him that? I knew I could have told him at the top when I was alone with him. Anyway, he'd chicken out, he always did, saying, "Let's go to my house for Ovaltine," hoping the cold would make us forget his cowardice.

God, he was actually crouching, getting on the sled. Even

Franky looked worried and shook his head. I wondered later if he would have heard us if we'd yelled then, at that exact moment. It would have been our last chance to have said we'd tried to stop him. My Pez dried up. He started down fast, faster, out of control from the start. As he got closer I could see he was lying on his sled like a bullet, making no effort to steer. He went straight down, gaining speed every second. His only hope was hitting a stump or a rock to slow him down. I hoped he'd had the brains to keep his head behind the steering mechanism so it wouldn't take the impact if he hit something. As he got near the Riverside Inn sign, there was no hope of a turn. He was mummified. He leapt off the pier like Superman on a board and hit the ice still moving. He shot out on the frozen Niagara River still travelling until he hit a brown patch of ice and stopped. He tried to stand, but the back of the sled sank. We heard a cracking, as though the world was unfolding like an accordion, and Trent McMaster was pulled under with his blue hat bobbing up and down like a forlorn buoy.

We stood there; my legs felt like two broken elastics. Dicky ran toward us screaming, "Cathy, get help!" I looked at the life preserver on a pole too high for me to reach. Franky looked off in the distance as though he were some kind of famous explorer, and Dicky was still negotiating his way down. How come I was suddenly in charge? I had to go into the Riverside Inn. My heart raced like a scooter. I didn't want to "get into trouble" like other girls who went in there.

Inside the inn, Dicky and Franky stood behind me. I smelled old beer. Roger, the bartender, ran toward me. "We saw. Call an ambulance!" he said to Mrs. Welsh. "I'll fish him the pole if I can," he added over his shoulder as he ran out with two other men.

Mrs. Welsh made three hot milks with little squirts from the big bottles with nipples on them that hung from the ceiling, and plunked the mugs on the dark mahogany bar. "Kate, sit down and warm your insides. You'll need it." As I drank what tasted like a turpentine milkshake, I wondered if this was how Sarah Welsh "got into trouble." As the three of us sat on the high stools, I looked down at my sawdusted red boots hanging limply.

"Who is it, darlin'?" she asked.

"Trent McMaster." I swung around on my bar stool once so I wouldn't see her face.

"My God, Mrs. McMaster will never survive the loss."

The loss? The *loss*. The Black Label sign flickered. Was he going to die? Surely that was just ridiculous "melodrama," the word my mother used to describe Dolores's carryings-on.

Everyone went to the bay window, and finally I ambled over as well. Roger, who also fixed radios and sometimes irons, was out on the ice with the others. They threw Trent a life preserver, but he never grabbed it.

"Hypothermia, muscles given out," said Jeffrey Hicks. He leaned back on the heels of his unlaced workboots and said, "What was you doin', little lady — up to no good with these here boys?"

Finally Roger gingerly walked out on the edge of the brown ice patch and we all took a deep breath, and one man with veins all over his nose like a road map muttered to the window, "Watch out, my man. Heaven's full of heroes." Roger himself was blowing across the ice, but he finally anchored himself and managed to get Trent to slither up on the pole like an inchworm. He was dragged across the thinnest part of the ice until Roger could grab him. He took off his parka and wrapped Trent in it. Only Trent's lifeless feet drooped out the end of the roll as he carried him in. Everyone moved aside and we were all silent.

"Clear the bar," Roger shouted, and laid him out on it. Trent looked patchy and blue. Mrs. Welsh put some brandy in his mouth, but it just dribbled along his cheek. I heard the screech of the siren through my numb heart.

One man at the bar looked at another and said, "Kids are such idiots, 'sa wonder more don't die." Then he knocked back a shot.

—

Trent didn't die; he had hypothermia. He hung between life and death until his body temperature returned to normal. He did, however, lose some fingers to frostbite. The doctor said he was lucky he retained his thumbs, which are the pincers that people really need. They said it was the wind chill factor when he raised his hands out of the water and clutched the edge of the ice that caused the irreversible damage.

After that I had to carry Trent's lunch to school every day and sit at his lunch table to click open his lunch box. I also had to hold the Kleenex for his nose because he now only had what looked like two hooves. He was in white oven-mitt bandages for months, and then had a series of operations in the years to come. As the months wore on and Trent was still in his bandages, my fantasy of what was under those bandages grew more terrifying with time. I'm sure nothing could have matched my vision of what he would look like when the bandages were removed. His hands, which in their bandages looked like two little golf clubs, earned him the nickname Stumpy. Trent didn't seem to mind the name. In fact, he began referring to himself as "Stumpy McMaster." Only his mother steadfastly held on to "Trent."

CHAPTER 6

anthony mcdougall

Every school had its sadist and ours was Anthony (named after the patron saint of lost causes) McDougall, the boy who was held back so many times he was mistaken for the janitor on parent-teacher night. When we did arithmetic, Anthony was especially rambunctious and our teacher, Sister Immaculata, relegated him to tidy the coat room and mop up the slush under the boot rack.

He had red hair as did his six brothers and one sister, and he had those kind of giant freckles that only redheads are blessed with that crowd their whole body, at least what I could see of it. I had little conjecture about the rest. His skin was as thin as it was white. His ears were like a replica of a newborn monkey's, so transparent you could see the veins and capillaries.

Catholics seem to have an inordinate belief in alphabetical order. Since my name was McClure and his was McDougall, he was always seated directly behind me. He was a perpetual fidgeting machine, either scratching, taking his pen apart and getting ink all over himself, or tapping his pencil. He led quite an impressive war campaign. He waged little battles on his desk, pretending his pencils were submarines bombing each other. He incessantly simulated bombing noises by blowing air out the side of his mouth, while simultaneously throwing his pencils in the air and ducking under his desk to avoid leaded shrapnel. All this activity made me feel as though I were in the middle of a war-torn country, and by noon I was suffering from battle fatigue. I eventually began to tune out "Anthony's Crimea," as Sister Immaculata termed it. But that was the least of my problems with Anthony McDougall.

Anthony was not pleased with my new policy of ignoring him. Apparently he preferred it when I turned around and screamed "Shut up!" as loudly as I could. He took to pulling my ponytail out in chunks. He would hold up fistfuls of blond switches with glistening roots that looked like yellow scallions. He would display these blond tendrils as though he'd won a lock of hair in some medieval tournament that only he was aware of. He would then carefully lay the tress trophy in the pencil indentation of his desk as if it had been specifically designed to hold his mane spoils.

Appealing to Anthony's sense of decency was not a rewarding activity, so I turned to my father, who suggested this was a case for the authorities. Sister Immaculata told me I made more of a fuss than Joan of Arc when she was burned at the stake. God was testing me, and according to Sister Immaculata, I was losing the fight. It was Satan who was always behind complaining. My father suggested I move up in the chain of command, so I appealed to the ultimate authority, Mother Agnese, our principal. She told me to offer up my sufferings for the poor souls in limbo. My father then suggested I ask for a seat reassignment. Sister Immaculata nixed that anarchistic suggestion, pointing out that if I flounced to another seat, then what would prevent everyone else from requesting a move based on some "inner longing." Eventually alphabetical order would mean nothing. She also pointed out the obvious dilemma that *someone* had to sit in front of Anthony McDougall. My mother suggested we invite Anthony to lunch, thus turning him into a friend. Needless to say, these suggestions only confirmed that I was on my own in finding a solution.

One Saturday when I was on delivery with Roy, he noticed that I wasn't leaning my head anywhere near the headrest because any pressure on my scalp sent electrifying pain from ear to ear. He asked me what was wrong. He couldn't believe it when he divided my hair and looked at the swollen red scales on my patchy head and my prematurely receding hairline. He shook his head when I yelped as he touched one of the reddish purple patches under my few remaining hairs. I couldn't even put it up in a ponytail anymore, because my bruised scalp could no longer stand the tension of the rubber band. Roy said it looked raw, and he didn't like the way I was cowering in the car when he reached toward my head.

I went through the whole saga of how I had appealed to every possible authority — even God hadn't helped. Roy shook his head and made the high-pitched sound — "emmm-hm!" — he made when things were either really good or really bad. He rubbed his five o'clock shadow, which he did when he was thinking of something to do or something was bothering him. He finally said that this was "no good" and that "Anthony needed a taste of his own medicine." Roy knew the McDougall family, as we had delivered medicine there for years. Roy agreed that there was no turning to Mr. McDougall, whom he referred to as "a tavern man," because he would just tell us to get off his property. Mrs. McDougall had, as Roy said, "lost sight of things many years ago." We both knew we delivered enough tranquillizers there to quiet a frisky colt. When Anthony was supposed to bring a dish for the May Day pageant potluck supper, Mrs. McDougall sent one devilled-ham sandwich wrapped in newspaper.

Roy assured me that when we were finished with the likes of Anthony McDougall, he'd shake in his boots so hard his freckles would fall off like filthy raindrops before he'd ever *think* of messing with me again. He said, "The guy's big, lots older, all them McDougalls is as skinny as six o'clock, but they're wild and wiry. Ya got to get in *once* and get him good. Maybe four seconds to get in and get out. You got but one chance — you miss the first time, you're scalped. You're not strong enough to actually hurt him by punchin' him. You got to use somethin' sharp and hit him where the body is packed with veins. Break the skin — that'll scare him. Go for the lip with the edge o' your lunch box or smash him in the hand with somethin' sharp — lots of veins there. When he bleeds he'll *think* he's been hurt a lot even if it's only a nick. It's your only chance. Remember, never cuff 'im when he starts up with you, he'll be on guard then. Hit him and hit him *hard* with something sharp in the lip or the hand when he's least expecting it, and instead of being the bloodsucker he is, for once he'll bleed. He'll bellyache like a baby for a while — you just walk away and that'll be the last time he'll pull your hair. Bullies are bad, cowards underneath, and you gots to end it on your feet — can't crawl away on your belly or you ain't never gettin' up. The good Lord punish the snake for temptin' Adam and he ain't never stood up since." Roy hit the dashboard and concluded, "I'd love to do it for ya, but then when you're alone with fast Anthony, he'd turn up that browbeatin' motor somethin' fierce."

Roy rarely gave advice, and he never gave bad advice. I bided my time. The following week Anthony pulled so hard on my ponytail the elastic snapped in half and flew into the P-through-R aisle. Now even my neck hurt when I turned it to either side. Still I waited to catch him unawares.

One morning we were learning how to bisect angles with our compasses. I glanced down at my gleaming metal compass with its sharp point perforating my paper, and I knew my moment had arrived. I buoyed myself up by repeating Roy's fighting words, "Seize the moment, act quickly, and get out." I suddenly turned around, looked at Anthony's see-through freckled hand, made a quick study of the vessels underneath which looked like a road map. I picked a major highway and jabbed my compass in, knowing I had no second chance. Blood gushed in the air like a geyser. Linda Low took it upon herself to tell Sister Immaculata (I guess she thought Sister Immaculata might miss the blood fountain spouting from Anthony's punctured hand). "Sister, Cathy McClure has fatally stabbed Anthony McDougall." (I was sure she got that line from *Perry Mason*.) Anthony stood up in slow motion, became paler, which I didn't think was humanly possible, looked aghast at the blood, and fainted dead away. As he fell he banged his head full force on the edge of his desk and was out like a light. Following Roy's instructions I ignored the whole thing and tried to go on bisecting my next angle.

Mother Agnese felt the quake one floor below as Anthony hit the floor. In fact, even the windows shook, and the purple construction-paper Easter bunny cut-outs whose ears were wedged between the frame and the glass fluttered to the floor. Mother Agnese came thundering upstairs and charged into our grade-three room.

As the ambulance siren whined to a halt, and we all heard the clatter of the stretcher as the fold-down wheels hit the cold tile, I felt eyes burning into my back as I swung large, carefree arcs on my graph paper. The volunteer ambulance driver was Brian Muller, who worked at the gas station. I heard Brian bark, "Let's get a tourniquet on him." Roger, the bartender from the Riverside Inn, who doubled as the volunteer ambulance sidekick, opened the huge red metal first-aid box, but added in his usual steady voice, "Probably fainted from the sight of the blood, and he hit his head." Sister Immaculata was now totally ignoring the prostrate Anthony and was whispering with Mother Agnese in the corner. Linda Low, with a never-ending flair for the obvious, took it upon herself yet again to tell Brian, "Catherine McClure stabbed Anthony McDougall. He was just sitting there minding his own

business. *She did it for no reason at all.*" Brian just shook his head
as though I were too much of a bad seed even to comment on. As
he approached the exit, he nodded his head toward me and
asked, "Mother Agnese, do you need help with *her*? Want me to
get the compass away?" Mother Agnese assumed the beatific smile
matched by the voice of chilling calm she appropriated when she
was in her "I'm but a vessel of the Lord" mode: "No thank you,
Brian, I'll handle this."

And "handle" it she did. My mother picked me up from school
in the car since I was too dangerous to be loose on the streets of
Lewiston walking, maybe stalking on my own. As I sat in Mother
Agnese's office counting the blood flecks on my royal-blue spring
uniform pleats, she chose to chide me with the following words:
"Well, Catherine, when a person's soul is empty, there is plenty of
room for the Devil."

The next morning when I tiptoed barefoot across the freezing
floor on my way downstairs to pick up my underpants, under-
shirt, and navy knee socks off the radiator where they were
warming in the cold dawn, my mother poked her pink sponge-
rollered head out of her bedroom, saying I might as well get some
more sleep as I wasn't going back to school until I had seen a
psychiatrist and he had pronounced me sane. I had no idea what
a psychiatrist was, although I could tell by my mother's expression, the same one she wore when they called the priest to bless
my dying grandmother, that seeing a psychiatrist must be worse
than a venial sin. It might be mortal. I heard the word *psychiatry*
referred to as a department when we dropped off medicine at the
Niagara Falls hospital, and thought it must be something like

mental extreme unction, the last hope before passing on to "another world." When I asked her what a psychiatrist was, Mother said it was the kind of doctor that Mrs. Poole and old Mad Bear saw. Now, I knew that Mrs. Poole thought people were trying to open her head with a hairbrush so she refused to stroke her hair until they took her with all her snarls to the loony bin. And old Mad Bear hadn't said one word or moved in years since he had his big attack or, as Dolores, our cleaning lady, said, "went on his last warpath." What my father referred to as Forest Avenue Sanatorium on his prescriptions, Dolores called "the laughing academy." This whole psychiatrist episode was shaping up to be a lot scarier than the work of the devil, in my possibly insane opinion.

My mother told me I must be "troubled" and that all I had to do was tell her the truth and everything would be alright. I was beginning to discern that all these understanding and kind words meant that I might be crazy. My mother asked me to sit down. She said in slow, measured tones that Mother Agnese was "surprised" that not only would I *plan* to hurt Anthony, but that I showed no "remorse." I wondered what remorse was; I certainly wished I had some. Maybe "*re*-Morse" was Morse code for retards. My mother saw my bewilderment, and asked me if I was sorry that I had stabbed Anthony. I was so relieved that all I had to do was to tell the truth that I quickly jumped in, assuring her with complete candour that I wasn't the least bit sorry I'd hurt Anthony. I could tell by her face this wasn't the truth she wanted to hear.

When she asked if I had planned it ahead, I was really disgusted by her naïveté and couldn't resist saying, with only a smidgen of the annoyance I felt, "Did Sugar Ray Robinson *plan* to fight Rocky Graziano or did they just run into one another in the ring?" When my mother asked, "Are those boys from school?" I shook my head and quickly switched metaphors, asking, "Did David *plan* to shoot a pebble at Goliath? After all, he was fighting a *giant* for his *life*." My mother's question was in the same league as her suggestion to have Anthony to lunch to befriend him. Anthony McDougall could bend the metal swings when he was mad. He was much older than me and twice my size. Of *course* I planned it ahead or I wouldn't be alive to tell the tale! No, I hadn't planned for him to go to the hospital with a concussion, I just wanted to draw blood.

The only thing that I lied about was the issue of planning it alone. I don't know why I lied about that but I had an unsettling idea that some people, like Constable Lombardy and Irene, the cosmetician at the drugstore, didn't fully approve of Roy. I didn't know why but I felt it. I thought maybe it was because he lived in Niagara Falls instead of Lewiston, which made him a bit of a foreigner. Truthfully I didn't know the reason, but I'd learned long ago not to share everything about my relationship with Roy with my parents. Besides, he was the only one who really tried to help me. If it hadn't been for him I'd have been bald by the time *they* stopped Anthony.

My father never once in my entire life alluded to what would eventually be referred to as "the Anthony episode." All he said on the following morning was that I should dress for work since there was no reason "to make idle hands the devil's workshop." He said I would work from 6:00 a.m. until the store closed at 9:00 p.m. and he cashed out at ten. Then I could come home with him. He said only one thing which chilled me: "This will be your schedule from now on *unless you return to school*."

The second I got to work I tore down the narrow stairs to Roy's makeshift office located in a nook under the sidewalk grate, separated from the rest of the storage room by orange crates. By this time I'd become rather frantic, and pictured myself sharing a couch with elder Mad Bear, and a hairdresser with Mrs. Poole. I'd be referred to as the girl with the third-grade education. Now I'd never get a chance to grow up and enter the Franciscan convent and become a scientist in the Congo like the sister in *The Nun's Story*. (I actually had no idea that was my life's ambition until I was sure that I was deprived of it.) I could see myself at Forest Lawn where we dropped off medicine to the guard with all the keys. I'd be their youngest patient and they'd have to shorten a little straitjacket especially for me.

Roy leaned back in his swivel chair, put his arms behind his head, and laughed his belly laugh when I told him what had happened. He hit his desk with his huge hand in actual fits of hysterics when I told him about the ambulance, and how I had to be driven home, and he was virtually doubled over when I got to the part about the psychiatrist. Actually, when Roy found the whole thing so funny I began to see the humour in the episode. We were laughing so hard I had tears running down my face before long. I did the whole imitation of Linda Low's tattle-tale speech and Brian Muller's bad imitation of *Dragnet*.

I acknowledged that I was fairly worried about the psychiatrist, and Roy assured me that most of them were just little guys, and a lot of them weren't even Americans. He told me that of course I was sane and that any psychiatrist would see that in about one minute. "I seen them headshrinkers and them places." (I should have known this — Roy had been everywhere and seen everything.) "They goin' to ask you the days a the week and if you be gettin' messages from other planets — stuff like that. You'll be home in an hour. It's like poppin' in to see Dr. Laughton, only it's for your head." Roy got out of his swivel chair with its leaking stuffing and jostled me by punching my shoulder. He hunkered down so we were eye to eye and said, "They just be jivin' you, girl. I know ya better than that psychiatrist be knowing ya and I knowed some psychos in the army and I can tell ya you ain't one. If *I* knows that then some head shrinker'll figure it on out." I sank into my chair in relief as he continued. "The upside is ya got a break from grade three. You already know how to read and write and do your figures and, what's more, I guarantee that Anthony McDougall will never mess with ya again. When he sees ya coming he goin' to roll out *the red carpet*." Roy acted out much of his speech and he began rolling out the dust cloth on his desk and laughing.

I felt the balm of reassurance, and for the first time realized how nervous I had been over the last twenty-four hours. I remember noting that Roy never asked me if I'd mentioned his name at any point when I was grilled during the Anthony interrogation. We both put our feet on the desk and ate a Nestlé's Crunch bar and sang one of our favourites. "N-E-S-T-L-E-S, Nestlé's makes the very best — *chocolate*."

Getting declared sane was not quite as easy or quick as Roy had predicted. First of all, it took three weeks to get an appointment. I was out of school until after I'd seen the doctor, so word travelled. As I sat on a bench outside Helms's Dry Goods Store one spring day, smelling the dew-soaked honeysuckle and licking my popsicle, I heard Mrs. Helms say to the butcher, who happened to be Mr. Helms, "Poor Janet and Jim McClure. Cathy can't go back to school until her nervous breakdown is over." Mrs. Johnson, who managed the shoe department which sold only overshoes in the winter, rubbers in the spring, and Keds sneakers in the summer (navy or white), piped in, "I always said she was too clever by half." Mr. Helms, not a man of many words, but one who only spoke to cap off others' statements, giving them a certain irrefutable finality, said, "They had her too late. Never a good thing." I decided at that moment that they had seen my last imitation of Ed Sullivan, to say nothing of Mr. Ed, Lucy and Desi having a fight, or bacon frying. Let them find someone else to entertain them, someone who wasn't born too late.

To compound the wait, my father wanted me to go to a Buffalo psychiatrist, presumably so I wouldn't be insane in front of any of the referring physicians from Niagara Falls that he knew, because he filled their prescriptions and ate breakfast with them. I suspected that finding a "child psychiatrist" wasn't easy since, as Roy said, they were little guys and mostly from other countries. I wondered how a child got the job — after all, it sounded as interesting as working in the store — but my mother assured me it wasn't a *child* psychiatrist, but an *adult* who studied children.

As my mother and I drove to Dr. Small's — I was as reassured by his name as I was impressed by Roy's amazing knowledge of how the world worked — she said, "Now just be yourself." I nodded my red-bowed, pigtailed head as I sat next to my mother in her crisp linen suit, white eyelet gloves, and navy hat. I looked down at what felt like a foreign body decked out in my red plaid pleated

skirt, red tights, patent leather Mary Janes, and a white blouse
with smocking and puff sleeves. My mother rarely took a stand on
anything; however, this particular morning she refused to let me
wear my cowboy suit, my holster, and my ten-gallon hat or my
boots with spurs. I'd worn them every other day, and all I usually
had to do was make a little fuss and my mother would relent on
the dress and the matching socks she had so carefully laid out on
my black rocking chair. Often the outfit was accompanied by
what she vainly hoped was the ultimate enticement — a matching hair band. However, today she stuck to her guns and made me
don this "Heidi goes to the psychiatrist" ensemble.

As we drove past Hooker Chemical Company we quickly
rolled up the windows or else we knew our eyes would start
smarting by the time we hit the Grand Island Bridge. While I was
baking in the car, my mother chose this airtight moment to drone
on: "Dr. Laughton has written a referring letter to Dr. Small, but
if I were you I'd be sure to tell him that you never *meant* for
Anthony to be hospitalized, and he fainted from the sight of blood
and hit his head."

I nodded. Trying to add a tad of levity, I said, "If Anthony
McDougall turns out to be brain-damaged from the fall, who
could tell?"

My mother said, "Well, for heaven's sake, don't say *that*. . . ." She
shook her head as though she were only beginning to realize what
a genetic mutant she had produced. I could see her apprehension
heating up until she finally managed to spill out, "Also . . . I don't
think it's worth mentioning the whole episode where you thought
the RCA Victor television was talking to you. I don't think everyone needs to know all our business." As she paid the parking lot

attendant, my mother's hand shook, and she dabbed little tears from the inner corners of her sunglasses, saying her allergies were bothering her.

The waiting room had no receptionist or nurse and I wondered what kind of show this Small guy was running. We each picked up our respective *Life* magazines; my mother chose "What To Do About Germ Warfare?" and I chose an issue with Dean Martin and Jerry Lewis splayed on the cover — they were jumping in the air with their hands covering their ears and their mouths were frozen in donut o's in terrified screams as though someone was sending electric currents through their brains. As I began browsing the article entitled "America's Most Successful Comedy Team," I snuck glances at the motley crew around me. I made the mistake of catching the unblinking eye of some kid who looked as though he was raised in an incubator, and still looked half-baked. He wore his corduroy pants high up on his chest in a kind of princess waistline with a big belt. He caught what I thought was one of my most extremely furtive glances and said, "What's your name?" sounding like a 78 record playing at 33. As soon as I said, "Cathy," he said, "Cathy, what's your name?" Not having a long fuse, I repeated my name with some irritation, and then he said it twice: "Cathy, Cathy, what's your name? Cathy, Cathy, what's your name?" His mother just kept looking at her *Life* magazine cover with a cheerful teenage girl and boy sailing entitled "Discovering the Fun of Being Pretty." My mother kept looking at her magazine as well, so I said, "Forget it." He continued in his staccato blast, "Cathy, what's your name? Forget it, forget it." And on it went.

Another boy sat there picking tiny pieces of invisible lint off his pants. His lips were all dry and peeling. Eventually we all ignored the parrot boy who wouldn't stop. There was another boy about thirteen years old who looked more normal than the other two. His mother had her hair done in one of those teased French twists coated with multi layers of hairspray that looked as though it housed spiders who burrowed and laid eggs in her brain before she ever washed it. She was furiously ripping out something from a magazine with Jack Paar on the cover. Her son spoke only once and that was to tell his mother that he had to use the washroom. She replied, "Well, you should have thought of that at home, shouldn't you," and continued ripping from her *Saturday Evening Post*. My mother and I exchanged glances over that one.

Finally Dr. Small, holding a manila folder, poked his head out of the door and called me in. He was fairly short with dark curly hair and glasses, but he didn't have a foreign accent. He folded his hands on his desk in front of his minuscule clock and didn't say anything for some time. I guess he was *looking* to see if I was sane. I wanted to be careful not to pick at any lint or repeat what he said. Finally, I began to wonder if I was supposed to talk on my own and tell him what had happened, but I didn't want to display any insanity. Since I wanted to make up to my mother for dragging her on this torturous excursion, I decided to follow her advice to the letter. The first thing I did was to tell Dr. Small that I never meant to hospitalize Anthony with a concussion, that he fainted from the sight of blood. Then I told him there was no point in going into the RCA Victor talking-television episode. Now that I'd cleared the decks, I could relax.

Dr. Small never alluded to the "Anthony episode" but began asking about my family. I told him the truth, that I didn't really have a family, just a mother and father. When he asked if they ever fought, I told him they never once raised their voices. He said that was very "unusual." The way he said the word *unusual*, I felt he was hinting that it might be insane. Then he wanted to know how my parents punished me. I wondered what he meant by *punishment*. If they never got angry, how could they punish me — for what? Then he suggested that possibly I'd forgotten it. He said that maybe when my parents got mad at me it was too frightening to remember. I couldn't argue with that.

Then he switched tactics and said it must be nice to live in such a pleasant home, and I assured him that it was. He then asked me what I did with my free time and I told him that I worked sixty hours a week in the summer and twenty hours during the school year. He seemed to think this was unusual, which he indicated by lifting one eyebrow and nodding slightly, so I told him it was doctor's orders. I then assured him that he would be receiving a letter from Dr. Laughton telling him I had a different metronome from other people and I needed to keep busy. When he said he had received the letter, I just stared at him — why was he asking me, then?

Then he asked me what my mother and I did together, and I told him that we watched *Queen for a Day* on television, and then we went to Schoonmaker's Restaurant together. He said, as though I had trouble following his simple question, "I don't mean what do you do on *special* days, what do you do on *most* days?" I told him we went to Schoonmaker's most days except for Ed Sullivan night and then we ate leftover food from the brunch at Schneider's after twelve-o'clock mass. He asked why we ate at a restaurant and I told him we enjoyed ourselves. Clearly not finding this a fruitful line of questioning for uncovering insanity, he moved on. When he asked if I helped my mother clean, I said she didn't clean because Dolores did it, and besides my mother had to work on her emerging African nations papers. He asked me if anything frightening ever happened to me, and I decided to leave Roy out of the entire conversation in case Dr. Small put two and two together and figured out that Roy had masterminded "the Anthony episode." I didn't tell about the death of the baby at Mad Bear's, the ice storm, or the time Trent McMaster lost his fingers when we dared him to sled on the whirlpools. I didn't tell about Franky Schmidt, who made us do daring feats to be members of the Bloods. I had learned "remorse" was the key issue, and I didn't want to look as though I was woefully lacking in it. Since I actually had no idea which one of these events showed lack of remorse, I steered clear of them all.

Then he asked me, if there was one thing about myself or my life that I could change what would it be. I was stumped. I felt my life was just great. I thought long and hard and finally just to fill the silence I said that I wished that I could be better and that I wished I had no sins to confess in confession and that I really wished Mother Agnese and Sister Immaculata would appreciate me in the same way people from my home and the drugstore cared for me. I was surprised when I heard myself saying this. As I heard the words coming out of my mouth they sounded a little shaky, as though they'd come from someone who lived inside my heart, but rarely made an appearance. You could have knocked me over with a feather as stinging tears started to pool in my eyes but, thank God, they didn't spill over.

Dr. Small said in a quiet voice that maybe my mother and father never corrected me because they were afraid of me. I asked him if he really thought that God, who designed a whole universe to work perfectly, would give children to parents who didn't know how to take care of them. Usually bringing God up was a perfect shield, but Dr. Small didn't seem fazed, and then came at me with the following curve ball: Did I ever wonder if other employees at work never corrected me because I was the boss's daughter? After all, they'd had to look after me since I was four. This was the most hurtful thing anyone had ever said to me. I had grown up with people at work, and felt I had always carried my own weight and they were like a family to me. It had never occurred to me that they had ulterior motives for liking me, or that Roy had been babysitting me instead of working with me, until horrible Dr. Small planted that seed. I looked right at him and said that I guessed he believed that if I was really bad or *insane* (at this point I decided to let it all hang out), my parents, who for some reason had no idea how to be parents, would be the last to notice bad behaviour, and the other workers at the store wouldn't correct me because I was the boss's daughter. So I guess the only people who were able to tell me *the truth* about me would be Mother Agnese or Sister Immaculata.

Dr. Small looked surprised that I had interpreted him this way, and he said that he was just trying to tell me that he saw my dilemma. He said I wasn't a child at home or at work and I had no rules in either place. It must have been hard at school for the teachers to impose childhood rules on me, and hard for me to accept them when I felt they didn't apply to me. He said he was only trying to sympathize with me and see things from my point of view. (Yeah, right, Buddy. I didn't usually feel this bad with so much sympathy.) That was the end of my cooperation with him.

Even Mother Agnese didn't come up with this kind of below-the-belt stuff. I simply stared at him steely-eyed until the end of the session.

He tried to weasel back into my good graces, but I'd permanently decamped. When he said it was time to go, I just sat there waiting for him to write my "sane certificate." To my shock he booked another appointment for "testing." I had no idea there was a "sanity test." He called my mother in and I remember what he said verbatim, since I was already in shock that I was not leaving with my sane certificate. I felt like leaping over his wide desk with his hideous family picture (his wife wore her hair piled on top of her head and looked like Bullwinkle) and stabbing him in the heart with an oversize compass — just in case he thought the only dangers were on the streets of New York. He said that he was sure my mother had been worried about me and he could certainly see that I had "a temper" which could lead to "complications." He continued, "Both Catherine and I believe that she needs more limits at home and some more time with female playmates."

What a liar! I began swinging my patent leather feet in rage while my mother looked totally nonplussed. She never said that I had a *job* with *responsibilities* and people *counted* on me to get things done, or that I had no desire to make tiny hard cakes from the Betty Crocker junior baking set with Judy and Susie Baker. Instead, she acted like this guy was the Father, Son, and Holy Ghost wrapped up in one. Stunned, I sat there like a lump of petrified wood as I heard my mother, the blue-linen turncoat, say, "Oh yes, Doctor, that is something my husband and I discussed, and we agreed on both of these suggestions." She lowered her voice and continued, "After the Anthony episode happened. It is just that she seemed so independent and happy that we left things too much alone."

—

The next two weeks of my life were unremittingly hellish. When not at work my mother arranged to have my neighbours, the Baker sisters, come over to "play" nearly every day. The first day they brought their Lennon Sisters paper-doll set. Although it was a beautiful morning with the river running, the lilacs in bloom, the magnolia buds strewn on the lawn like giant confetti, I was a prisoner in my own home.

The staccato blasts of the Bloods wafted into the open windows as they sped by on their bikes. I could hear the tat-a-tat-tat of the playing cards they had placed in their bike spokes with clothes-pins so their wheels would make gearchanging noises. I felt the rhythmical beating of the cards calling to me to run with the pack; yet I was chained to my scissors for *hours* on end, shackled to the Lennon Sisters paper pile. The Schmidt brothers bustled back and forth playing Dick Tracy with walkie-talkies made from two orange-juice cans connected with clothesline which *I* had care-fully constructed.

I watched them through the leaded glass bars of my parents' living room window as I sat cutting out the Lennon Sisters dresses that were paper replicas of those worn on the *Lawrence Welk Show*, where the sisterly gaggle warbled weekly. Susie actually made us sing a medley of their songs. I was great at doing one task and could smoke with concentration; however, I never mastered doing two tasks simultaneously. As we sang "Kay-sa-rah-sa-rah, whatever will be will be," and the Baker girls' favourite, "Whip-er-will whip-er-will you and I know, Tammy, Tammy, Tammy's in love," I cut mine all wrong and snipped off all the tabs that held the clothes on the cardboard figures. Judy and Sue Baker were disgusted with me for having wrecked three evening gowns. (As my mother said, "Haven't they ever heard of tape?") Cutting out the pleated skirts with those jagged edges was a true exercise in patience. My fingers were tired and blistered by the time we finished snipping the entire wardrobe from the large paper sheets. I thought *then* maybe the fun would begin. I had a desire to be sane and if playing Lennon Sisters paper dolls was the ticket, I was willing to pay my admission.

Susie, the eldest of the sisters, placed each of us on the floor of my living room and we each had a home for our Lennon sister under the skirt of a wing chair. We had to keep our clothes in neat piles, with casuals in one pile and formals in another. The skirt of the chair kept knocking my apparel askew and the heating vent behind the chair kept blowing my wardrobe from one end of my wing-chair home to the other, creating a storm that rivalled the one in Kansas at Dorothy's house in *The Wizard of Oz*. However, Judy's and Susie's seemed perfectly organized. Susie had the eldest two Lennon sisters, Judy the middle sister, and I had the youngest. Susie held her doll in the middle of the floor and said we were all going out on "a convertible date." Everyone got dressed. So we all had to find a paper dress and hat and fold our tabs back on our cardboard figures. Then Susie held out her doll and walked around the room. I guess that meant we were on a driving date, although there were never any men dolls. Then she said, "Oh, we're going to a debutante ball where I'm going to be on the throne commit-tee so we have to all wear strapless gowns. . . . Oh, except for Cathy. Her Lennon sister is much too young for strapless. She will have to wear capped sleeves." *Great.* There was a lot of flurry and we all went back to our skirted wing chairs and changed paper dresses and emerged to admire Susie as her Lennon sister lay on the coffee table inert — apparently she was on her throne. Since she couldn't bend at the knees, I guess she had to be a reclining debutante queen, sort of like Cleopatra. Then it was time for the "splash party" after the dance, and now even *I* guessed that we had to scurry back to our chairs to change our Lennon sisters' clothes yet again and this time we had to don our bathing suits, wrap covers with matching hats, and gold wedge high heels.

On it went, day after gruesome day, until the day arrived when I heard the insistent whine as the Baker sisters leaned on the doorbell, and I ran out the back door and locked myself in the car and beeped the horn whenever my mother tried to talk to me. Finally she gave up. Believe it or not, the Baker sisters didn't get the hint. They simply stood stunned in the gravel driveway in their matching flowered sundresses with the thick straps. I heard my mother saying that I wasn't myself. Still they stood. Finally my mother had to tell them to go home. They seemed shocked by the news that they were not wanted.

—

The testing week was even more silly. I was now used to the waiting room at Dr. Small's office, and was not nearly as shocked as I'd been the first time. In fact, the term "nuts" never shocked me again. My only concern was not becoming one. I actually took to doing imitations of "parrot boy," "Mr. Lint," and "twisted French mother" on our way home from Buffalo, and my mother couldn't help but laugh.

The testing took place in a room off what Dr. Small referred to as his "consulting room." (Strange name since he never consulted with me.) This room had separate stations in it where you moved from one activity to another while he held a stopwatch like the TV show *Beat the Clock*. In the centre of the room there was a little table and two chairs with decals of Humpty Dumpty falling off the wall while looking terrified in mid-air. Dr. Small was lucky he was so puny so he could fit into the little chair without much of a squeeze. Sitting at the diminutive table opposite me, he said, with what I thought was a speech impediment involving the letter R, but my mother assured me was a New York accent, "Well, Catherine, now here I have a number of cards with pictures of Blacky the dog. Blacky lives in a family just like you. He has a mother and father. I'd like to show you some pictures of Blacky doing different things and you can tell me a story about Blacky and what *you* think he is doing and why."

I nodded, feeling my shoulders lighten with sudden relief. All I had to do was tell a story about Blacky and I was out of this laughing academy and declared sane. One thing I knew about myself — I was a good storyteller. Everyone listened as I spun yarns at the post office. Even adults stood transfixed by what Dolores referred to as my "tall tales." I had a routine at the post office of ripping open an innocuous advertisement from Sears and Roebuck and pretending that I'd received mail from Howdy Doody and Roy Rogers, and my speciality was the invitation I got from Walt Disney who ran the Mickey Mouse Club requesting that I replace Annette, the most popular Mouseketeer. I also did song-and-dance numbers. One of my most popular was bobbing up and down on imaginary Trigger as I imitated Roy Rogers singing "Happy Trails," and for an encore I sang one of his earlier songs from his radio days, one of my favourite bright red 78s entitled "Don't Fence Me In."

The first card Dr. Small placed before me had a dog, presumably Blacky, drinking milk from his mother's body. That was really disgusting, so naturally I chose to ignore it and said that Blacky had seen a scary movie and was hiding under his mother and closing his eyes until the film was over.

"Oh," Dr. Small said noncommittally. "Could you tell me more about that."

"Sure," I went on. "Blacky had just been to see the movie *Old Yeller* and was really upset when the dog had to be shot, so Blacky hid under his mother." Dr. Small looked sceptical so I added, "You know that would be a scary movie for a dog to watch."

Dr. Small wasn't giving up on this one. He said quietly, "Some people actually think that Blacky is drinking milk from his mother in this picture."

"God, I wouldn't want to meet them," I answered in a tone I was sure would reassure him that I had seen nothing like that to cast doubts on my sanity.

"Let's try another picture."

I looked at a picture of Blacky baring his teeth and chewing on a collar that had the word *Mamma* on it in big bold letters. I was getting the dawning realization that these were trick cards. The idea was if you saw Blacky doing these sick things then you were insane. In order to look as though I was travelling with a full deck, I'd have to put a different spin on Blacky's activities. "Well, Blacky is really a good dog. He is carrying his mother's collar for her because she got a crook in her neck in her doghouse, which is too low. Blacky is offering to carry it for her."

"Why is he snarling and growling?" Dr. Small snarled.

"Oh, he isn't. He just doesn't want to get it all wet so he is keeping his lips open. Who wants a drooled-on collar?"

On it went. In each picture Blacky was doing something more vile than in the last. I really started to sweat when Blacky made a giant bowel movement in front of his mother's house and in another when he licked himself "down there." (In my family we used what my mother called "medical terms" to refer to bodily functions if we mentioned them at all.) I made sure that Dr. Small didn't have any idea that I had those "insane" thoughts and I kept the whole thing on the up and up. I said Blacky had dropped a Dairy Queen chocolate-dipped soft-ice-cream cone right in front of his dad's door and he was burying it so his dad wouldn't know he's been careless and wasted his ten-cent cone. Unfortunately he'd spilled some ice cream on himself (I cleverly didn't mention where) and in order to be a tidy dog he'd been embarrassed but had to lick it off.

Although I stayed on my toes, the test never seemed to end. I was sure God didn't test this much before he opened heaven's gate. Nor did Joan of Arc have to fight so much for her sanity. If her inquisitors had been this relentlessly devious, it was no wonder she finally said, "Just burn me at the stake."

The next week Dr. Small had set up a little dollhouse on one table and a farm and barnyard on another. He took the mother doll into the dollhouse and put her in front of the oven and asked what she was cooking. I drew a blank. Finally I said that she was drying mittens. We were very near to dropping the thin veneer of politeness we had precariously maintained throughout the Blacky caper. He asked if we were going to eat the mittens and I couldn't resist saying that I didn't want to pull the wool over his eyes but people who lived outside of New York City didn't eat mitten stroganoff. They ate in restaurants.

He seemed a little taken aback by the mention of him as a New Yorker and he moved on to the toy barn. In front of a pig stall was a little girl doll in blond pigtails that stuck out at a ninety-degree angle (speaking of insane), wearing a red gingham dress. He asked what she would do with the pigs. Would she feed them, he asked leadingly. I knew better than to wallow with the swine on this one, knowing what a sane person would do. I said I'd kill all the pigs before they ate any more food, cut them up, and sell pork chops in a stand by the side of the road. I'd make sure I was out selling them during rush hour. I added that part just to let him know that I wasn't so stupid I'd stand out on a country road all day with no traffic. After all, I'd been selling newspapers outside for years.

On it went. I think I acted as "sane as the next person," as Roy said when I regaled him with my responses to the Blacky dog cards, dollhouse, and farm set. Finally, after my mother had several more visits with Dr. Small (my father and I were working so we couldn't go), I was declared sane!

It wasn't that I exactly admired Dr. Small. In fact, I thought he was appropriately named. Yet the *job* appealed to me. However, I'd get a nurse and larger furniture instead of that Munchkin stuff. I liked the idea of being the deity who decided if you were sane or not. It sure beat being on the other side of the desk trying to look sane for the Dr. Smalls of this world. I found it far more comforting to switch chairs. If I couldn't beat Father Flanagan or Mother Superior, at least I could find a role that was safe from them.

I was to return to school the following Monday after five weeks away. I knew that people had been counting my marbles and it was a little nerve-racking going back after so long. Anthony had his stitches out but was still wearing a filthy bandage just for effect. Roy, realizing that I was edgy, said the most important time would be the first five minutes of my return. He said I had to act as though I'd had a purpose in what I had done, and my mission had been accomplished. I had to confront Anthony right away to show him and the rest of the class that I wasn't buying into the sane/insane red herring. "You gots to profile by Anthony the second you're back and let him know right off the bat that you're back for good. Let him know he ain't won this round. Take *nothing* from him." Roy swaggered up to me in the stockroom and stared at me in what my mother would have called an "insolent" way. He walked too close and I had to move back. "Make him move out of *your* way. He needs to know the compass only the beginnin' and you ain't buyin' *none* of this insanity jive." Roy said a battle of the wits is no different from a battle in the ring. You have to maintain dominance and never let up. He told me to refer to my time off as my "spring furlough."

So I strolled into school the following Monday wearing all new clothes that my mother was only too happy to buy, tossed my lunch box on the rack above my coat hook with gay abandon. It barely cleared Clyde Ayers' head and everyone turned to look at me as they took off their yellow rain slickers. I said I couldn't believe that I was back in this dump. I said I'd had a great time burning the midnight oil watching *Gunsmoke* and *Have Gun Will Travel* and going to bed whenever I pleased. I paraded into the classroom and felt all the eyes burning into my back. Anthony was standing in line at the pencil sharpener. I got my pencil and strode purposefully over to the pencil-sharpening lineup. I cut right in front of Anthony and said, "I'm next." There was a silence. I waited with my back to him. Sister Immaculata stopped correcting papers at her desk. The room went dead quiet and Anthony waited behind me while I sharpened my pencil to a fine point. It was over.

CHAPTER 7

marie sweeney

Roy had time for everyone. Work got done but it didn't always

seem to come first. If Mrs. Glish, who ran a bakery out of her back

kitchen, invited us in for warm pastry, Roy and I always had the

time to sit at her table for a chat and a slice of hot kugel. We just

pushed our delivery schedule ahead, and watched her flabby

triceps quiver as she rolled out pastry dough. If Roy was invited in for life-sustaining libations — for "Christmas cheer," a shot for "the damned cold," a cool beer on a hot day, or a patriotic toast to the "I Like Ike" campaign — we relished the hospitality of others. As Roy said, quoting the great Seneca, "Nothing is ours except time." (Although I could "tell time," I hadn't quite figured out exactly what I was measuring since my father's approach was to quote Ben Franklin's line "Time is money" whenever I was "lolly-gagging.")

Christmas was my favourite delivery season because of all the outdoor decorations and the festive atmosphere. In our customers' homes I was always warmed by the wafting scents of ginger and cloves that met me at the door. I basked in all the kitchen bustling, the stoves heating the rooms to the point that condensation dripped from the windows. It seemed strange yet magical to me that cookies could be made in a home kitchen of all places, and that so many people seemed to do it really amazed me. When I told my mother about what I'd seen, she seemed equally amazed, pointing out that I hadn't even witnessed the shopping or the cleaning up!

Roy and I were frequently given gifts of assorted homemade cookies and candied fruit squares that had exotic names like "conga bars," "grumble bars," "Hello Dollies," or "fly catchers." They were placed in neat layers of waxed paper in Currier and Ives covered tins. We devoured our favourites en route, the ones with the frosting, the coloured sprinkles, and silver beads, and then took our daily leftovers into Shim-Shacks Tavern and placed them on the bar, where everyone eagerly congregated to poke through layers of Santas, snowmen, bells, and stars of Bethlehem.

I took it upon myself to hand out the type of cookie that I thought each patron would enjoy. Roy suggested we simply leave the canisters open on the bar, but I told him they were *our* cookies, so I could decide who got what. I matched the personality of Buzz, the bartender, with Rudolph, because they both had red noses, Black Cloud got Grumble bars because he never talked, and on it went. Roy warned everybody, "Careful! In this bar you can always tell a man by his cookie." While we ate our bounty, Buzz gave us all Irish coffees on the house as a Christmas treat and proposed a toast to "wash down the holy wafers of Christ's birthday" and we all clinked glasses. Buzz taught me to dip my ginger snap into my coffee until, as he said, "the *exact* second when it loses its snappiness, but still isn't mushy."

Roy laughingly told Buzz he should *never* tell me to do anything *exactly*, or he would be unleashing a monster. Tapping the side of my head, he continued, "She'll be hell-bent to get it done *exactly* right." Roy assured the chuckling bar patrons that he had not heard the end of the *exact* moment when you should dip your ginger snap into your Irish coffee. No one could do imitations better than Roy. He caught every nuance and blew it out of proportion until you were forced to laugh at yourself. This time it was of an evangelical tent preacher: "*Lord, Lord,* save me, please," he said looking heavenward. "Do you know how many ideas, then theories, and finally rules — *yes rules, Lord* — I'm goin' to hear? Why, they'll be more *rules* than McClure's Drugs got pills. You think I'm not goin' to have to learn from Catherine McClure, the archangel of exactitude, as to how long the whole world should dip their ginger snap into their Irish coffee?" Roy's arms lifted heavenward and his voice went up a full octave. "You miss that moment, Buzz my son, and you is dammed *exactly* to the wrong side of the river of Jordan." Even the Indians laughed, as they had seen me gauging angles off the boards in the electronic bowling game and measuring to make sure my opponents' steel puck was not touching the red line. After all, things looked different from different angles and we had money on every game.

There were several reasons why that episode stands out in my mind. It was fun and relaxed. I must have had some premonition that life doesn't have that many warm, wonderful moments when everyone is having a good time, so I squirreled that one away. No one asked if *I* should have an Irish coffee — it just got poured. I had no idea it had liquor in it (boy, did I warm up quickly and the saying "a shot for the cold" suddenly came alive for me), but I knew I was doing something that made me totally acceptable as an equal, as I sat with my short legs swinging on the impossibly high bar stool. I realize, in retrospect, that those people had a bit too much Irish in their coffee, but still it is a freeze frame of perfection in my mind.

I also loved ritual. We did the Irish coffee toast every year (I got mad at Buzz if he changed even one word of his testimonial) and I shared the cookies and felt as though everyone knew me and accepted me along with my cookie-matching and my "bossiness" (a word originally introduced by Dolores that made me cringe, but was echoed by Irene and on rare occasions my mother, who whispered to me as she dropped me off at kindergarten, "Don't forget to take small bites at snack time and don't be too bossy").

This episode has stayed with me because I had a revelation in Shim-Shacks that Christmas Eve of 1952, as the jukebox played Bing Crosby's "White Christmas." I understood for the first time that not all the world shared the values of my family. I thought it was *inherently* good to be exacting. Everyone in my home and environs seemed to revere punctiliousness as a trait approaching godliness. It would not have been strange to say, for example, "He or she is a good person, very meticulous, precise, religious, and honest." For the first time I saw that Roy, the Indians, and the other people at Shim-Shacks didn't value exactness or precision, at least not in the way I had learned it. In fact, they thought it was a neurotic manifestation that they tolerated because they liked me, but in itself, *exactly* measuring and labelling things was about as useful as flying a plane into the sky to try to see Jesus. Up until this point I had realized that some people were lacking in precision, but felt they knew they were falling short of the mark. I suddenly realized that something I thought was inherently good was really only a trait peddled by a relatively small, albeit powerful, circle of people in my life.

I guess we all remember moments in time when we realize some truth about the world, something much bigger than what is happening to us at the moment. My small town suddenly fell into perspective and became a dot on the globe. Alas, Lewiston was a town that for me was showing its first signs of shrinking.

—

Roy and I drove around in the dreary snowbelt that seemed to get slushier and dirtier every day as winter wore on, but in December there was a spectacular transformation. The once austere lines of white clapboard colonials, or stolid Germanic brick homes, were softened by leafy cedars which waved to us in the winter wind and welcomed us wherever we went. The homes were bedecked in ruby and emerald enchantment which came alive at sunset.

When I read the story of Sleeping Beauty, the part where she woke up and all the overgrown courtyard turned into lush blossoms, it reminded me of sleepy Lewiston that awoke at Christmastime. Even nature cooperated and offered a fresh snowfall as a clean backdrop.

There was a contest in Lewiston for the top three outdoor Christmas decorations, and nearly everyone participated. The only notable exception were the Wolfsons, where the father was a physicist for Bell labs. My father shook his head when their lack of participation was mentioned. He said he thought their behaviour had "un-American leanings." This was a particularly scary bit of information since Mr. Wolfson had worked on the atomic bomb in Los Alamos before moving to Lewiston. I assumed that the U.S. government didn't know the Wolfsons would be the type who wouldn't participate in Christmas decorations, or he never would have had security clearance. I told my father at The Horseshoe Restaurant, in front of the other businessmen who always ate breakfast there, that mother had said the Wolfsons were Jewish, and may not feel comfortable putting up Christmas decorations. My father said, "Well, they had no trouble eating a turkey on Thanksgiving or coming to the Fourth of July fireworks, now did they?" And Abe Wallins, my father's buddy, who had a clothing store close by the pharmacy, said, "Jewish, bluish, it's a national holiday. We're all Americans, for Christ's sake."

One prize was for the best Nativity, one was for beauty (I guess the judges thought Nativity and beauty couldn't go together), and the last was for originality. Roy and I considered ourselves local experts, since we drove around all day and were conversant with decorations in the hinterlands of nearly all of Niagara County. The only thing we loved more than the decorations was gambling, or as Roy referred to it, "the science of risk." We placed wagers on the best decorations and then again on who we thought would win the prizes. Of course we had to take handicaps into consideration, such as the politics of choice, who won last year and couldn't win two years in a row, who were the judges, etc. Roy was very good at predicting what *others* would choose, and he knew that Seymour Knox, a benefactor of the Albright-Knox Art Gallery in Buffalo and an aficionado of modern art, would be one of the judges. Roy was sure that the other members of the committee would kowtow to him and something "way-out" would be chosen. Over the years I came to understand a more sophisticated minimalist aesthetic through Knox's choices, after getting burned the first few years by choosing "tinsel flash" or old-fashioned 'Twas-the-Night-Before-Christmas stuff. When you're staking a week's wages you can learn anything quickly. The contest took up all kinds of time at Mom's Hamburger Shoppe and at The Horseshoe, although no one seemed to care at Shim-Shacks. I had placed heavy odds on the traditional Duponts of nylon fame, and Roy had bets on the more unusual Hookers of Hooker Chemical.

I still remember entering the circular drive of the Dupont home (actually, the wife was said to be the Dupont; although the family had another surname, the family home was always referred to as "the Duponts'") on the edge of the Niagara Escarpment overlooking the frozen village and the Niagara River, winding along below the American and Canadian escarpments like an albino snake. I loved seeing the Christmas boughs held up by twenty-foot red-ribbon bows which festooned the eaves of the Tudor mansion. All the huge conifers were covered with coloured lights that peeked through a blanket of snow. It took two men to hoist the wreath onto the wrought-iron hooks on the studded double doors with the big black handles. The keyhole was so huge that a matching black cover swung over it when the key was not in use. A spotlight shone on the doors, catching the glitter of the gold-sprayed foot-long pine cones from the coulter pine trees of the west coast. The Duponts' dog, a black boxer named Holly (whom Roy addressed as Joe Louis), had her own doghouse with a stained-glass window depicting St. Peter holding the keys to heaven, and her own little wreath made of — you guessed it — holly, and tiny white lights on her swinging door. She sat outside her mini-mansion barking until Roy and I came over and made a big fuss over her decorations, and Roy shadow-boxed with her.

I dreaded going to the Duponts' door alone to deliver the Dilantin, phenobarbital, syringes, and other paraphernalia for their daughter, so I usually made Roy accompany me. No one I knew had ever seen her, but Dolores said that her sister-in-law from the Falls, who had cleaned house for the Duponts, told her the daughter wore a harness, and there was a house rule that no one could look her in the eye or she'd go after your peepers like a hungry buzzard on the Kalahari. Roy said that if he had to wear a harness, he wouldn't want anyone, least of all Dolores's loose-lipped sister-in-law, gawkin' at him either.

Mrs. Dupont always invited us in during the Christmas season to see their tree, saying I was about the same age as her daughter, who was "indisposed at the moment." The tree which stood in their cathedral-ceiling living room was the most magnificent I'd ever seen. Each year since the 1800s the family had added a new ornament representing something topical for that particular year.

Roy and I had to guess which was the new ornament and what it represented. Roy was far better at the game than I; he was never in the room for thirty seconds before he spotted it. In 1952 he picked out an ornament at least thirty feet up, the Maid of the Mist Ferry ensconced inside a dome of water which, when heated under a tree light, sprayed a mist. Who was about the size of a pinky nail in one of the tiny portholes, wearing a Santa hat? None other than Marilyn Monroe! Roy said with nonchalance, "Why, Cath, look, there is Marilyn wavin' out at us, probably promotin' her new movie, *Niagara*."

As the years rolled on and Mrs. Dupont gradually became more impressed by Roy's astounding visual acuity, she made the game progressively harder. By 1962 she greeted us at the door saying she was sure she could stump us. But as soon as she slid back the parlour doors and we saw the tree with its hundreds of ornaments and lights, Roy's eagle eye cut right through the Christmas cacophony and spotted a tiny red-and-green plane with glittering wheels, near the top of the tree. The pilot had antlers and the cockpit was full of Christmas presents. Not missing a beat, he said with calculated insouciance, "Why, that there would be the U-2 spy plane that crashed this year over Russia during a reconnaissance mission. That ain't no Rudolph. Why, I'd know Gary Powers even without his antlers. Must be drop-liftin' Christmas presents to Khrushchev." Incredulous, Mrs. Dupont asked how he knew. Roy looked perplexed, as though it was obvious: "Why, it's built like a jet and has the body of a glider. Got to be a U-2."

Later, when we had left the Duponts', I asked Roy how he had developed such a memory for detail. He said when you can't read and you need to remember how to get places in the delivery business, you have to be able to remember exactly what a spot looks like so you can retrace your steps. You had to remember each turn by a visual detail and, as he pointed out, "I didn't always have you." What I didn't understand was why, if he could tell the tiny features of planes and never forget the minutiae of any *three*-dimensional object, didn't he simply learn the twenty-six letters of the alphabet. I knew better than to ask him, because it was one of the few things I could tell embarrassed him. He'd come up with elaborate ruses to hide his illiteracy.

For twelve years neither Roy nor I ever once laid eyes on the Dupont daughter when we delivered her bags and bags of medicine. Dour nurses in white uniforms carrying gleaming steel utensils covered in white towels crept up and down the winding staircase and looked distinctly relieved when we arrived, the phenobarbital-toting angels of mercy. Mrs. Dupont would take us through their dark wainscotted hallways and show us her daughter's train set, which Roy referred to as "Grand Central." She had her own engine, so huge you could sit in it and drive around. It had a pull whistle, and made chugging noises. You actually passed scenery, and big plaster of Paris cows, and chugged by miniature road signs, and you could pull into a train station. Roy and I played on the train to make Mrs. Dupont happy, but kept our eyes on the door for fear the daughter, Lewiston's Boo Radley, would swoop down the stairs and pluck out our eyes. Once you got past the living room, there was such a pall cast upon that house that we always wanted to get out of there as soon as we felt it was polite to make a graceful exit.

The first few years Mrs. Dupont tried to give Roy a tip or Christmas money, but he wouldn't take it, saying that he got wages. I wondered why Roy didn't take the money, but as the years went on I understood he had his own rules. When she gave him a big green-ribboned fruitcake soaked in rum, he took it gladly, saying there was nothing like a hot toddy and a fruitcake snack on a cold delivering day.

I had a great affinity for labels. I had particular ardour for what my father called "binomial nomenclature," and labelled all my specimen jars, or dead animals, as Dolores referred to them, in Latin and English. Whenever I asked my father the name of anything, he gave me the general parameters and told me to look it up, and then always checked back with me the next day to see if I'd found it. We shared little binomial-nomenclature jokes, like when moths ate my mother's woollen winter underwear he said they had been "licentious lepidoptera." He taught me how to distinguish the phylum, species, genus, order, and class of my various wildlife. I still remember the day he told me to look up Homo sapiens and I found it was me! Whenever we found a stray pill behind the scale or the typewriter, he taught me to trace its origin by looking up its image in the drug compendium. He seemed enormously pleased if I found its exact spot in the universe. However, I didn't do it just for him; it was also a natural inclination of mine to label the world. It gave things an order which I found reassuring. Otherwise things just seemed to be a big buzzing jumbled mess which sometimes closed in on me.

As we dove down the steep hill from the Duponts' home in Lewiston Heights, into what was known as the village of Lewiston, I told Roy we could figure out the Duponts' daughter's disease if we looked up phenobarbital and Dilantin. I knew the former was to quiet you down, since Roy and I had been late in delivering Elder Mad Bear's once, and he'd gone on a rampage. I knew Dilantin was for epilepsy, because we had to deliver it to Belinda MacIntosh's house after she had a seizure in the lunch-room and almost swallowed her tongue, and knocked over the statue of St. Francis of Assisi, birds and all. Roy thought about what I said and replied, "I ain't so sure knowin' the name goin' to make one lick a difference. We all God's children no matter what we got. It's *one* tragedy that a man could invent nylon so all the women in this world could be happy wearing stockings again after the war, yet he couldn't invent a cure for his own daughter's disease." As he drove along he added, "Just one a life's little tricks, I guess."

As we headed down from the icy escarpment in our lowest gear, with our tire chains making sparks on the sanded incline, Roy announced the next stop would be Marie Sweeney's. I always liked going to Marie's house because it was definitely a way to step off the page of my own story. We usually had to spend a bit more time at Marie's place, because she needed Roy to help her put on her cortisone cream for what she referred to as her "devil's disease and flaming joints." Her hands were crippled up with arthritis and looked like gnarled roots that had grown in a pot that was too small. She usually held them up on her chest, cradling them next to her heart, to offer them the only comfort she could give them.

As we reached the foot of the hill and headed into the outskirts of town, I was reminiscing about what we'd been doing exactly one year ago that night on Christmas Eve. Roy and I had been barrelling out of the store on our last-minute deliveries when we passed the revolving door of last-minute shoppers who were barrelling in, mostly men, swarming Irene's cosmetic counter to buy whatever she recommended, which was always Evening in Paris perfume accompanied by what she felt was the ultimate enticement, "After all, *I* wear it." Roy once said the only good thing about being an astronaut and landing on the moon would be not having to smell Irene's Evening of Paris perfume. Ted, one of the other pharmacists, said he had never considered that angle before, but he could now justify the government spending for the space race. My father said, given what the store smelled like, he would be surprised if Evening of Paris was not the first thing the astronauts would smell upon taking their first step out of their capsule. Irene simply looked at us all nonplussed and said she assumed *part* of our problem was that none of us knew what Paris smelled like.

Roy had been waylaid by the cash register on this busiest of Christmas Eves and surveyed the impulse items. He held up a cheap stocking-stuffer candle in the shape of a red Santa Claus that had been sitting there eyeing the customers since early November, but was now finally making genuine eye contact with guilty last-minute Christmas shoppers. "Hey, boss," he asked my father, who was emptying the cash register and placing the money in burlap bags, "mind if I give this candle to Marie Sweeney when I drop off her Percodan — might be her only present." My father hesitated in his counting for a minute and Roy pressed on, opting for plan B: "Hey, it'll only be half-price after Christmas." My father continued his counting, but nodded his approval, and we were on our way. I grabbed a Christmas card for Marie and signed all our names to it, except for Irene who said she was "abstaining."

Christmas Eve last year seemed so long ago. I felt almost twice as old now. I understood so much more about the world. Last year I was shocked that a cheap candle would be Marie's only gift. After all, she lived in America, had a visit from Santa, to say nothing of her own nine children who would be bringing her presents. I now realized that Christmas bounty wasn't always fair. In fact, I wasn't even shocked by it anymore. What I still hadn't figured out was why God, who was good, would let Marie suffer with no presents. I was sure I would figure that out before I made my first communion next year.

Marie lived in a small flat above the Monte Carlo Hair Salon, which was connected to the angel-brick facade of the shabby Buena Vista Motel. Her stairs smelled like a combination of decaying fish and saturated kitty litter, which became more pungent the higher you climbed. Roy and I used to plug our noses and run with watering eyes to Marie's door, where there were paper signs written in nail polish saying, "Stay out." One also said, "If you're a Fuller Brush man — don't knock unless you want a brush with death."

Roy knocked on the unfinished plywood door and Marie grumbled with her Lauren Bacall gone-to-seed rasp, "Git movin'." When Roy rapped again she said, "Understand English or are ya from Canada?" However, when Roy said, "McClure's Drugs," she changed her tune, knowing that on the other side of that thin door were her painkillers and her cigarettes. Cockroaches pinged around the kitchenette counter sounding like rain on a tin patio roof. The room was always dark with long black velvet curtains shutting out the present. The furnishings were canvas lawn chairs assembled in a pathetic conversation circle. On the floor were indoor/outdoor carpeting samples donated by Hansen's Hardware.

Marie remained a murky figure in the corner who refused to

turn on the light. She only came into focus when *we* accommodated to *her* dark. She was so thin and wrinkled she looked like a yellow balloon that had been forgotten at the Volunteer Firemen's Peach Festival and had slowly shrivelled. Upon our arrival she tore open her Chesterfield carton and had Roy tap open a pack on the arm of her chair. She smoked by balancing the cigarette in the crook between her thumb and index finger. Once she got the cigarette to her lips she could grasp it tightly, a service her fingers could no longer perform. She held the cigarette exactly in the middle of her lips, while drinking from the right side of her mouth and talking out of the left with no apparent difficulty. Then she quickly pawed through the bag until she found the Percodan prescription and Roy helped her "wash it down" with a few Johnny Walkers while I had a Coke and Hostess Twinkies. I thought Roy was brave to apply the cream to those mangled stubs. When I told him later that he was like Jesus anointing the lepers, he shook his head and said, "It ain't so easy to lose your looks when you ain't got a backup plan." When I informed him that *everyone* got old, a favourite line of my mother's, he answered, "Poor Marie was sittin' on her groceries." I thought that this strange habit explained Marie's thin and withered look. Obviously she *sat* on her groceries instead of *eating* them. It was many years later when I heard a Joni Mitchell song about a prostitute "sitting on her groceries" that Roy's line jumped back to my mind.

As we all had our "Cokes-and-smokes chat," as Marie called it, she would reminisce about her life when she was a girl. I really liked that part. She told me not to be a ninny when I was in high school like she had been. I'd never heard a grown-up claim to have made a mistake, let alone own up to being a *ninny*. She said she was a shameless nincompoop to marry ol' Jim when she was still shy of fifteen, and have a baby, forever after referred to as "young Jim," by her sixteenth birthday. She looked disgustedly at me. "Can ya imagine what it felt like when I woke up from that nightmare and it weren't no dream and I weren't goin' nowhere. No siree! My ma said I'd made my bed — so now I could just lie in it. I had four more babies 'fore I knowed that it weren't God that was givin' em to me." Puzzled, I asked Marie who was giving her the babies. If it wasn't God then maybe it was the Archangel Gabriel of the Annunciation. "Oh, that would be ol' Jim hisself and he weren't no angel, I can tell ya that much. That was way back when he could still bully me, before he lost his legs to the sugar an' the drink and his mind was pickled in the hard stuff," she said, holding up her glass for Roy to refill. "Yep, I was one blind dimwit. Thought his tattoos from the navy and the way he leaned on the pickup was sexy as hell."

Sex was an interesting word I'd never heard before. I somehow had an inkling the word had something to do with magazines that only Roy could put on the top shelf of the magazine rack. The entire magazine was ensconced in a brown paper sleeve so that you couldn't see any part of the cover nor could you open it. I found it humiliating that *my* father had such things in his store. No one ever said anything about them, but I somehow knew that it would be wrong to exhibit any interest in them. It would be a mistake to ask Roy about them, and a bigger mistake to ask my father. I was quite sure my mother had no idea such things existed so there was no point in even mentioning it to her.

I wondered how ol' Jim ever managed as a father since now he was just a torso sitting in front of the post office on a rolling four-wheeled platform an inch from the ground, yelling dirty words at people. Sometimes he sold things like painted metal frogs that jumped an inch at a time if you wound them up with a key. He usually had a grubby little demo model. If you didn't buy one of his stupid frogs he yelled obscenities at you when you walked down the street. My mother always bought whatever he had to offer and told him how much she needed a metal pet frog. Seymour Knox was not invited back to the Christmas-decoration selection committee when he awarded ol' Jim the Nativity scene display first prize in 1955.

I was amazed that Marie and ol' Jim were once married. I had no idea that leaving a husband was even a possibility, outside of Hollywood, by any method other than death. It seemed particularly ironic to me that Marie literally kicked ol' Jim out when he had no legs and she had no hands. They could have been quite useful to one another. I also wondered if Marie knew that she was going to hell after committing mortal sins, if she hadn't figured it out yet, or if she genuinely didn't care, having given up on the whole business. I had never met anyone who had given up on it all; someone who said that she didn't care if life was only a breath compared to eternity, she was at least going to have a good time breathing.

I was also amazed that someone as lowly as ol' Jim, a person who even young Jim, who cleaned the septic tanks, didn't say hello to when he walked past the post office, could be in *charge* of giving out babies. I thought about the story of the good Samaritan, how God dressed as a beggar to see who would help him. On the way home, when I shared this idea with Roy, he said that I was probably right, and there were people who passed ol' Jim every day and never saw the God within him.

Marie became quite worked up when ol' Jim was mentioned, and started to wave her atrophied hands in front of me, saying that she got the "devil's own disease" because she had to work cleaning up other people's sins. Noticing my appalled look, she picked up momentum. "That's right, I had to clean the confessionals at church and all the floors back in them days when they never heated the church, exceptin' on Sundays. Dr. Alderman says I get this scourge from havin' my hands in cold water for years. When I had my knees operated on, the surgeon said I wored 'em away on that floor. He said that knee bone was thinner than a parchment paper by the time he got to it. He told me the light shine right through it. I scrubbed that place from baptismal to confessional while ol' Jim threw that money down his gullet at the Riverside Inn as fast as I earned it. Dr. Alderman told him he goin' to lose hisself to the drink, but he only keep on. Finally when the drink got the better o' him and he was sittin' on his hip bones, I just slide his platform right out the door and down the Lewiston Hill toward the river. He want to go to the Riverside Inn, so I got him there by the fastest route." Marie, Roy, and I were laughing at the image of ol' Jim speeding as he headed down the steep hill. "His hands get mighty brush-burned that day, let me tell ya," Marie said as she took a deep drag on a much-needed Chesterfield, and daintily picked a little bit of tobacco off her lip.

I said, "Well, what goes around comes around," a favourite line I learned from Irene, the cosmetician of Evening of Paris fame. I was thrilled to have a chance to use it. Roy laughed and slapped my hand, and Marie was laughing so hard she almost tumbled off her lawn chair.

When we calmed down a little, she asked Roy if he was the

bartender because "We ladies want our drinks freshened." I took to a lot of Marie's phrases and used them when I could. In fact, the next day at breakfast I asked Loretta to "freshen" my orange juice.

When Marie was what Roy referred to as "feeling no pain" (I was relieved the Percodan had taken effect), she moved on to the second phase of her life, which she called her "golden era." "He was one mean drunk, that one was, I'm here to tell ya, knocked me from one wall to another. Dr. Alderman knowed what's goin' on. He seen it on the x-ray pictures and let me stay in the hospital, sometimes for a week at a time, just to have a break from him. When I got rid o' him, I figured I mights as well make money from what I had to do with him. Let me tell you, Roy, there were men who were willing to pay for me in them days." She asked us to flick on a switch over a picture on the wall. Most of her pictures were of little children with unblinking eyes in rangy clothes with black velvet backgrounds, but she had one large oil painting of herself with a light switch placed on the upper edge of the ornate gold frame.

When Roy turned on the tiny spotlight, a young, beautiful, and truly voluptuous Marie came into focus. She was wearing a strapless black taffeta evening gown accentuating a tiny waist. Her hair was in a French twist. I told her she looked more beautiful than Stupefying Jones in *L'il Abner*, and her face resembled Lana Turner on the Toni permanent-wave box. I could tell Marie liked that image so I continued telling her that she looked like the French royalty she was descended from. "Dolores told my mother that you were a *Madam*." Marie's eyes narrowed and she took a big swig of her drink and then a long drag on her cigarette. I quickly realized she didn't want Dolores referring to her French ancestry.

"Dolores couldn't make a dime in my line of work if she only wore her apron." I tried to picture Dolores in only an apron. "Let the likes o' Dolores clean other people's houses. I can tell ya I saw her husband a lot more than she did and got a lot more money from him in one hour than she got in a week." She sank back into her chair and turned her gaze back upon the portrait. "Ya see that twenty-three-inch waist. I had that waist and that thirty-eight inch bust after nine children. Tell Dolores to kiss my you-know-what. Father Flanagan ran his confessional and I ran mine. We're the only ones who know the underbelly of Lewiston and the Falls."

Roy agreed, saying, "More people heard o' you than the Maid of the Mist."

She leaned toward Roy and I as though she was telling us both a secret. "Ya know, when I hired my own girls, sold the drinks, and the Canadians came by the truckful, I was makin' $2,000 a week on booze alone. They came in from Fort Erie after the races. We were jumpin' on Sundays. I had a licence to print money when the Power Project was in full swing. Why, thousands of men poured into town like water over the Falls. That's without the tax man knocking on my door — for money, that is. Now my business, my body, and even a chunk of the Falls is dried up. It happens faster than ya think."

Roy shook his head in admiration. "Umm-mm, I'm sorry I missed them days. Must a been a sight."

Marie said, "Ya know I never could hire from you folks, Roy. Them girls want to keep them babies when they get in the family way."

I really didn't understand why Marie couldn't have hired us and was feeling mildly offended. When I later expressed my consternation to Roy, he said she wasn't hiring anyone, so it was one less thing we had to concern ourselves with. Yet the phrase "keep them babies" haunted me. I had no idea people didn't keep their own babies. What if *I* wasn't my parents' baby? Maybe I had been left in the bulrushes like Moses. After all, my parents were older and I was an only child like Moses. . . . Sister Agnese *had* called me a "bad seed." Maybe Roy Rogers and Dale Evans, now a childless couple, were my real parents and they left me with my favourite beloved little cowboy suit when they gave me up to go on television.

As I was piecing together my possible lineage, Marie broke into what was not to be my last thoughts on the matter. "Ya can't do the same thing forever, ya know. Ya get older. Gotta pay the piper. I changed lines — got into fixin' girls in trouble. I was always good with my hands" — she didn't look that good to me — "and I could fix 'em better than anyone in these parts. In fact for miles round right up through Montreal they called what I done right there on that pinochle table 'gettin' sweenied.'"

Marie looked over at me and asked if I knew why she kept her curtains closed. When I acknowledged that I had no idea, she said it was to keep the hypocrites out. "This town is crawling with 'em. Marie is *this*, and Marie is *that*," she said, mimicking the tone of a gossipmonger. "Till all them country-club girls from the heights played at more 'n golf and suddenly needed my help. Then there ain't no one like good ol' Marie. Lemme tell you that!"

As we were about to leave, my eyes had finally adjusted to the dark, and I saw on her makeshift side table, an upside-down orange crate, that she had her Santa candle from last year that Roy had given her resting on the card we'd given her. The card had red candle drippings and Santa's head had already melted away from its last Christmas burning. I wanted Roy to know she'd saved it even though she hadn't made much of a fuss over it when we had given it to her, so I mentioned Santa's headless condition. "Don't worry," Marie said, dragging on her cigarette, "them reindeers knows the way here by heart. Besides, I never met a man who used his head for anything more than a hat rack, anyway."

I had never heard anyone say anything bad about men, although the comment did resonate with something within me. I thought men were the top of the heap. They made the money, were in charge, forgave us our sins, and were the altar boys. I glanced at Roy to catch his reaction. He bellowed out his infectious laughter and said, "Now that's the truth!" I also began laughing and felt thoroughly relaxed and realized that although Marie was sort of worn-out, she had guts. Maybe having guts wears you out.

I told Marie that before we left we should light the candle and sing a Christmas song since, after all, it *was* Christmas Eve. She said, "Sure, whatever. This'll pretty much wrap up my Christmas cheer." She didn't say this in a sad tone, but more as a throwaway line. Roy lit the headless Santa, and I asked Marie to pick a carol. I figured she would pick "I'm Getting Nothin' for Christmas 'Cause I Ain't Been Nothin' but Bad." (For some reason that song scared me.) But she didn't. She picked "Silent Night." Marie, Roy, and I sang all the verses. Roy sang in a rich baritone and Marie's voice was so sweetly different from her speaking voice I was amazed. They harmonized beautifully together. Roy kept his hand on Marie's shoulder for the last verse because she was looking kind of misty.

We drove along in silence as night fell and I tried to put together the things Marie had said into one cohesive picture. Why, if she was royalty, did she live in a dump? Why, since she had nine children, did she not see them on Christmas? Why had she seen Dolores's husband more than Dolores had? I guess when she fixed people they told her their secrets just like they told Father Flanagan in confession. I also wondered how girls could get in trouble when it was usually boys, as far as I could see. Why was no one helping her when she had "fixed" so many others? When I expressed these sentiments to Roy on the way home, he said, "People think that some favours are best forgotten," but he agreed with me that Lewiston had been ungrateful to Marie.

After both of my parents had died and I'd moved away, an article appeared in the press about several famous women, including Gloria Steinem and Catherine Deneuve, who agreed to go public after having had illegal abortions in the fifties and sixties. A few of these well-known women named Marie Sweeney as their abortionist. Marie, if she had still been with us, could have flung open her black velvet curtains and become, however briefly, the toast of the Lewiston avant-garde.

Marie opened the creaky door to the world a bit for me. She didn't seem to care about the town's hierarchy that my mother so rigidly adhered to and I had come to believe was inviolable. When she laughed at the priest, missed mass on Sunday, wore white shoes in the winter, lipstick over her natural lip line, and called her husband a "no-good layabout" (no one I had ever met called their husband anything but their Christian names), I found it all inexplicably liberating. When I asked Roy what a "hypocrite" was, he said it was a person who did one thing by day but another when the sun went down. I pictured the people of Lewiston scurrying around like nocturnal rodents doing inexplicably awful things in the shadows of moonlight.

—

A few weeks later my mother was having her bridge club, with several tables of four set up in the living room, dining room, and front parlour. It was my job to supply the coasters to each guest so their highball glasses wouldn't leave a ring on my mother's unblemished cherry bridge tables. Dolores was darting back and forth placing bridge mix, hors d'oeuvres, and tiny white Wonder Bread sandwiches with no crust arranged on a platter like the floral clock in Canada. As we were all bustling around, my ears pricked up when I heard Mrs. Aungier say that her teenage daughter Cindy, a ballerina (she travelled to Niagara Falls for dance lessons), needed to have her feet fixed; however, there was no one in Lewiston or the Falls to do it. Since I had a never-ending desire to be part of the conversation while handing out gratuitous advice, I suggested to Mrs. Aungier that Marie Sweeney could fix Cindy. After all, I pointed out, she had fixed many girls from Lewiston. Mrs. Aungier paled when I mentioned her daughter's name in the same breath as Marie Sweeney's. After she'd recovered sufficiently she said that Cindy was not in *that* kind of trouble. Not having any idea what she meant, I attempted to give Marie some legitimacy in Mrs. Aungier's eyes so I forged ahead. "Marie could fix anything — why, she's seen more of Dolores's husband than Dolores ever has."

The cards stopped shuffling, the bidding came to an abrupt halt in all the rooms, and Dolores disappeared through the kitchen swinging door. In the sudden silence all that could be heard was the swish of the air as the door kept swinging. My mother scurried after Dolores, and asked me to go upstairs and feed my caterpillars. In a voice that I could hear was fading, was losing its grip, the one she used when she said she had a headache and was going to lie down, she told me that she would speak to me *later*.

I was enraged to be sent away when all I was doing was trying to drum up some business for poor old Marie. Why did we scour the African missions in search of poor people when we had Marie smack dab in the middle of Lewiston? What about all those film strips that we saw in religion class, on the rare occasions when Sister Immaculata could figure out how to run the projector, which preached that God walks amongst us and He tests our faith. Are you the good Samaritan if you only help Miss America, but ignore the Marie Sweeneys of this world?

Engaged in these religious conundrums, I dragged myself to my room and took the rhinestone clip-on bows off my Mary Janes, threw them out the window, and watched as they sank into the snow. I couldn't resist a spiteful grin, thinking how much my mother adored them. My bow suicide never packed the wallop I'd hoped for since no one ever noticed they were gone except Roy. My mother actually found them in the spring when she was checking for the crocuses and they were perfectly alright. Instead of being angry, she said, "Well, this bow episode should be used as an ad for the Stride-Rite shoe company."

—

Some years later, when my mother was dying and we were reminiscing about good times ("After all," as my mother wisely said, "what's the point of talking about how you're feeling when you're dying — as it's kind of a one-note song"), she said she wanted to talk about the "Marie–Dolores debacle," as it had become known over the years. I guess that's what she meant when she said she wanted to talk to me *later*. She recounted one more detail in my day as a social pariah that I hadn't remembered at all. The human memory plays interesting tricks; it's fascinating what the unconscious chooses to let float to the surface and what stays subterranean. As Dolores was going to pieces in the kitchen, sobbing into the asparagus roll-ups, my mother said that although she made some appropriate clucking noises, all she could really do was look on helplessly. She knew Dolores's reputation was lunch meat in Lewiston. Small towns give you warmth and recognition, but sometimes that warmth is red-hot and burns you, and the recognition, if it's a juicy piece of gossip, is more painful than a public flogging. At least a flogging ends. Gossip lives on for years, and in a town like Lewiston, it grows like moss on the north side of a rock.

As happens in any emergency, everyone thinks of themselves. That day my mother's feelings for Dolores faded into her own worries. Who was going to heat and pass the food? Who was going to make the cocktails? Who was going to play *masters* bridge in my mother's foursome while she bumbled along with the food? While my mother was contemplating this horrendous situation, she flew into a tizzy matched only by Dolores's. The fallout was such that Dolores never helped at social gatherings again, which became a moot point since my mother never entertained again for the rest of her life, and Dolores never forgave me for the rest of hers.

As it *actually* happened, after the bridge-club banishment, I didn't go directly to my room, but made a quick stop at the curve in the stairs and leaned my head through the spindles and yelled at the thirty-six players below. "You're all hypocrites and I'm closing my drapes so I never have to see any of you." My mother, never one to criticize, said of the whole event, "I was amazed that at the age of seven you knew the word *hypocrite*." Mother said when she re-entered the dining room to try to get the party on the rails again, all the chairs were vacated and the bridge players were tumbling out of the house, the ones most eager to escape already down the walk. They were terrified they were going to be mentioned next so they hightailed it out of there, leaving a ghost town of bridge tables. As they scattered in all directions, they said over their shoulders that poor Dolores must need to have some time alone. Mother said she was so relieved that I had managed to smoke out the whole hive of them. She pointed out that last-minute emergencies abound in home entertaining, and it was all too much for her. She was infinitely grateful to me for getting rid of everyone just as Dolores had taken a powder.

CHAPTER 8

cold

I woke up to radiators that were hissing at the cold and clanking to beat the band. My slipper socks and underwear were, as usual, waiting on the radiator for me as I tiptoed across the cold pine floor to reach them. I was tired today since I'd stayed up listening to *Fibber McGee and Molly* and *Gangbusters* on the radio that I hid under my covers to muffle the sound.

I got set for our usual predawn routine. The frozen long under-wear came off the line like cadavers in rigor mortis and the flannel sheets had to be carried in like coffins. I usually donned my favourite outfit, which my mother referred to as my "western coordinates," blue jeans lined in cream-coloured flannel with a pattern in burnt-orange silhouette of a cowboy lassoing a bucking bronco. I cuffed the jeans exactly four inches, which revealed how stylishly the flannel lining of the pants matched the flannel shirt. If it was above zero I was allowed to wear my cowboy hat of black felt; however, if it was below zero I had to wear my wool hat with ear flaps.

First of all my father and I would start the motor, shovel the driveway, sand the ice, and scrape the windshield. Then when the car was warmed up we'd drive to Niagara Falls and have break-fast at The Horseshoe, ordering from the "early riser" menu. I had an Italian delicacy called "Quaker Oatmeal" and my father had the "get crackin'."

At 6:00 a.m. it was my job to stock the royal-blue newspaper box and wait outside and sell the *Niagara Falls Gazette* until eight-thirty. The paper cost seven cents and customers almost always gave me a dime. I couldn't make change with my mitts on and I can still remember all the faces who smiled and said, "Keep the change," as well as the rich men in cashmere coats and homburgs who waited patiently while I took off my gloves to find their three cold pennies.

We spent untold hours fighting the elements. We lived in the snow-belt, where ice could fell a tree as though it were a pencil. There were no snow tires, only chains, car batteries gave out when it was more than fifteen below, plows took longer, salt was scarce, and sand didn't always do the trick.

Weather in the 1950s along the Niagara Frontier laughed at the faint-hearted. We had the ice jams of 1955 on the Niagara River in Lewiston that chewed up wooden houses and spit them out like sawdust. Even brick ones were ground to fine orange soot and sprinkled on top of huge chunks of ice that leapt over the Niagara Gorge with the power of the Falls behind them.

The snowstorms could bury cars in record time and we had only chains on our tires and batteries that needed heating just to turn over. Most kids my age stayed home and made snowmen in their yards with their moms watching them out the window to make sure they didn't wander or get frostbite. However, no matter what the weather, I knew we had to make it to the far corners of Niagara County. Every morning it was my job to scrape the ice off the forest-green Nash Rambler delivery car and make sure the insignia of the stork holding the prescription in its mouth was visible below the thick yellow letters that spelled McClure's Drugs. I then had to start the car and warm up the engine. I still remember that dull grinding thud when it was too cold to turn over. I had to keep my foot on the gas and slowly let out the choke or else we stalled or flooded. This was not an easy manoeuvre with the short legs of an eight-year-old. The car had to idle for fifteen minutes before it was slammed into drive, and those were the longest and coldest fifteen minutes of my life. When Roy arrived by nine, I'd have the car loaded with prescriptions, having mapped out our route for the day on a clipboard. I made sure we were near several "watering holes," as Roy called taverns, at crucial parts of the day. As soon as I saw him coming up the alley,

I'd punch in the lighter, knowing he'd want his cigarette as we pulled out of the loading dock. He'd bring the paper and I'd read the weather aloud. If it forecast blizzard we still forged ahead, so I really have no idea why we ever checked the weather — it made no difference to our plans.

Roy and I found ourselves for hours in places where we had only meant to spend a minute. We dug ourselves out, lit Sterno packs, set up flares on country roads when our battery was dead so snowplows would see us in the dark. On a few stormy occasions we worked all night, dropping off our last prescription as we drove into the dawn light. But we always got the insulin, the morphine, and the Digitalis there on time. Sometimes people would be pacing, pale, and shaking by the time we arrived, but mostly their overriding emotion was amazement and gratitude that we'd made it.

This morning seemed somehow different than any other that I remembered. The light seemed clearer and it was colder. My mother's African violets died overnight on the windowsill from the cold-air drafts. The battery of the delivery car sounded as though it were full of glue, then it made no sound at all. My father had to have Vincent's Garage come over and jump-start it. Mr. Vincent always smelled like gasoline and wore a "Happy Motoring" blue jumpsuit. He came in for coffee and a cigarette to warm up, but stood at the back door blowing into his mittens, saying he had too long a list to sit down. "Yup, it's the worst cold snap since 1928. We even made the national news, minus thirty-two and falling, not including the wind chill factor, says Eric Sevareid. Even the antifreeze is hard as a rock. In all my born days I never seen the oil on the lift freeze. Why, you couldn't lift a car this morning for love nor money."

"Might be time to invest in a heating block for the Nash and the Lincoln — don't want to crack the engine block," my father suggested.

"I wouldn't jump the gun on that one," Mr. Vincent advised, "but I can tell you that they have warnings out today to stay inside if you can, and if you have to go out, stay no more than ten minutes at a time. Wind chill takin' her down to minus seventy-eight! Otherwise they're goin' to need an ice pick to thaw ya out!"

My mother said, "Well, I for one will not take one step out of this house." We all laughed, knowing it was not a great personal sacrifice for my mother not to take a step out of the house. In fact, the weather conditions had to be near perfect for her to venture past the front parlour.

As I put on my boots, I told Dad that I might have to sell the newspapers from *inside* the store today. I also reminded him to leave the car running while Roy loaded up the deliveries, just in case the battery couldn't handle the load. Father nodded in agreement.

Mr. Vincent tousled my hair and said, "I'm waitin' for the weather that slows this one down." Laughing at his own joke, he continued, "I bet you've been prayin' for that cold snap."

My father smiled and said, "She's my right-hand man." He stubbed out his cigarette and donned his Hudson's Bay red boiled wool jacket with the big black stripe. He usually only wore that jacket when we went to the hardware store, shovelled the snow, or cut the Christmas tree. I'd never seen him forego his topcoat when he wore his suit. This breach of decorum is what told me it was really cold. When he donned his wool cap with the ear flaps instead of his homburg, I knew it was a national disaster.

As we walked to the garage we were accosted by the cold. The clothes on the line swung at us like dancing mummies. It hurt to breathe, and the hairs in my nostrils, of which I was previously unaware, were immediately coated with ice. I felt as though I were breathing through stalactites and stalagmites. My breath froze on my upper lip. When Mr. Vincent hopped up into his tow truck he spit, and it was frozen by the time it hit the ground with a ping, and shattered.

As we pulled into the store's alley and onto the loading dock, the boss told me to keep my foot on the gas pedal and make sure I didn't change gears. I had to slouch down in the driver's seat to make contact with the gas pedal. I was really getting cold and was shocked that the heater wasn't managing to heat the car. I kept putting my hand on it to see if it was working, and it was indeed sending out hot air, but it couldn't keep up with the cold wind. Finally, through the rearview mirror I saw Roy walking up the alley. I knew right away to push in the lighter. Roy, true to form, was what he referred to as "lidless." He refused to wear a hat, saying it made his hair nappy. He got into the car with a cigarette behind his ear, which he immediately handed to me and I lit with the lighter. I always took a drag like the women on *Alfred Hitchcock Presents* before I gave it to him, saying, "We're loaded. Let's hit the road, Jack."

Roy made a whistle like Wolfman Jack and said, "Whoooo wee, it's nippy out there. You drive to work today?"

I loved it when Roy did this. He wasn't like my parents' friends in how he joked. "Yup. Dad blew away and froze to a telephone pole and I had to drive all the way up on my own."

"No trouble with the alley?" he asked as he glanced at the clip-board with the day's deliveries.

"None. I just went slowly." He nodded his approval. As we were about to back out of the alley, "Rock Around the Clock" by Bill Haley and his Comets blasted on the radio he brought with him, and Roy made it clear that cold weather would not deter us from our usual merriment. As they sang, "One o'clock, two o'clock, three o'clock, rock," Roy put the car in reverse. "Four o'clock, five o'clock, six o'clock, rock," and he slammed it into forward. On he went, shifting to the music, and off we lurched down Falls Street, singing and laughing in the face of the drop-ping thermometer.

After we'd done our local deliveries, we headed out to a farm in Wheatfield, on the outskirts of the county, to make our last delivery. Mr. Vincent had reminded me to tell Roy that before we went out to Wheatfield we should fill up the tank because it was pretty desolate out there and if your gas tank is even half-empty in this weather you can get ice in the gas line and clog the carbu-retor. He'd also said to watch for snow out there as it was the eye of the snowbelt in those parts. I had to get out the long county atlas to figure out where this farm was and where we had to drop off this expensive ointment that we had to keep next to the heater because it cost a fortune and its label read "Keep at room temper-ature." We were really in the sticks and some of the roads weren't on the city *or* the county street guides. Finally we figured we made some wrong turns on farmers' unmarked back roads. Anyway, we got back onto the highway and decided to try again.

It was now dusk, snowing, and we were both eager to find someone to ask directions. The snow was blowing on what looked like a lunar landscape and we hadn't passed any sign of life for miles. Suddenly Roy hit a patch of black ice and we did a 360-degree turn and headed onto the shoulder and into a drainage ditch. We didn't even have time to get scared. Something under the car had ripped on the grey ice ledge the snowplow had left on the side of the highway. The motor ground to a halt. Roy got out of the car and saw we were tilted forward and the back wheels were off the ground entirely. The tailpipe had ripped off on the ice mound and the muffler lay perfectly sawed off under the car, as though the delivery car had given birth to it and was now too spent to even turn over, no matter how much Roy fiddled with her choke.

It was dropping from dusk to dark as we walked around the car, assessing the damage. We were dug in. It would take a truck to pull us out. As we got back in the car Roy said, "Well, the good news is we didn't hit no one and we're not hurt, and the bad news is it's colder than a witch's tit." The land was flat and cut into giant squares by an electrified fence. There was nothing in sight but frozen clumps of cultivated ground dusted in blowing snow like confectioner's sugar on molasses cookies. We sat in silence for a few minutes as I presumed Roy was planning our exit strategy. "Well . . . well," he finally said again. "Well, we don't have many choices. It's too cold to walk to the next farm."

I piped in, "Wherever that is."

"It's blowin' like a whistle out there and we'd get turned around, not knowing north from south in this here whiteout." I didn't say anything, so he continued, only this time he tried to cheer me up, which I certainly wasn't above needing. "Well, Cisco, we'd best be sittin' tight like two bugs in a rug in this here automobile. The boss is one organized hombre. He gots a copy of our schedule and when we not back on time, he'll call everyone on the list and see who didn't get their medicine and then when he gets a hold of the Ryder farm and they say they ain't seen hide nor hair of us, he'll know just where we are. Nothing get by that man. Besides, someone is bound to drive along this road. It's a highway."

I thought for a moment. "Roy, what if the lines are down or what if the Ryders, people we've never ever laid eyes on before, don't have a phone. Lots of farmers think phones are newfangled."

"Yeah, maybe on *Gunsmoke* or *Have Gun Will Travel*. Sister, this is 1956! I bet you one day's — no, one *week's* pay — that we get outta here . . . in one piece."

I could tell what that pause was about. "Sorry, Pancho, I'm not taking that bet. By the way, did you ever hear a short story called 'To Build a Fire'? It's about a guy who freezes to death."

Roy started laughing. "Oh, I'm not goin' down that road, man."

We had no heater and it was unbelievable how quickly the temperature was already dropping. There was no point in saying anything more about it. I knew what kind of behaviour got on Roy's nerves. He didn't mind all the talk in the world or even all the demands, but he couldn't abide a whiny kid. The kind that goes on and on about things made him as mad as all get out. I'd seen it when snivellers came into the store.

After we sat there awhile, Roy said, "Put up your hood and leave it up. Loosen your boots so there are no tight parts and your skin isn't pressed anywhere. Keep your fingers moving slowly in your mittens and hold your hands close to your chest or put them under your armpits." The wind rocked the car slightly making noises like hungry wolves, and our seats were leaning forward as the car was nose-dived. Roy said, "The time'll go faster if we keep each other entertained and if we don't talk about the *weather*. Notice I didn't use the word *cold*." I nodded. My ears were beginning to hurt but we had decided not to mention it. He suggested, "You name the topic. Oh, by the way, Cisco, I sure as shootin' don't want to hear none o' that freezin'-to-death-gotta-build-a-fire kinda story. Let's hear somethin' warm — *hot* even."

I thought for a moment and then suggested we revisit what had become known as "the Marilyn Monroe saga." We had actually made a real visit to Marilyn Monroe over two years ago. Roy agreed that was a good one and said I had the elephant's memory, so why didn't I tell it. I informed Roy, in a moment of sudden inspiration, that I was going to tell it in the form of a "true fairy tale."

⌒

Once upon a time in 1952 when Cathy was four years old and Roy was . . . already big, a movie called Niagara *was being made in one of the seven wonders of the world called Niagara Falls. As chance would have it, these Falls were only a few blocks away from McClure's Drugs, where Cathy and Roy toiled happily. Marilyn Monroe was the star of the movie and her manager called our store to say that she needed sleeping pills. The boss of the store said a doctor had to call in the prescription and then McClure's would fill and deliver it.*

When it came time to deliver it, the boss said he'd drop it off on his way home from work that very day. Cathy, the girl who toiled in the drugstore, told the boss, who coincidentally happened to be her father, how unfair it was that he should suddenly deliver the morphine and Nembutal prescription, when for years it had been the job of Roy, the deliveryman, and Cathy, his assistant. After all, Roy and Cathy had delivered to some pretty ornery people in their travels, but when they complained that they had a tough time on the reservation or anywhere else for that matter, the boss assured them it was "all in a day's work." Cathy asked why delivering to Marilyn Monroe wasn't part of their day's work instead of his. After very little ado, the father agreed, after his favourite daughter made him see the error of his ways.

One July day when it was so hot that the Niagara Falls Gazette had a picture of a man frying an egg on the sidewalk, Roy and Cathy walked hand in hand over to the movie set. They couldn't take the delivery car because of the herds of rubberneckers. As they walked they played a game which they entitled Squeeze That Tune, where Roy squeezed Cathy's hand to the rhythm of a song and she had to guess the title. They were amazed by the throngs of people who were roped off from a set of trailers and a movie set with a motel called Rainbow Cabins that only had a front held up by stilts, but no real rooms.

Cathy went up to the guard and said that they had a prescription for Marilyn Monroe. The guard said that he would make sure she got it, but Cathy informed him of the narcotics law in New York State which maintained that the person whose name was on the prescription had to sign for the drug if it was listed in the registry as a narcotic. Low and behold, the rope was moved, and the crowd parted like the Red Sea when Moses divided it, and Roy and Cathy were led onto the set. They went over to the chairs where Henry Hathaway, the movie's director, and Joseph Cotten, the leading man, were sitting. Joseph Cotten, a man, was wearing makeup that even Irene would have thought excessive.

Henry Hathaway seemed relieved to see Cathy and Roy and said, "Thank God Marilyn's medicine is here. You've saved my bacon!" He reached for a megaphone and yelled, "Let's call those extras back to the set in one hour please."

Jean Peters, another actress, who was leaning on the motel set having a cigarette under the "No Vacancy" sign, threw her cigarette on the lawn and seemed kind of in a huff. She said, pointing to Cathy, "Well, she's the only natural blond on the lot."

Henry Hathaway laughed and told Cathy, "You never know. You may be our next star."

Joseph Cotten said, smoothing his tweezed eyebrow, "After all, Betty Grable was discovered at Schrafft's and her hair was only half as blond as yours."

Cathy was thrilled. Henry gave the security guard the go-ahead for them to go to Marilyn's room in the Sheraton Brock Hotel. Because of the crowds who were waiting for Marilyn to get off the elevator, the guard had to take them up in a special freight elevator that had quilts on the walls.

Cathy knocked on the door, but no one answered. One thing Cathy and Roy knew was that when you deliver narcotics, people are happy to see you. That much she'd learned practically in her crib. She leaned close to the door, tapped, and murmured, "Nembutal for Marilyn Monroe."

That was the open sesame. Marilyn popped her head out of the door looking like a ruffled white rooster with hair askew and smeared ruby red lips and muttered, "Oh, I'm not quite dressed yet. I know I have to sign — pardon my attire and the mess and come on in." She opened the door fully and the delivery pair entered, not without trepidation, for Marilyn was in her slip. There were clothes all over the floor, and cigarettes with red ends that were hardly smoked were overflowing the ashtray and getting mixed in with piles of makeup in more colours than an artist's palette. "I just have two more nails," she said, hastily applying Revlon Night to Remember nail polish on top of chipped old red polish.

Her tight slip wasn't doing a good or even adequate job of covering her body. The scanty eyelet undergarment was white, but her long-line brassiere, garter belt, and pants were black. The cups of the bra were lace and had concentric circles sewn in top-stitching, and were shaped like sugar cones for ice cream, pointing straight out. Now, if the facts be known, Cathy wouldn't have been caught dead in a room with another woman, let alone a man, in that getup. Cathy gave Marilyn a look which let her know that Roy was a man and that maybe he should wait outside.

Roy carried the maroon leather narcotics log and held it out for Marilyn to sign, pointing to the spot where the morphine was listed. As he leaned over to give her a pen, she flopped down on her vanity stool and prepared to sign, scowling as though she'd signed more of these than she cared to remember. Suddenly her mood and body seemed to loosen up, and she said in a little-girl kind of breathy voice, "What's that smell? Is that Juicy Fruit?" She leaned close to Roy's face, sniffing. Roy didn't say anything. He just got out his Juicy Fruit and casually handed her a piece, but she said he had to peel it because her nails were wet. As he took off the yellow wrapper and foil, she gave the signed narcotics log a big squeeze against her chest, which made parts of her body come up over the top of her slip and slide all around. Then she handed the book back to Roy, saying in that same gushy voice, with her eyes open wide, as though she were shocked or something, "Now, that was a sneaky way to get my autograph." Then she smiled at Roy and her face really lit up. Her whole sort of pudgy sour face turned radiant.

He remained calm, as though he were talking to the Duponts or Warty or Marie. Roy had a style that didn't change with the wind. He said, "I go all over these parts, givin' out Juicy Fruit sticks and gettin' autographs. Why, yesterday we got . . . who was it, Cath? Ava Gardner, wasn't it? But she wanted Doublemint." He beamed back a smile right at her.

Marilyn didn't wait for Cathy's share of the joke. "Well," she said, raising her shoulders and everything else that seemed connected as well, except for her slip, "I guess you can't satisfy everyone."

Roy was quiet and never moved away after getting the book back. He said, "So I've heard tell."

For some reason Cathy didn't feel included. Marilyn hadn't even said hello to Cathy and now she was ignoring the fact that she was in a slip in front of a man. Dolores would have said she had no shame at all. Cathy moved toward the door to give Roy the hint that this was really too silly for words and then Marilyn asked him, "Do you have any Photoplay or any full packages of Juicy Fruit with you?" Roy smiled and shook his head like he'd been caught out and this was a normal question. Did she think he travelled with an arsenal of gum and magazines? "Say!" she said as though she'd just had a flash of genius. "Do you think you can drop by later with the latest Photoplay, and a big package of Juicy Fruit?"

Roy indicated that wouldn't be a problem as he and I walked to the door. With the door opened, he turned and said, "I'll be droppin' them sundries off around nine tonight." Before you could say "Bob's your uncle," Cathy and Roy were in the hall, sinking into thick carpeting that silenced their steps.

Cathy waited for Roy to say something when they were in the elevator; however, he was silent with no perceivable expression on his face. "You know what I think, Roy?" He looked down to hear Cathy's opinion. "Well, I think she was a floozy."

Roy lifted an eyebrow. "That's a new one on me," Roy ventured.

"Well, I guess I'll have to tell you what a floozy is. Dolores said Mrs. Sapider was a floozy because she wore shorts to the post office. Isn't that sort of like wearing a slip in front of a man?"

"Why, was that a slip? I thought it might be an evening dress."

"Roy!" was all Cathy chose to say as they got off the elevator.

They walked along on this scalding night, when even the katydids were too hot to fiddle, past the coloured lights of the Falls, where they lingered, allowing the cool mist to cover their faces until it dripped off. Now, Cathy knew when to let things drop, especially when Roy was concerned, but for some reason she was like a dog with a bone with this one and couldn't help but ask, "Roy, did you notice she had dark roots — longer than Irene's — and her nails were all chewed?"

"Nope, didn't notice."

"Well, I thought since she's a movie star she'd be more polite or more — ladylike."

He put his hand on Cathy's shoulder and said, "I don't know if she was ladylike, but she was sure a lady I liked," and he started laughing.

Cathy remained miffed and marvelled that she had never had a feeling quite like the one she felt as she was cooled by the mist of the Falls. She decided to just go with her grouchiness and let Roy laugh alone.

As they approached the drugstore, Cathy was already planning her imitation of Marilyn, and how the actress had implored Roy to peel her Juicy Fruit. Now, Roy had worked with Cathy for many years and, smoking out her plans, he said, "I'm goin' to ask you for a favour. I think it's my first. You let me know now if you can do it."

Cathy was so shocked you could have knocked her over with a feather. She snuck a glance up at Roy, but he looked fairly relaxed with the if-you-can-do-it-fine — if-you-can't-fine kind of expression. Still it was totally unlike him to ask for a favour. He usually played his cards close to his chest. "No matter what it is I can do it," Cathy said, with the confidence she felt.

Finally he said quietly, "When you is doin' your routine of the Marilyn delivery for the staff — and by the way, I'm sure you'll have a heyday with that imitation at Coke break — don't ever mention the part about me bringin' back the Photoplay *or the* Juicy Fruit.*"*

"Your wish is granted," was all she said.

Cathy and Roy walked back to the store together and lived happily ever after.

———

As I finished my story and looked over at Roy, his hair was now frosted and resembled a lamb's-wool bonnet as his head bobbed up and down with laughter. "Lord, you's a fox in the chicken coop!" Howling, he said, "Lord above, I got to tell ya that story really warm me up. No one in their right mind can say Cathy McClure cannot spin one good yarn. Someday that memory of yours is goin' to get ya in trouble." Still chuckling, he continued, "You never took to ol' Marilyn. Now that is a *fact*. You two just didn't see eye to eye." He laughed so hard he had to lean on the steering wheel.

"Roy can I ask you *one* question?"

"You always just got *one* more question."

"Well?"

"Go on. Hit me."

"Did you go back to the Sheraton that night? If you tell me, I'll tell you a secret about Ted. . . . Something I saw him doing."

"You know somethin', Della? You been watching too much Perry Mason. One thing a gentleman learns is never tell anything about a lady, especially to another lady, or you ain't no gentleman."

As usual the world was too much for me to figure out. Even though I was now two years older than when the Marilyn Monroe saga transpired, I *still* couldn't help but wonder what was right and what was wrong. I tried to sort the issue out logically and present myself with the facts. My mother and father made this big fuss about being ladylike. When I showed Ted, one of the pharmacists, my red petticoat under my strawberry party dress that I wore for the employees' Christmas party, my father said it wasn't ladylike. Everyone makes a fuss about how you sit in a chair, how you chew your gum, the words you use, bright yellow hair dye, women wearing shorts to the post office, Gretchen Prince's older sister who sat too close to her boyfriend in his convertible and "parked" with him. Dolores called her a "hussy" and Irene called her "cheap." Roy said men pack .44s and women pack a reputation and both can kill you. Once I heard a customer telling Irene about a woman who wore an ankle bracelet. Irene shook her head and said, "Once you get on the wrong side of the tracks, there is no way home." That scared me because I wasn't sure what catapulted you to the wrong side of the tracks, and I didn't want to inadvertently put myself there on a one-way ticket.

The weird and incomprehensible thing about the Marilyn Monroe saga that both confused and actually alarmed me was the seemingly obvious contradictions. Didn't she wear what my mother called "provocative attire"? Who answers the door in underwear? Didn't she have bad hair dye? Didn't she stand too close to Roy to be ladylike? Wasn't she messy and tardy, holding up the whole crew? Didn't she look like she was from "the wrong side of the tracks"? Yet my father wanted to deliver her medicine. *My father.* My mother *laughed* when I said she was in her slip. She said, "Oh my word!" Everyone crowded around me in Helms's Dry Goods Store as I told the story of Marilyn Monroe's Nembutal delivery. Marilyn was treated as royalty. Thousands of people stormed the Maid of the Mist lineup to see her. Yet wasn't she everything that people in Lewiston warned you *not* to become? I didn't get it. Maybe when you go so far over the wrong side of the tracks, you come full circle?

The Marilyn Monroe saga was just a loose string on a tangled ball of yarn. There was something about women and their relationship to men that I didn't get. I knew that much. I also knew it was bigger than Marilyn Monroe. It had something to do with everyone. Yet it was deeply camouflaged. It was somehow connected to the magazines in the store that were well-hidden in manila sleeves on the top shelf of the rack and sold like hot cakes — but only to men. I knew that everyone was secretly involved because my mother had a black long-line getup similar to Marilyn's in the bottom drawer of her bureau, hidden under beaded evening bags and pearl opera glasses. I tried it on sometimes when my parents were out. I sauntered around alone in the empty house wearing the long-line bra stuffed with Kleenex, teetering in *peau de soie* black high heels, holding unlit Camel cigarettes while looking into mirrors.

The whole Marilyn-Monroe-as-a-goddess enigma paralleled the phoney battlefront photos that Mr. Harlan passed off as his own, when everyone knew he spent the war right here at Fort Niagara. If lying was really bad, then why was it okay to lie about being in the war, and why did my father, Roy, and the chamber of commerce go along with what they called a "white lie." Sometimes the world seemed so complicated, I felt as though everything were spinning, like a ride at Crystal Beach Amusement Park, and I was barely holding on for dear life. What puzzled me was why *I* seemed to be so troubled by all these irregularities and exceptions to major rules while others blithely marched ahead.

—

As I snapped out of my reverie and flashed back to the chilling situation at hand, I realized Roy was, as usual, right about telling the story. I had miraculously forgotten about the cold. Now I noticed that the inside of the window was covered with my frosty words which had condensed then frozen the second they hit the windshield. Frost had begun to creep onto the dashboard in shapes of cracked crystals and hairy sticks and was moving toward us like frozen lava as the minutes crept by. Our breath was literally closing in on us.

"You know," I said, "I was just thinking about all those times Irene told you that you weren't dressed for the weather and you were going to catch your death. . . . Well, here we are." (I was a true I-told-you-so fan.)

"Yup." I wished he'd said something more reassuring. Reading my mind he lightened his tone. "Yes siree, Bob! I always said Irene got enough makeup on to keep her warm. Not even the cold would go near that much Evening in Paris perfume."

I was really starting to feel cold, especially in my ears. I looked over at Roy and he had a little white spot on his nose, sort of like the scrap of paper my dad puts on when he cuts himself shaving. I reached over and touched it to brush it away, but it was his skin.

"Roy, are you cold?" I asked.

"Hey, is the Pope Catholic?" was his answer. After a moment he perked up and hit the steering wheel with his gloved fist and said, "Now it's my turn for a story, but the trouble, as I see it, is I could never top your Marilyn Monroe tale. I don't remember all the who-said-what-to-who the way you do."

"You're just trying to get me to do another story, but I'm not falling for it."

"Give me some ideas?" he implored.

"OK. Think of your happiest childhood moment," I said, imitating Dr. Small, the child psychiatrist. "You *have* to include your mom and dad and your brothers and sisters and the whole story has to have hot weather."

"The hot weather is easy 'cause I grew up down south. The rest . . . I don't know." He rubbed his face, which he did when he was figuring something out or he was a little nervous. "Ya know, I'm thinkin' of the strangest thing when you ask me about my happiest childhood moment? I haven't thought about this in over twenty years."

Roy told a story about when he was a little boy and his mother took in laundry. It was his job to keep the fire going under the barrel which held the white clothes that he stirred with a magnolia stick. He said that sometimes he would sweat so much he'd put out the fire. One blistering day a delivery truck pulled up to his back shed and unloaded a wringer washing machine. It turned out that Roy's dad had ordered it as a surprise for a certain young lady he was gallivanting with down the road; however, it was mistakenly delivered to Roy's mom. Roy said his mother was so upset when the washing machine was taken away, she fell on the unpaved driveway, clutching dirt in both hands, and gave birth to her ninth child, a sister who had water on her brain. Roy said her huge head carried the troubles for the whole family. All of Roy's brothers and sisters blamed the father for the sudden tragic birth. No one in the family ever talked to him again and Roy's older siblings ran him off the property whenever he tried to come by. Roy said he saw him in town once or twice after that, but out of respect for his mama, he never gave him any heed.

While my head was reeling about what it would be like to ignore your father for the rest of your life, to actually cut him dead on the street, and how God could have made such a mistake as to give Roy's father nine children, Roy went on to tell what was ostensibly the point of the story.

Even before the loss of the washing machine, Roy's mother had admired a wooden wagon with red sides in the window of the general store. Although it would have been perfect for delivering the laundry around town, they couldn't afford it, even by pooling the incomes of his eldest two sisters who "worked out."

Roy built a soapbox derby car out of junk parts and won a Fourth of July soapbox derby in his town. He marched right over to the hardware store and plunked down his prize money for that red wagon for his mother. Roy said his mother, generally "not one for words," because she was so busy and suffered from back pain due to a bad case of "the dry bones," recognized his efforts to make up for the phantom washing machine, saying it was the nicest surprise she'd ever received and he had not one drop of bad blood in him.

—

Roy rubbed his hands together and shivered. "Now that was one long time ago — and I can still smell the new rubber wheels on that wagon, and I can still see the red fence sides — how they fit in them grooves."

"You know, you've been a driver ever since. You love driving if it's a car or a truck, as long as it has wheels."

"You know I never thought of that, but you're onto somethin' there."

"You even love the dolly on the loading dock. Why, I bet you'd even marry a forklift. You know, like the one at Veverett Lumber?" Roy just shook his head when I got what he called "carried away."

It was really cold now and dark, so dark there wasn't a light in the sky. Not even a star or the moon. My father had a telescope so I knew a little about the constellations. I couldn't believe they didn't even have astronomy in Wheatfield. There hadn't been a car or even a rabbit since we were stranded, which had now been a long time. I was beginning to feel tired, as though everything were a big chore. Even talking seemed sort of exhausting. My ears had hurt a while ago, but now I couldn't feel them when I touched them. When I bent my hand, my mitten was hard. I'd never heard of wool freezing. I felt like I was wearing woollen casts on my hands. "Roy, do you think we'll be found?"

"Yup." He wanted to be enthusiastic, but he could barely manage a whisper. I was dressed more warmly than he was. When I suggested he have a cigarette, which had always rejuvenated him, he said he was too tired to light it, right then. *Jeepers!* I thought. He started talking to me about how nice it would be to have a hot toddy at Shim-Shacks. "Wouldn't that be a great wagon." *Wagon?* Roy was drifting off, but his eyes were open.

"Roy, Roy!" I yelled. "Roy, son of a sea cook!" That's a phrase my father used when he hammered his finger when doing carpentry or if something really made him angry. "This isn't funny. Cut it out and let's make some *plans* here." Roy was breathing heavily and leaning back on the headrest. I realized there were not a lot of plans to make. It was windy outside and we were starting to freeze. I could press in the lighter but what would I burn? Then I started to imagine things. I saw a big red light spin in the sky and then it came closer and closer like a pink tornado and then I blinked and realized a police car had pulled up behind us.

The police knew who we were. In fact, they were looking for us. They had us get out of the car. I wondered why, since we were already freezing, did we have to step out into the wind chill factor? Roy whispered that he was getting ready to cross the river Jordan as he stumbled out.

The Wheatfield police told us to put snow on our faces and hands before we got in the cruiser. They said we were "subject to frostbite" and that we couldn't thaw out all at once or else all the blood would go to our frozen parts and "bust the vessels." The policeman said we were "welcome to thaw," but it had to be very slowly. I stood up in the wind and put snow on my nose and hands and then got in the cruiser. By the time we got to Niagara Falls we were in more pain than I can ever remember having. My ears and feet started to pound like the Telltale Heart and it got louder and louder and I truly believed my ears would burst. Then they felt hot, prickly, and itchy. The nurse in emergency told me not to touch them, but as soon as she left the room I scratched my right ear. I guess that's when I lost a little chunk, or maybe it was earlier. Roy had to be wrapped in a special blanket, and they told him in the future he would be more susceptible to frostbite and that from now on he always needed to wear a hat. When they said his nose would never be quite the same, he smiled and said, "There's nothing wrong with a little change."

CHAPTER 9

warty

It was a spring afternoon in 1958. Sputnik had just been launched into space, and I was stuck on earth in the same spot I'd been in for years — stuffed into a small desk with its attached chair. I really couldn't listen to Mother Agnese, my teacher, any longer. I looked longingly out the window at the yellow forsythia that waved, begging me to come outside. Purple lilacs were in bloom along the chain-link fence. I was sure God did not want us to be sitting in the same spot seven hours at a stretch or why would he have given us legs?

I daydreamed about pioneer days, my favourite era. I imagined myself on a farm in the backwoods of Tennessee. There was no school because it hadn't been invented yet. America was too busy for that kind of thing. It was my job to trap for the family, so I set off in my coonskin cap with my rifle and my dog, Ol' Yeller, at my side. I waved goodbye to my mother, who wore a long dress and made pies in the kitchen. As I tramped blissfully through the rough, smelling the wet earth and sweet grass, I popped open milkweed pods and blew the seeds into the air to see which way the wind was blowing.

My reverie was disturbed by the laughter of my classmates. I looked up to see Mother Agnese looming over my desk. "Well, Catherine, I'll ask you *one* more time what you think." What I thought about what? I had no idea what she was talking about. I didn't even know what subject we were on. I quickly worked backwards. We had already had lunch, lined up for the washroom, and parsed our sentences. Anthony McDougall had already been sent to stand in the coatroom for making "ungodly noises," which had to take us to about two o'clock. This must be history or social studies. We never actually had social studies that didn't have to do with God or Mother Agnese's view of the world; everything was one big fat subject entitled The World According to Mother Agnese, an as-told-to version — told by God to Mother Agnese.

Oh well, I guess I had to own up to not having been paying attention. If you didn't pay attention you paid in other ways. As if eight hours locked in school wasn't bad enough, you had to stay even longer to clean the chalkboards and sweep after school. As I saw it, I had three choices. I could be honest and say I wasn't listening and take my punishment like a man; or I could wing it and say something general like "I believe it's true" or "God has his reasons that are not for us to question." However, that was risky since I could make a fool of myself if she'd asked something specific. I opted for the third choice, which was answering a question with a question. This was also a risk since Mother Agnese was a lot sharper than the other nuns. That's how she'd made it to principal which, at Hennepin Hall, was top of the heap. I asked, finding the perfect combination of righteous indignation and genuine confusion, "How come everything interesting has already happened? For heaven's sake, we missed the Renaissance *and* the Reformation. Everything in history is old news. How come there are no saints now? Who are the Joan of Arcs or the Saint Theresas of Lewiston?" Some of the kids around me actually perked up and nodded their interest in this filibuster.

"As usual, Catherine, you are looking for the glory, the great deed. *God* will decide who is a saint. *You* must find grace in every-day life. It is you who must decide to live a holy and selfless life. When Saint Theresa was accused of knocking over a vase of flowers and she knew she hadn't done it, what did she do?"

How would I know? For sure this was a trick question and the answer wasn't going to be the obvious — whoever spilled it should clean it up.

Linda Low raised her hand and said in singsong perfection, "She fell to her knees and prayed for God's forgiveness as though she had dropped the vase. She found redemption in her humility.

That's why she is called the Little Flower."

Great. I could see where this was going.

Mother Agnese picked up the ball and ran with it. "It was many years later that the Little Flower was canonized, but that does not mean she wasn't a saint in her own time."

"How can you be a saint if you're not canonized?" I asked.

Mother Agnese looked perplexed, as though I were not seeing the obvious. "There are great inventors who have walked silently among us; who, for example, invented the wheel?" (She ignored Anthony McDougall, who shouted, "Chevrolet!" between the slats of the coatroom door.) "Why shouldn't there be saints who do the same? Recognition is the least important part of sainthood. Canonization is only so we may have registered examples to follow." Mother Agnese took a deep breath, readjusted her wimple, and turned her penetrating gaze toward the rest of the class. "In fact, Catherine, your unusually dispirited vexation comes at an ideal moment, since we are about to embark on a unit in English called *journalism and interviewing*. As you know, all of our work is done for the love of God. Perhaps we could kill two birds with one stone. I would ask each one of you to find someone who lives amongst us, an adult you admire, as Linda admires the Little Flower, someone who gives to God every day by small but cumulative sacrifices. Those Sarah Bernhardts amongst us," she said, looking at me, "who are looking for the grand gesture, will have to revamp their idea of sainthood along more humble lines. Now we will make up a list of questions together, and I expect you to have selected your local saint candidates by Friday. Naturally, boys will interview men and girls will confine themselves to women. I would suggest you do not choose any relative since we already know their habits, holy and otherwise. It is important for all of us to help Catherine understand that we are not studying history but that we are part of it. As George Santayana said, 'Those who cannot remember the past are condemned to repeat it.'

I didn't know who George was, but I liked his ideas. I perked up, seeing myself as a part of history, and the idea that there were future saints around me made a spring day cooped up at Hennepin Hall slightly more bearable.

The saintly sleuthing became quite an event in Lewiston. Father Flanagan gave a sermon on the topic on Sunday. He announced that he, with the help of our good Lord above, would pick the winning essay and read it aloud at our May Day Procession in honour of Our Lady. This definitely upped the ante because I thrived on competition of any kind and revelled in public speaking. If I had to beat the bushes, I was going to find the one true saint in Lewiston.

Naturally Linda Low chose Mother Agnese. Several boys called my home that night and asked my father if they could interview him. Although he said nothing, I felt he was flattered, immediately inviting them out to "a breakfast meeting" the next morning. Two girls chose my mother, I guess since she arranged flowers near the tabernacle for the Altar and Rosary Society, and put up plaques on historical buildings telling who had slept there. I didn't see that as exactly *saintly*, but as my dad said, "Someone has to do it. And besides, any job done well has honour in it." He said it was up to me to decipher the difference between "honour" and "sanctification."

As far as finding a saint went, I was stumped. I read over the criteria again and again. *Did nothing for self-gratification, worshipped God in their every endeavour, both independently and through their church affiliation, and would perform good works no matter what the influences or what the personal sacrifice,* etc. I showed the list to Roy and he was equally baffled. We couldn't come up with one woman who was independent except for the five Kelly sisters who lived together in one house. They were independent, in that none of them married, but they didn't do much other than grow really old, breathe, eat, break their hips, and live in the big house that they grew up in. The Hooker family was a possibility because they had helped slaves cross the border to Canada, but that was a hundred years ago. I didn't think modern-day saints could live on the laurels of previous generations. There was Mrs. Aungier who taught piano and played the church organ. Unfortunately I had already had a run-in with her in my brief time on earth, when I suggested her daughter get "fixed" by Marie Sweeney. Mrs. Glish, the local baker, was always in a good mood, but I didn't think she'd do well on the questions about how she'd overcome adversity. She was too happy to have made a lot of sacrifices. Her worst day was when a cake failed to rise.

I became completely obsessed with this project, and talked over all my possibilities with Roy as we drove to the garbage dump. One thing I had to admit was that Mother Agnese had forced me to think about what a saint really was. I wondered aloud if you could be a saint if you had no adversity in your life.

Roy said, "Everyone has their own cross to bear, and the saint part comes depending how you carry it."

I told Roy I'd do him as my saint if he wasn't of the male persuasion. He thought that was a scream and could hardly drive the car. He said delivering wasn't his "only prowl." He said he committed all his sins after I'd gone to bed. I knew he was kidding because he never took praise well. I didn't understand why he shied away from compliments while I loved them. I basked in the light of praise as a cold-blooded lizard absorbed the heat from the sun. I told him how he always put on Marie's joint cream, and he always got a coffee for ol' Jim when we picked up the mail. I was a little embarrassed to say these things to Roy, so I tried to make them straight facts with no tinge of the admiration I felt. I told him it was the *gospel truth* that he made others happy. He said that he only bothered with people he liked, so that wasn't saintly. I retaliated, "When we're bone-tired after delivering Mr. Harlan's Digitalis, you always listen to his war stories."

He protested, "Come on, I love them stories about Saint-Mihiel, how he was talking to the guy next to him in the trench and never knew till the next morning he was stone cold dead."

"Roy! You know Mr. Harlan had a bad heart and never left the supply depot at Fort Niagara. I would have told him to stop being so silly, but you always listen to the same yarn about how he got trench foot in the Marne and lost two layers off his foot. You even *ask* him about the time he met Pershing." Roy shook his head, unconvinced. Not one to give up, I plowed ahead. "You even showed justified anger like God showed in the temple when merchants tried to sell their wares in God's house of worship."

Roy looked puzzled. "Now when was that? I swear you can conjure up whoppers to put Pinocchio out of a job."

"I got you this time," I retaliated. "Remember two years ago when Mr. Clifford — you know, the guy on the escarpment who gets the thyroid extract and is always working on his rock garden — wanted me to sit on his lap and I said no, and he kept going on and on about it and then started to pick me up? Well you stepped in front of him and said, in a real back-off kind of voice, 'She don't like that kind of thing.' Old man Clifford scurried mighty quickly right back to his rocker."

Roy looked at me, surprised that I'd remembered, and said, "Land sakes! Why, you're an elephant in a dress."

As we headed into the long narrow bumpy road to the dump, Roy said something I'll never forget. "Who you think is paying my salary when I doin' all this stuff you think is so good? Who you think pays for Marie's medicine, or ol' Jim's or anyone who havin' a hard time? *I* ain't in charge of that running tab. You check the prescription ledger and see who pays for what." I was shocked into silence, which for me was fairly shocked. Roy pushed ahead, seeing it was his chance to get a word in edgewise. "You know the Parker Pen set we delivered to Mr. Harlan that said 'In apprecia-tion for the war pictures,' signed 'From the Chamber of Commerce.' Everyone knew they weren't of Mr. Harlan. Who you think sent that pen set? You think it was the Chamber of Commerce?" I nodded, indicating that I thought they had. "Think again. They knew those war pictures were cut out from *Colliers* magazine and then mounted in Mr. Harlan's scrapbook. Why, they even had print on the back. They just threw them out. Who you think got that pen set, paid a pretty penny for it, and had Irene wrap it and write the card? I'll give ya one hint. It weren't me. I'll give you another hint. You think one of those boys at the breakfast meeting will ever hear any of that?"

"No," I said quietly, realizing Roy was not the only one who didn't need the limelight.

As we drove along I tried to figure out the world. It was like a map that I could see but for which I had no legend. I *thought* it was wrong to lie. Yet Mr. Harlan was a *normal* man, retired from Niagara Mohawk where he worked at a desk job, had a wife and grandchildren, owned a home, cut his lawn, decorated for Christmas. Yet he lied, actually told whoppers about the trenches and the time Pershing inspected his unit, and even foisted this bilge onto the Chamber of Commerce. For some reason Roy thought that was OK, and so did my father. It was incidents like this that made me realize how complicated morality really was. Was Mr. Harlan sinning? Obviously he had some kind of need to have fought in the war, and making him feel better was more important than his actual presence in France in 1917. Did each situation have to be judged individually or what? Who judged them? How much *time* would it take to judge each situation? I liked rules and I was happy to live within them or *know* I was disobeying them. It was the same in high jumping. I could make it over almost anything if I knew where the bar was, but I hated it when the coach kept moving the bar.

Noticing I was lost in thought, Roy said, in a precautionary tone to bring me back to the scene at hand, "Listen, girl, I hope you separated that garbage. I can't abide the wrath of Warty. You know she sent Irene's husband home last week with his tail between his legs, toting his garbage, telling him he best read the signs about sorting." Roy stopped in front of the locked gate that said Lewiston Dump. Roy knew the rules. He beeped the horn and waited. "Lord, she's coming toward us now," Roy said as he rolled his window up except for the top inch and braced the steering wheel with his long arms outstretched.

Warty, her real name, even on her prescriptions, lived and

worked at the town dump. She had a truly astonishingly grotesque appearance. Her skin was covered with brown lumps varying in size from warts to baseballs. The lumps were a much darker colour than her skin. It looked as if someone had spilled hot coffee on her and her skin had puckered and then shrivelled in those burned spots. Some of her larger skin tumours had the consistency of cauliflower. A number of the growths were on top of the skin and some grew under it, stretching the skin on top, making it smooth. Her head was so misshapen one could only tell its function by its location on her shoulders. Her cranium had a number of cauliflower protrusions that were so large they flopped over from their own gravity. Her skull looked as though she permanently wore a Harlequin hat with a pointy floppy crown. Her matted black hair grew around these lumps and looked as though it may have been naturally curly at birth, but had become too tangled to move, let alone curl. She had a fibrous growth below one of her eyes which pulled her lid down, exposing the red capillaries of the socket. This made her eye gape, and ooze like an open wound. Her other eye was masked under a floppy growth that looked like a wad of rolled-up pie dough protruding from her eyebrow. Yet she knew exactly who we were from fifty yards away, and she could tell any car horn from "the lot," as she called it. She had some growths on her back the size of footballs which were porous and looked like shrivelled heads. Some people in town said they were suitors who had kissed her and immediately shrivelled. Her spine had grown in an arc like a croquet wicket, instead of straight up, and she was so bent over that she used her hands for balance on the ground when she had to. Living on the steep shale escarpment was ideal for her condition because she could climb anything steep. While most of us teetered on the edge of the cliff, she scampered up the rocks with ease. Her feet were wrapped in filthy bandages to hold in her lumps of flesh so she could fit huge men's rubber boots over them. She was very tiny, and her voice had an unearthly pitch that frightened dogs and made them tilt their heads. Her voice sounded as though she were being choked and this was her last moment on earth. She also exuded a terrible strange smell. It was hard for her to keep the entire surface area clean and she would always have some infection. Maybe that's what caused the odour. In fact, that was why we were at the dump today. We had Mycostatin anti-fungal skin cream to deliver to Warty.

As I reached into the back seat to get the medication, the cyclopean Warty shambled toward us almost doubled over. She asked Roy if he had his garbage separated. Roy assured her he did and got two boxes of empty pill vials and crushed ointment tubes from the trunk. She opened the gate, and he waved as he went through. He said out the crack in his window that we had her ointment, and she screeched that we should throw the bag to the right and proceed on into the dry lot with our garbage. The closest she ever got was twenty feet from the car.

The garbage dump was a totally orderly sight where every wayward piece of garbage had its own home. Everything was divided up by substance and then further subdivided by use. (As it turned out, her obsession with garbage order and recycling was ahead of her time.) She never let anyone into the dump who didn't have everything sorted by bottles, paper, organic matter, large objects, dead animals, etc. She had an uncanny sense of smell and could tell if you'd cheated on the organic matter. If you didn't have everything sorted neatly, she simply didn't open the gate. She knew the cheaters and refused to let them in again, and they had to drive to the Niagara Falls dump.

To me the dump was an amazing, almost enchanting place. It was like a huge castle of many rooms with invisible walls filled with different glittering objects. I loved the heap of glass, especially in the sunlight when it glittered like a mountain of pirates' bounty. The pile of tires, when covered with snow and ice, looked like a glistening Tower of Babel. The old furniture was set up in room arrangements of couches, end tables, and various conversational areas. Sometimes when you drove through in autumn, the "rooms" would look beautiful with the red, orange, and yellow fall maples forming magnificent wall hangings and the fallen leaves forming soft carpets. As you drove to your destination you'd catch tiny Warty in a rocking chair swinging with the leaves. She'd wave and smile as you drove by.

All the roadkill was lined up flank to flank at the edge of the gorge so the smell would be carried away by strong wind from the river breezes coming from the Falls. The animals were lined up according to size and at a certain point of decomposition she'd cover them with ashes she obtained from burning the papers, to prevent rat infestation. All organic mass (*compost* was an unheard-of word in the fifties) was turned over regularly and made into what she called "Warty gold." (Roy said maybe "Warty" was short for "Rumplewartkin.") She used it as fertilizer on her four hundred tomato plants. No one had bigger or juicier tomatoes than Warty and she always gave some to each storekeeper who had helped her out in the winter. She also turned a profit on old appliances when she sold them to a scrap-metal dealer who came all the way from

New Jersey once a year with a cavalcade of trucks.

Warty was the self-proclaimed administrator of the town dump. She greeted all cars with authority that no one questioned, because if you did then you'd have to deal with her personally and *no one* wanted to do that. There wasn't a soul in Lewiston who didn't know Warty, since everyone had garbage and everyone had to dump it. Besides, she stood out in any crowd. Every family I knew had a box in the basement marked "Warty" and they put all their used clothes in it for her. She could wear children's clothes since she was so tiny. Once I saw her in winter with one of my outgrown orange toques hanging off one of her head growths. It looked as though a carrot was growing at a forty-five degree angle on her head. In the post office there was a big cardboard Modess box labelled "Warty" and everyone put their used clothes or canned foods in it for her. If someone had a party and there was food left, it was dropped off to her. At the Volunteer Firemen's Peach Festival there was a "go fish" booth with prizes donated by the Chamber of Commerce, and the profits went to Warty.

Although the town took care of her basic clothing and food needs, people were frightened of her. Not only was her appearance terrifying, but people were most afraid of catching her "warts." She was often used as an example of what a child could grow into if she disobeyed her parents. Mothers would say, "If you don't want to grow up to look like Warty, then you'd better wash your hands before eating."

Warty had twelve Dalmatians who always barked at the gate of the dump, and they alone didn't seem frightened by her high-pitched squeak that sounded as though she'd swallowed helium. Warty said she had Dalmatians because her spots looked like theirs.

Some carried this further and said that Warty was half-Dalmatian.

The janitorial nun, Sister Bridget of Kildare, wore a different habit from the other nuns, a blue-and-white pinafore for cleaning. She couldn't teach anymore because something had happened, I never knew exactly what, when she was up north in Canada teaching in some Indian school. Knowing that dirt terrified her, we sometimes tore up to her with mud from the playground on our hands. This infuriated her and she picked me up by my ear, which rang like the angelus bells for weeks. In her thick Irish brogue she told me, "If you like filth then you can have warts like Warty, and as one filthy lie after another spews from your lips, then your warts will grow with each lie told." She assured me that eventually I'd be the new Warty. When I laughed this off, she terrified me by saying, "What do you think that face of freckles is about, Miss Dirty McClure? It's just the beginning of the warts — mark my words."

There were various stories that made the rounds as to Warty's origin, since she had no family that anyone had ever seen. Some said she was born on Halloween — lightning hit some rotted cauliflower in the organic garbage pile, and Warty sprang to life. Some said that her mother was bitten by a lizard when she was pregnant with Warty, and that she was half-lizard. Some argued this point and said that she was half-skunk which accounted for her odour as well as her colours. Jim Mackay, a volunteer fireman, said that he'd heard that when she was in her mother's stomach, the poor woman stood too close to the flames of the Wheeler barn fire on River Road long ago, and Warty sizzled inside and she was born burned and popped.

Nee-Nee, my teenage babysitter, had the most terrifying birth story I'd ever heard. First of all she made me promise not to tell, assuring me that only she knew the real story and would know if I told anyone. She said that Warty was born to an unwed teenage mother who tried to hide her pregnancy by wearing a tight belt and hitting her stomach every day with a trowel, trying to kill the baby inside. When "her time" came, she went to the school washroom and gave birth to Warty. She took one look at Warty, wrapped her in the white pull-down towel with the blue line from the lavatory wall, and dropped her off at the dump, and the mother was never seen in Lewiston again. Although I didn't follow all the details of that tale, I was speechless with terror. For about a month after hearing it, every time my stomach growled I went into the garage and hit my stomach with a tin watering can.

There was a religious fanatic named Marian, who Dolores described as "pure as the fresh-driven *slush*," living on Ticonderoga Road, who had signs on her lawn quoting scripture which she changed monthly. She had no trouble with the short ones like "For the wages of sin is death"; however, she had problems planning ahead when writing the longer ones, like "He that toucheth pitch shall be defiled therewith," and had to scrunch the last few words at the bottom. I listened as Mrs. Helms told my mother that Marian stood up at town meetings and said that Warty was "original sin" and God sent her to earth to remind us that we were expelled from Eden as punishment for our own lust. Mrs. Helms, the town mayor, said it was only Marian's opinion, not town business, and she was getting the "lower element" of the town all excited with her "doomsday claptrap." I had previously thought the Helms were communists so I didn't know what to think when my mother wholeheartedly agreed with her.

Touching Warty was a risky proposition. Anthony McDougall

had warts on his hand and Clyde Ayers said that Anthony had touched Warty and she *planted* the warts on him — in fact, that's why they're called *plantar's* warts. Whenever Anthony came near anyone on the playground, we all screamed and ran away. Once when I was loading up for deliveries, I saw salicylic acid, Anthony McDougall's wart medicine, and told my father that Anthony got the warts from Warty when he handed her the garbage.

My father stopped in his tracks, saying these theories were ignorant and he had no intention of his daughter participating in such medieval nonsense. The word *ignorant* took me aback as my father never spoke that way to me or used words that would in any way cast aspersions upon me. Humiliated, I snapped to attention as my father continued. He said that Warty had Von Recklinghausen's disease (the name was later changed to neurofi-bromatosis, the disease made famous by *The Elephant Man*), which caused café au lait spots and tumours to grow on or under the skin. Her voice was strange because some of these growths had constricted her vocal cords. Her odd crooked walk was caused by enlargement and deformation of the bones and curva-ture of the spine. She probably heard sounds in her head, a condition called tinnitus, caused by the growths pressuring her ear drum which accounted for why, on occasion, she suddenly grabbed her head. It had nothing to do with being possessed by the devil or hearing voices. The reason she smelled peculiar was because it was impossible to clean between the protrusions, and when she did clean it was impossible to get all the surface area dry which caused the fungal growth and smell — to say nothing of the fact that she had no running water.

No one spoke after my father had explained all that. I loaded boxes and Roy carried them to the car. Ted counted pills and we all kept our eyes lowered. Irene, who had heard only the tail end of the conversation while ringing up a sale at the cash register, came back into the long narrow prescription room and said, "No matter what she's got, she's not right in the head."

That set my father off, I could tell by his thinning lips and the way he spoke with a kind of controlled patience that had rolling waves of agitation under it that I'd never heard before. "Of course she's not right. No one has talked to her for almost all of her abandoned life, so how would she know how to act normal? She has no frame of reference." He continued to pound a white powder with a mortar and pestle as he went on. "Not only does she have growths all over her, but people have made her feel as though she has been the cause of her own disease. Her illness was translated into evil, or into communicable disease that could corrupt or infect anyone near her. No matter how much Anthony McDougall touched Warty, he would not get the disease. Von Recklinghausen's disease is *genetic*, which means it's inherited, and is unfortunately autosomal dominant." I had no idea what he meant. Usually in situations like that I asked for clarification of all the details, but in this case I simply wished he'd stop talking about it. After pounding for a while in silence, he continued. "That means that if one parent has the disease, each of their children has a fifty per cent chance of inheriting it." He lowered his voice and said, "If anyone were to be interested in the truth, they would have found out that Warty's mother had the same disease and died young, leaving Warty on her own. With all Warty's been handed, does she ever ask for a thing? *No*. What about all the people who have arthritis in one finger joint? They come crying to me every day. What about all those Helena Rubinsteins who drum up cosmetic bills they've no intention of paying and come to me crying the blues about how they have had bad times? Has anyone ever heard a word of complaint from Warty or has she ever asked for a dime? *Never.* She has given unstintingly to this town while being ostracized by it." As he added his crushed powder to an emollient with a spatula, he said as an afterthought, "I think she deserves a medal for getting up in the morning." Roy and Ted nodded, but Irene just kept busily unpacking her free samples from Revlon.

I opened the thick steel-lined door, blinded with bright spring sunshine as it bounced off the loading dock. Blinking like Paul on the road to Damascus, I too was thrown from my horse by blinding revelation: *Warty was the Saint of Lewiston.*

My guilt and humiliation faded and actually turned mighty quickly into exaltation when I began to make my plans. I'd found Warty's permanent state of grace and would be responsible for having her canonized when I wrote about her and won the contest. (Humility wasn't my strongest suit.) I also knew that I had to interview her as a penance. I had laughed when Warty got on the bus. I'd run to the back with the Baker sisters when Warty's smell wafted our way. Warty had always appeared oblivious and it was only now that I let myself feel how cruel I'd been. I, like Mother Agnese, would kill two birds with one stone. I would win the contest, get Warty canonized, and atone for my sin at the same time. Why, this wasn't two birds with one stone, it was a virtual scattergun of good intentions. Although frightened, I knew I had to do this completely on my own, as Warty was on her own. If I went with Roy it wouldn't count as a penance. It would be hard not to tell him, but I knew it was necessary.

No one knew where Warty lived. It was somewhere in the woods up the steep escarpment rocks with no road or path entry. It had to be somewhere near the rock quarry which was used as the dump. The first thing I realized was that I'd have to skip a day of school. This would take a whole day and I worked on weekends. I couldn't come up with anything other than a birthday party that would let me off work, and Roy would take me to those and pick me up afterward.

I started out early for school on a crisp spring morning, when the dew was still threatening frost. I'd packed my plaid flannel-lined dungarees and matching flannel shirt in my Ponytail tote book bag. I also put mittens in my lunch box in case I had to scale the rocks on the escarpment. I hoped her home was on the road side, instead of the river side, as I had no desire to hang on to rocks with whirlpools below me. God, I was nervous about finding it, and I'd never been as far away from home on my own before. The night before, in my own toasty little room, I confidently told myself that it was within walking distance of the dump; but in the clear cold light of morning I acknowledged that I had no idea in what direction her house was from the dump.

As I passed school on the other side of the street, I saw all the kids crowding into the double doors of Hennepin Hall at nine, like sheep to the slaughter. I wondered why I'd never thought of skipping school before. Why, I could take a bus to Niagara Falls (not that I'd ever really do that) or go the library and read Nancy Drew mysteries. I could go shopping on my own and even buy a straight skirt like Nee-Nee had with a kick-pleat and a buckle in the back. After all, I had my own money.

When I'd woken up that morning I'd felt terrified at the prospect of actually talking to Warty. First of all, her wheezy little squeak was really hard to understand. I tried to remind myself that all the people in the town were superstitious about germs and acted as though they had never heard of the twentieth century, as my father had said. I gained confidence as I walked out of the village toward the huge shale escarpment. I started up the Lewiston hill on the road and realized I'd been walking a long time. I kept looking over the edge, and all I saw were whirlpools below me. Finally I saw a monorail track which must have been the remnant of the abandoned pipeline to Canada. I decided to follow it, figuring it couldn't be too rugged or narrow if a train could get through. If they were going to build a pipeline they would pick the most direct route through the escarpment. Still, I had to hold on to huge shale juttings and pull myself up to keep hold of the rusty old monorail. The bottoms of my feet hurt from bending them around rocks and tree roots as I climbed straight up through the foliage.

I decided to sit down, have my lunch, take off my shoes, and rest and dry my feet in the sun. I sat amongst the blowing Queen Anne's lace and opened my Fluffernutter that I'd made myself that morning. Usually I went to a restaurant for lunch, but I knew I'd be too far away today. A magnificent panorama unfolded as I looked down the escarpment and across the river to Canada. Gulls dipped into the river, landing like Sky King's plane. I was convinced I looked exactly like Penny, the female pilot on that TV show, and made my mother fix my hair in exactly the same braids as she wore, on the off chance I would be mistaken for her. The sunlight on the swift current made the river appear covered in

floating blue fireflies. On the Canadian side of the gorge, the landscape above the escarpment had cherry trees in white blossom,
accented by a saucy petticoat of pink flowering almond.

I was transported to my favourite era, the pioneer days.
Suddenly I became Hawkeye, the explorer in *The Last of the
Mohicans*. I pretended to share my Fluffernutter with Uncas, the
brave Mohican of the title, and I could tell by his expression he
had never tasted a Fluffernutter before.

As I sat on the steep canyon slope, I thought of how this spot
called "the portage," a title still used today, was named by the
French fur traders long before the Mayflower landed. It was the
only French touch, or what I thought to be a cosmopolitan flair,
within Lewiston and I liked pronouncing the word with a French
accent. We enacted this portage route every year in our school play
with me as the narrator. (Dolores said I was always given the star-
ring role because I had the biggest mouth, but my mother said it
was because my voice had resonance and I knew how to read with
expression.) I pointed out to the audience of parents, who had
seen this play every year since the year dot, and "visiting digni-
taries," Mother Agnese's term for a priest from a neighbouring
parish, that many years ago there was no way anyone could travel
through the interior of eastern America because of its dense bush.
The only means of travel was through the waterways and we were
lucky that God had thought to connect the Great Lakes. The only
problem was that every traveller had to portage around Niagara
Falls and carry all their belongings to lower ground. Whoever
controlled the portage, the land of Lewiston along the banks of the
river, controlled trade from the St. Lawrence to the Mississippi.

I then quickly darted behind stage and changed from my

moderator first-communion dress to my French costume and led the portage. Father Hennepin, our school's namesake, played by Patrick Hyla, the angelic head altar boy, was a Franciscan explorer who came here as a missionary to convert the Indians. Our class loaded up our white cardboard canoes with some of our mothers' old furs, fox pelts worn over their suits in the fall, replete with feet and heads. We wee Frenchmen, in our stocking caps and knickers, all the girls dressed as men since there were no roles for girl explorers, were paddling along, in our folding chairs with the cardboard canoes attached and suddenly we would find ourselves on the edge of the Falls. The great cataract was represented by a fan behind a blowing blue curtain. Father Hennepin and Father Jacques Cartier would pray to God who, just in the nick of time, would inspire Father Hennepin into suggesting portaging around the Falls through Lewiston. Then we would march around the lunchroom holding the canoe over our heads reciting different passages from history. One year I was a Seneca fighting the Mohawks, another I was a Brit during the French and Indian war. This past year I was an American colonist fighting the British.

The play came to life for me today as I crawled over those rocks. I realized how hard it must have been to portage on this cliff carrying your canoe over your head filled with everything you owned. I wondered how many must have gone over the Falls until they figured out the rushing currents and how early you had to get off the river before being swept away. I thought of all the countries and wars fought and lives lost over this portage that has again reverted to wilderness. Now no one valued it except for Warty.

Little did Warty or I know that the steep Lewiston hill and its dramatic escarpment would disappear within a few short years.

The only thing left of the geology is the memory of it. Even the fossils that lay buried in the earth, the layers of sea life, the dawn of man, the Indians, the portage, the geophysical remnants of civilization up through the 1950s, were dynamited for the New York Power Project. Even the Maid of the Mist would have trouble finding her way because the Falls has been rerouted.

It hadn't occurred to me that it was noon already, and if I walked home right then I could barely get there before school was over. On I trudged, chatting to Uncas, darting behind trees, ducking the redcoats until I emerged in a clearing where wild crocuses had been trampled, and I smelled smoke.

Suddenly Dalmatians came running toward me, showing their fangs and shaking with rage. Surrounded by barking, I was sure I was going to be eaten — I'd wind up another carcass in Warty's pet cemetery. Anyone who had ever been this close to Warty's before, and that couldn't have been many, because I had to squeeze between two rocks which no adult could have done, would be frozen in their tracks by these hounds. One of them had white foam in the edges of his mouth. It was moments like this when I wished I'd travelled with dog biscuits like Alexander Hamilton, the bread man. I remembered Roy said that when a dog barks at a customer's door, never look it in the eye because that's a challenge. So I looked up and stood still. Looking around, I realized Warty had built a brilliant fortress high on a stone cliff with whirlpools beneath her. The pass was hard to find and too narrow for an adult to get through. Once you scaled the wall there was the modern equivalent of a medieval moat. Her dragons were spotted and leapt out over the rocks. I was too terrified to descend, and my legs were shaking like a newborn colt's. Finally

I heard a shrill whistle from Warty, and the dogs begrudgingly returned to the house.

Warty, still fifty feet away, motioned me to go away with her arm as she turned to walk into her house. I knew it was now or never so I piped up, "Warty! Warty, it's Cathy McClure." She turned around, nodded, as if to say that she *knew* who I was, but still wanted me to go away. "I'd like to talk to you for a minute." Suddenly the idea of interviewing Warty as a saint seemed really far-fetched, to say the least. Warty kept walking away into her diminutive shed, which I later surmised was her home. It looked like a dormitory for the seven dwarves, no more than four or five feet high and long, like a chicken coop. The dogs followed her to the door but circled outside whining, hovering, and scratching at the earth, waiting for Warty to tell them they could attack me.

I didn't know what to do since she had gone in, and the dogs — I counted nine — would never let me approach. I inched my way toward the house where the dogs stood, eyeing me. Finally I must have taken one baby step too many, and they went berserk. I imagine I'd been closer than anyone had ever been to the house and the dogs vacillated between rage and shock. Warty walked out and shooed them all away from the door and motioned me to come in. I must have been standing outside for about twenty minutes and she figured it had been enough of a standoff. I walked up to the white cinder-block shed that probably had been used as a depot for the gas company many years ago. The whole place was no bigger than my bedroom. This one-room home boasted no modern amenities. It had no electricity nor any kerosene lamp, no running water, and no bathroom. For some reason she had three ladders going to the roof.

I tried to explain why I was there, but for one of the first times in my life, words failed me. The climb, the dogs, the proximity to Warty, the wacky saint idea had finally caught up to me. I fumbled for an explanation but wound up mumbling incoherently. I had no way of making myself understood. I made several introductions — I had come to visit her . . . to talk to her . . . to interview her. Finally I ground to a halt as I looked at the terror in her one visible droopy eye. Her pupil had dilated and she was breathing as though she were about to engage in a battle to the death. My assumption, which I was rapidly revising, had been that she was lonely and would ultimately welcome guests. It had never occurred to me, until I smelled the fear in that tiny room, that Warty might be as frightened of others as they were of her. It hadn't occurred to me, until I was standing there, that she might not *want* company. After all, her space was all she had. Probably no one had talked to her before, and I'm sure no one had visited her before.

One of the things fear does is speed things up, and that includes learning. Suddenly I realized that if no one had been nice to Warty, of course she wouldn't miss them. She probably stopped longing for guests, friends, or any human company, about five minutes after she was born! Boy, had I been stupid. It hit me that I had tried to imagine what Warty wanted, but only from my own perspective. I had no idea before that moment that there were different vantage points. People had been nice to me so I'd miss them. Loneliness was a concept totally dependent on one's previous experience. I was shocked to realize that yet again the rules were falling away. "Everyone needs a friend" or "All the world is lonely" are lines for samplers, but that was about it as far as *truth* went. I had a feeling of vertigo and didn't want to look over the edge of the escarpment again. How would I get home? I felt myself slipping. Everything depended on something else. At that second, a line from one of Roy's jazz songs came into my mind. The line was sung in a defiant staccato at the end of each verse and Roy and I used to sing it together — "Real, compared to what?" I understood what that line meant at that exact moment in Warty's house.

I decided to back off from explanations and just look around until she got a little used to me. Her chair was two potato sacks filled with straw, one for the cushion and one for the back. The rest of the furniture was from the dump. The bed was old and had obviously been thrown out when a child had outgrown it, for it had been painted white and was covered with decals of nursery rhymes on the headboard. There was a blue cow jumping over a yellow moon. The bed was topped with an air mattress, the type I used when I floated around on Lake Erie, drinking a Coke in the summer. When I saw the nursery-rhyme decals, I recited aloud pointing to the illustrations. "Hey diddle diddle, the cat and the fiddle, the cow jumps over the moon." Warty's face softened slightly, so I continued, pointing in sequence to the decals of the dog, the dish, and the spoon with legs: "The little dog laughed to see such sport, and the dish ran away with the spoon." She stopped looking so frightened and smiled and pointed to another one of an egg in a tuxedo jacket with skinny legs perched on a wall. I said, "Humpty Dumpty sat on a wall, Humpty Dumpty had a great fall. All the king's horses and all the king's men, couldn't put Humpty together again." She clapped and smiled her toothless grin. Her one eye was dancing merrily.

We went around the bed and I did "Little Jack Horner," "Old

King Cole," "Mary Had a Little Lamb," and "Old Mother Hubbard." Then she pointed to them again and we did it all over. By the third time she was humming the rhythm with me and nodding her head as the floppy growths on her skull moved from side to side. I wondered if this was the only thing she remembered from her childhood. Maybe her mother had told her nursery rhymes before she died, or left her, or whatever. Maybe Warty had been looking at the decals for years and wanted to put words to the pictures. It would definitely be hard to make a story of an egg with legs, an old woman who lived in a shoe with children hanging off the shoelaces. I thought these characters might have been her only friends. Who knows? Maybe she just liked the rhythm of the nursery rhymes. That wasn't so weird. After all, I certainly did and so had thousands before me.

Her cupboards were empty appliances. She had taken the doors off old fridges and put the fridges in a row and now kept blankets and food in them. Cans that had been dropped off for her at a range of fifty feet had been carefully unpacked and sorted.

She had obviously picked things she liked out of the garbage and had quite a collection of stuff. She made an expansive gesture with her arms, encouraging me to look around. I found a pair of mother-of-pearl opera glasses which I held up and peered through. She then opened a box and displayed a pile of used binoculars that were in cracked, old leather cases with ripped satin interiors. I realized that looking out for enemies was a big thing for Warty. That's probably why she had the ladders up to the roof. When she was up there she could see anyone coming from a long distance if she could see over the cliff. There were three more old dogs in the shed with us; one had white frosty eyes, while another limped with stiff hind legs, and the third never moved at all. Warty poked him and laughed and recited in a tiny squeak that I had to listen to with all my might in order to understand, "All the king's horses and all the king's men couldn't put Humpty together again," and we laughed. I told her that the next time Roy and I came to the dump we'd bring her a book of nursery rhymes. "Roy don't read." She swallowed air to say words.

"How did you know?" I asked.

"He always asks Warty when the dump is open and it's on the sign. People don't talk to Warty unless they have to."

Even after I'd been there what seemed about half an hour she hadn't asked what I wanted, and as time went on I had less and less of an idea of how to bring it up. Finally I decided to just lay it on the line. "Warty, I have to write a paper for school and I have to interview someone I admire, so I chose you." Warty just laughed and then showed me her pulley system for pulling cans out of the hot fire outside. I didn't know what more to say since she had obviously dismissed what I'd said as ridiculous. She must have understood the words, for she understood the nursery rhymes. I decided to forge ahead as though she had said, "Oh, an interview, what a lovely idea, I'm flattered." "Some people chose Father Flanagan, some chose Dr. Laughton," I explained. She made a face when I mentioned his name and I mimicked it in agreement. "Isn't he the worst? He always acts like I'm crazy or something." She nodded in consensus. I told her the story about how Dr. Laughton said I was hyper, and how I'd wound up at a psychiatrist. I told the story of the disgusting dog cards and she really laughed out loud, a normal-sounding laugh, and she wanted me to tell the story about the disgusting dog cards again.

She never spoke in a full sentence but seemed to understand everything I said and could say it back to me. It was difficult to understand her because her speech was sort of belched in a high-pitched squeak. As if the growth-laden oesophagus wasn't enough, she had tumours on the roof of her mouth preventing her from forming certain words properly. She also had no available lower lip so she couldn't make a P, B, or M sound, each of which required the lips to meet. I had noticed she pronounced Humpty Dumpty "Huy Duy."

She said, "When Warty went to Dr. Laughton, he shooed Warty out. Warty only went once when she broke her foot. Warty just wanted a cast. Instead Warty was an outcast."

We laughed at this play on words. I wondered why she referred to herself as Warty instead of I. I didn't know if I should say anything, but I really wanted to help her. "Warty, you can say, 'I want a cast.' It's the same as Warty when you are talking about yourself." She responded with a faint smile as though she really didn't understand what I meant, so I let it go. (I later found out that if a child suffers extreme deprivation, like the Wild Boy of Avignon, or Kaspar Hauser of Germany, who were isolated from birth for ten years or more, then they will have the peculiar permanent linguistic impairment of not being able to refer to themselves through the first person. Kaspar Hauser's teacher reported that Kaspar himself had no idea that he was indeed Kaspar Hauser. No one knows if the problem is linguistic, philosophical, psychological, or all three.)

"Can you follow Warty's words?" she asked.

I knew I had to be truthful, as I could tell she was a lot sharper than she appeared. People must have been dismissing her for years, assuming from her garbled speech that she was retarded. "I'm following more than half and the rest I'm filling in from the gist of things. I guess talking isn't the most important thing if you have no one to talk to." I'd mean that as a comfort, but it hadn't come out right.

"Warty's got friends outside," she said, walking out into the spring air. She showed me her collection of bees and her beehives. "Don't even use gloves or smoke. They know Warty's their friend, never been stung. These are Warty's girls, and those," she said, pointing to the Dalmatians, "are Warty's boys."

As we returned inside, I timidly got out my notebook and offered to share my Three Musketeers bar with her. She said, "Warty eats alone." I realized, looking at the pendulous growth on her lower lip, that she might not be able to keep her mouth closed when she chewed and she had no desire to embarrass herself. I wondered what it would be like to never share a meal with another human.

Finally I just dove in. "Warty, your life has been pretty hard." She made a face pooh-poohing that idea and looked around the room as though for an escape route. I realized I needed more of an opener. "Warty, I'm doing a paper on a woman in Lewiston who is good."

"Keep looking," she said, cackling and shaking her head.

I could see her eye was starting to get its wariness back so I changed tactics. I decided to say nothing good about her at all, as she just saw that as fawning at best and outright lies and attempts to humiliate her at worst. Best to just ask her straight questions which I believed she would cooperate in answering. "How did you start out at the dump?"

"Warty's not leaving. Warty got squatter's rights here. Lawyer Scovell told Warty so."

After assuring her that no one wanted her to leave, I asked, "Did you come by your garbage system all on your own or did you learn it somewhere? My dad says you're ahead of your time on waste disposal and the streets would be littered with roadkill if you didn't go around town with your wheelbarrow and pick them up.

"Warty likes studying rotting things. Warty knows that anything that doesn't rot in the summer will freeze in the winter and we've got to start all over again. So Warty arranges the live stuff to get sunlight. Warty puts everything for the rag picker in one pile to get paid for by the bag and Warty uses the old appliances to store things like tools. Warty doesn't mind doing the garbage but she's not going to handle a big mess that can cause diseases or catch on fire."

"Who set up your clothing box in the post office?" I inquired.

"Mr. Scovell."

"It must have been before I was born. How did Mr. Scovell get involved?"

"He was the lawyer when Warty came here and the county was after Warty for this and that."

"Like what?"

"They wanted Warty to move on, but Warty got him to write that Warty's needed in Lewiston and filling a job that no one else can do and they went away."

"Mr. Scovell's a good man," I ventured about the venerable lawyer who was what my mother referred to as "civic-minded." People turned to him in a dispute whenever there was a legal question like wills or how big signs should be, but they also turned to him in moral disputes such as when Niagara University fraternity boys made Vinny Carmichael, who was pledging for them, eat raw meat and he choked to death. It never went to trial. It was Mr. Scovell who settled issues like that. Warty remained quiet. "Don't you think?" I prompted her.

She looked away and said, "He got paid."

"By whom?" Not wanting to say more, she again cackled in her high-pitched caterwaul. I knew that I was onto something. Warty had not been evasive up to this point. Why be evasive about who paid Mr. Scovell?

Warty began rifling through old rusty junk. Then she opened one of her old freezers which she used for documents and brought out two sheets of cardboard that were used for dry-cleaned shirts when they were folded.

"He knew that Warty wanted to be on her own." She pulled out a picture of a woman who looked remarkably like her, only less deformed. The woman in the picture had the smooth warts but not the giant cauliflower growths. It was a professional picture taken at the Peach Festival by a barker-photographer with a back-drop of Niagara Falls. On the back of the picture it said in black fountain ink, *Scovell 1908.* "Mr. Scovell gave Warty that picture."

"Who was your father?"

"A local man."

"Is it someone in Lewiston?"

"Yes it is."

"Who?"

"He paid Mr. Scovell to be Warty's benefactor and he thinks Warty doesn't know who he is but Warty knows. He doesn't want to know Warty . . . so . . . that's the way it is. Do alright on Warty's own. Kept it quiet this long, might as well keep on. Only living soul that knows is Mr. Scovell and the only soul who knows Mr. Scovell knows is you."

"Warty, I'll never tell anyone. I promise."

"It doesn't matter to Warty, he'd just deny it."

"Everyone has all these silly ideas about how you came into the world. Wouldn't it be better if they knew the truth?"

"Warty don't care what they think. If Warty cared she'd be dead long ago." She didn't say this with malice but only as a point of fact. She *had* to give up caring for the kindness of others. I suddenly saw her point. If she needed anyone they wouldn't be there for her. It was better to never need them. I guess she trained herself not to care the same way I trained myself to high jump — by discipline.

"Did you want friends when you were little?"

"Not that Warty remembers. Warty went to school until Warty couldn't do it anymore. They thought Warty was stupid because of the speech which was a lot better then, if you can believe it," she said, resuming her cackle. "Warty was meant to be with her spotted boys." She smiled and petted the cataract-fogged Dalmatian. I realized that to have asked her about loneliness would have been ridiculous. She only felt an absence of pain. "Stayed long enough to read and then got out, but brought a dictionary, and Warty used to sit in the post office mailroom when crazy Eddie let her in and Warty'd listen to people and learn how they talked." She looked at the picture again. "Ma sounded like Warty."

"How long have you been on your own?"

"Long time."

"Where did your mom go?" I asked timidly.

Warty laughed. "She got more warts than Warty and died when her growths took over her lungs. She choked when one took over her windpipe when Warty was little. Warty's been here since."

"How little were you?"

"Young. Don't rightfully know."

As I prepared to leave I wanted to say I was sorry for hiding under the covered porch at school when she walked down Main Street. As I started to rhyme off my apology, Warty looked stern for the first time and said she didn't want any of that stuff. Changing the subject, she said, "Your daddy's a good man. That's why Warty let you in today. One day years ago, before you were born and he'd just started up the store, he dropped off his garbage and surprised Warty by handing her some medicated cream. Warty never asked for it, but it helped a lot. He told Warty about the disease and about how it gets passed on if Warty were to have youngsters of her own. No one ever told her that before. He gave Warty something to help with the smell for Christmas every year. He dropped by a beautifully wrapped bottle." She walked over to an old oven and pulled out a blue bottle of Evening in Paris. "Even Artie, the Niagara Falls bus driver, said Warty smelled better."

For some reason the sight of the perfume bottle brought tears to my eyes. Warty tried to comfort me, hardly the point of my visit. "Warty's got a good job, her own boss, useful to everyone in the town. No matter how high and mighty you want to be you've got garbage. Warty never degraded herself. Only other people tried to do that. Why, Warty remembers once the Erie County Fair people found her, came all the way from Hamburg, when she was about your age and offered her a job in the freak show as 'Lizard Woman.'

They said they'd pay her good if she'd nab live flies with her tongue and snap them in her mouth like a lizard. But Warty wasn't going to be someone else. Warty was born in the dump and she knew enough to stay here and just be Warty. God gave her the calling and she's done it to the best of her ability. There's good in that."

Overwhelmed, I poured out, "Warty, how did you never get mean? Why didn't you figure you should treat people as they treated you? You know, an eye-for-an-eye kind of thing."

"You know Saint Francis?"

"My God!" I said excitedly. "He's my favourite saint."

"Saint Francis had to wear a hair shirt to suffer. Warty only had to wear her skin. He loved all the birds and the little creatures and they were his friends. So we have the same friends. Saint Francis had to get rid of all of his possessions, his clothes, and cover his good looks with stigmata. She had none of those problems." We laughed at that. I could tell that both of us had been taught by the Franciscan nuns. We chatted on about Saint Francis because for both of us he was a hero who had sustained us each in different ways. She told me that she went to mass, for her a very long walk, every morning at six, sat in the back, and left after the consecration. During these daily visits she stood praying at the foot of the side altar of Saint Francis, beneath the statue of our favourite saint who looked on compassionately. She shared her feelings with him, the saint who helped her solve her every problem and never allowed her to be lonely. As she said, "No one could have a better friend."

—

I had to walk home in the dark. Warty and the dogs walked to the tracks with me and I followed the monorail to the road going down the hill. I had a hike ahead and my legs were already scraped and spent from scaling the escarpment. When I started down Main Street, Constable Lombardy pulled over, motioned me in the front seat, and proceeded to tell me that they were getting ready to dredge the river for me. I'd seen him in action before, so I wasn't overly concerned, as I knew he liked to ham it up. When he asked me how school had been, he used his *Father Knows Best* voice, so I knew better than to fall into that trap. I told him I hadn't gone to school. I said I had hid in the woods and played Davy Crockett and lost track of time. As he drove me home he said he'd let my mother deal with that big fat fib and that maybe I'd like to remember that it was against *the law* to miss school.

When I got home, I found my mother sitting in the dark, rocking in a chair in the dining room, clutching her rosary, looking out the window with tears streaming down her face. She said she had called Constable Lombardy after she called Maureen Toohey, who said that I hadn't been to her father's restaurant for lunch and in fact I hadn't been at school. I realized I'd caused my mother pain and worry but I was fairly determined not to say where I'd been. I knew if I mentioned Warty it would somehow be her fault and I didn't want that. Although Mom tried to poke holes in the pathetic Davy Crockett story, it matched the scrapes on my legs. She said she was disappointed because, although I was difficult in some ways, she had *thought* that deep down I was sensible. She sat silently rocking for an amazingly long time while neither of us spoke. She knew she hadn't approached hearing the real story, but said that if I needed a day off from my routine, she wasn't going to lose sleep over it nor had she called my father to worry him. (I guess she'd rather call the police.) Her only request was that in the future I call and say that I'm alive or will be late. She never mentioned going out for supper so I just wandered through the dark house, went to my room, and curled up in my flannel sheets, trying to get warm and fighting off hunger.

When I wrote my essay on Warty, entitled "A Saint Walks Amongst Us," I compared her to Saint Francis of Assisi and said she had offered up all her sufferings to Christ and she bore her own stigmata. Plus she forgave all of her tormentors, who were not the Romans, anti-Catholic kings, communists, or other atheists, but the people of Lewiston who felt she was possessed or contagious, when she was neither. While Warty crept through the dump, the catacombs of Lewiston, she was a martyr in that no one had more sufferings to offer up to God. Not only did she do it, she did it with grace.

I never mentioned our interview, Mr. Scovell, her mother, or her father who was *not* a saint, but was amongst us. He was one of us who passed her on the street. Yet she never blew his cover, not for her own revenge, nor for longing for a family or someone to assuage her own loneliness. Now, *that* was true sacrifice.

I thought it was the best thing I'd ever written. I wrote it in one sitting with tears streaming down my face. I said that no one can be a martyr unless there is suffering. I was one of the people who had been cruel to Warty, but she forgave us as Christ forgave his tormentors. She echoed Christ's words to God the Father: *Forgive them for they know not what they do.* She used her suffering to cleanse her soul, which was only one of the features that made her a saint.

——

Two weeks later we had a May Day procession for the blessed Virgin Mary since May, the month of renewal, was dedicated to her. The winning essay was to be read aloud by Father Flanagan and offered up to the Blessed Mother. Each girl carried flowers for the Virgin Mother. I hauled all the peonies in the procession since my mother donated most of the flowers for the May Day altar. Peonies were my favourite flower. I loved to watch trade-offs in nature and one of my favourite was how the plant was crawling with ants that chewed the wax off the buds in early May, allowing the flower to blossom each year exactly on time for the May Day festival. The procession commenced at dusk and we all carried lit candles as we proceeded from school to church singing "Ave Maria."

I had insisted on a new outfit and straw hat (not yet ready for a hair shirt) so I could be ready for the presentation. Even though I didn't tell my mother, I was sure that I'd win the contest. Father Flanagan would call me up to the altar, and my essay would be read aloud. I wanted to wear something no one had ever seen before. As Roy said, women couldn't remember how to change a tire, but they never forgot one another's wardrobes. I bought a new yellow dress and wore satin yellow ribbons in my hair and white gloves with yellow trim. The dress had a beautiful pale green satin cummerbund with a yellow satin rose rakishly placed to the side. The rose was protected from being crushed in the shipping and on the rack in the store with cardboard edging. (Dolores actually believed the cardboard edging was part of the dress!) I tried the dress on for everyone at the drugstore for a dry run, and they all agreed it was spectacular. It must have been really frou-frou because even Irene liked it.

On the hot spring night in church with a standing-room-only crowd, the girls led the procession, shortest in front, tallest in back. I was always the farthest back (we had learned in practice to silently count our steps with the word *steamboat* in the middle to slow us down). The boys shook the incense and rolled the statue of the Virgin Mother, resplendent in her white robes on her own little gurney. Hennepin Hall School filed in and sat in the reserved seats in the front of the church. During the rosary I glanced around and caught the eye of my father in his spring seersucker suit and my mother in her flowered shirt-waist and with her big-brimmed straw hat with the silk gardenia. I wanted to know where they were sitting so I could catch their eyes when I went up to get my prize.

After we had knelt for endless Hail Marys, we were finally allowed to sit in our pews for the presentation. You could feel the electricity in the air. I took off my gloves to receive my prize. When Father Flanagan began, I was sure he was looking at me so I smiled back. He began by saying that he had never realized that there were saints outside of Ireland. This got its requisite laugh and then he adopted his deep slow voice, the one he used when delivering the gospel. "These essays were the most profoundly moving documents I've read in years. When they say 'innocence from the mouth of babes,' they know from whence they speak. It reminded me of why angels are portrayed as children. Someday when we are all in heaven — at least I hope that will be our vantage point — we'll look down on the goings-on in our own little Lewiston and realize how wonderful and holy it really has been in its blessed innocence. Everything that *seems* to be run-of-the-mill, even boring, in the present, will one day be sacred to us. The change of the season, the little kindnesses, the milkman who stops his cart to congratulate you on the prize lamb."

There are no milk carts or lambs in Lewiston. He's waxing eloquent on County Cork in Ireland again. Wrong country, wrong county, wrong town, I thought. Sometimes his face was red, his voice was more booming than usual, and he didn't seem to know he was on this side of the Atlantic. I wondered if anyone else noticed it. I'd never mention it since I knew it was uncharitable to criticize another person, and a sin to criticize a *priest* since he brought us the word of our Lord. On that note I forced myself to tune back in.

"The small touches again and again are what make a life worth living. When Frank Beatello gives the extra penny candy, Jim McClure gives the pills for your pain and not your pocketbook, and Crazy Eddie delivers your parcel for once unopened! Mom's Hamburger Shoppe gives you the hamburger of your heart's desire and the Good Lord gives you the lilac air to breathe in the love shared throughout the town. I will never feel the same about any one person mentioned in these essays nor on the sanctity of Lewiston. I had a devil of a time choosing a winner, so in this trough of plenty I was forced to declare a tie. Would the two champions of canonizations please come forward and read their essays aloud: I welcome Patrick Hyla, our first-place winner who wishes to award Robert Moses, the engineer in charge of giving us power as the chief engineer of the Niagara Falls Power Project. As Patrick so beautifully pointed out, it was God who gave us the Falls but 'the saint is the man who takes what God has given us and shapes it into progress for mankind.'"

The church oohed and aahed over Patrick's words.

Father Flanagan stepped back up to the pulpit and announced that "Edward Fitzpatrick should come forward and read his essay on the saintly Nick Amigone. We knew the entire family of Amigones, who have been in the funeral business for three generations, had a calling when God named them 'Am-I-Gone?' What other vocation could the Good Lord have had in mind with a name like that? As Edward has so eloquently stated it, Mr. Nicholas Amigone is the first man in this town to see when a man changes from man to angel. Not only does he *em*balm, but he bombs the ball as the little-league convenor. Never one to ignore the need for Christian charity, he donated the uniforms for the Cataract Midget Baseball League. The Amigone brothers, Nicholas being the eldest — a devoted Yankees fan, I might add — have buried our bodies and watched our souls rise; they have given of their time and opened their tills. So, my good parishioners, whether these men will be canonized or not is up to Rome and to the future, but it has made me see God's light shine upon them."

My heart was pounding as I sank back into my pew. I felt my face suddenly heat up and blush as only a fair freckled complexion can do and I developed raspberry-stain blotches up my neck. I was fighting off tears that threatened to make my internal humiliation public, terrified that they would spill over and I would bring shame upon my whole family. I had no Kleenex, so I dabbed my eyes with my gloves and then focused on putting them back on, covering each finger with care while the boys read their saintly essays.

CHAPTER 10

the reservoir

In 1957 I was nine years old and the editor of my school's news-paper, *The Franciscan*. I had no idea what Saint Francis had to do with the news, but there he was prominently displayed on the upper-right-hand corner of the masthead, wearing his brown-hooded dress, talking to a bird as it perched on his wrist. I finally figured out that since he could talk to the animals and they understood him, maybe he was the patron saint of interspecies communication.

My mother, who rarely took an interest in things that other mothers seemed concerned about, such as food, my exact where-abouts, and bedtimes, was passionately interested in my newspaper and my editorship. Since the nuns were too busy offer-ing up novenas to relocate souls who had been marooned in purgatory, my mother volunteered to be the adviser on the paper. We had only two staff members, three if you include Saint Francis: Gordon Deede was the sportswriter who always rooted for his team and covered the World Series with breathless anticipation two weeks after it was over; the other was me, the editor-in-chief in charge of international and local news, businesses, the women's section, as well as all editorials. I had no idea I was supposed to assign editorials to anyone but myself so I cranked up the mimeo-graph with my purple prose each Monday covering "My Week in Review." My editorials ranged from "Why girls should be allowed to be altar boys" to one of my mother's favourite topics, "What *really* happens in the African missions." Fortunately I was not hindered by having on-site interviews such as actually going to Africa, but instead completed all my investigative journalism by relying upon my previous nine years of having lived in Lewiston.

Once, in 1956–57, the sleepy town of Lewiston was actually shaken by an issue of national importance and we hit the big map. We were all mesmerized to see ourselves and our little town spoken about in curt dramatic sentences by Huntley and Brinkley on the national news. Edward R. Murrow sat in his chair, smoked a cigarette, and talked to us, the town of Lewiston. Finally the

Supreme Court became involved and the greatest minds in the land debated about us, wrote opinions about *us*!

The participants were Lewiston and the Tuscarora Indians, and the issue was the same as it was when America was settled — land rights. It was the first land battle with the Indians to come to light since Wounded Knee.

In the 1950s, Lewiston Heights was the chosen site for construction of the largest water-driven power plant in the world. Its location just north of Niagara Falls made it an ideal spot for a hydroelectric power plant. The project required thousands of workers, effectively doubling the population of Lewiston, to chop away the rocks of the escarpment and eventually rein in the power of Niagara Falls and build the largest turbines to date, which would disseminate hydroelectric power for hundreds of miles in all directions.

The man in charge of this massive undertaking was Robert Moses. Naturally he was highly thought of by the town's Chamber of Commerce since their coffers filled as Lewiston filled with yellow hardhats which landed like canaries on every high wire. Moses was known for his efficiency; he actually completed the project within his budget and, to give you some idea of his time management, he was finished on the projected date of completion, which had been forecast seven years earlier. These traits of restraint and reliability were thought to be the paragon of American virtue. As my father said, "You have to hand it to the guy." This sentiment was reflected by Nelson Rockefeller, who immortalized him by naming the power project and a highway after him.

Naturally, such a punctilious man would be upset when he ran into a snag in his game plan midstream. He needed a great reservoir which would act as a gigantic storage tank for water that could be used in peak hours to supplement the flow from the conduit and drive the big turbines at the foot of the cliff. Moses wanted a good chunk of the Tuscarora Indians' land from their reservation because he did not want to disturb the white residents of Lewiston and take their land. The taxes that the whites paid would be lost if their land was expropriated. Moreover, it would be prohibitively expensive to purchase the homes and pay the owners for the move. Moses thought the best solution was to take the Tuscaroras' land, much of which was unused. The Indians paid no taxes and their homes were simple. Moses was certain their land would go cheaply. He estimated that the total costs of expropriation would be far less than moving the white residents of Lewiston and he would stay within his budget.

In 1957 the Tuscaroras mounted a campaign that Moses never anticipated. He expected the Indians, none of whom were well off, to jump at his financial offer. Instead, they unanimously voted to veto it, and as the negotiations dragged on, Moses doubled the sum, but the Indians refused to budge.

The Indians had a few supporters among the townspeople, most of whom were on the historical board, who said that Moses was bullying them. However, that trickle of support dried up when Moses pitted the townspeople against the Indians, saying one of them had to give up their land. No one wanted *their* house uprooted and moved on a flatbed trailer to the middle of nowhere, despite the offer of a paltry sum, a new basement, and a spindly sapling for their yard. Not only would people be uprooted, but the town would have a gigantic reservoir with dirt sides obstructing the view of those who remained. The town, which had wavered only slightly anyway, was suddenly solidly behind Moses, their prophet of progress who could indeed part the waters.

The villagers of Lewiston believed they had a central core or "business district" surrounded by well-ordered streets replete with homes, while the reservation had no central core and only a few dilapidated houses placed randomly throughout what appeared to be largely unused land. In addition to doubling the price of the land, Moses offered to name a generator after the Tuscaroras (the Indians laughed at the idea of firing up the "Tuscarora") and build a "recreational hall" for them, which left them bewildered. The settlers of Lewiston believed the Tuscaroras were "holding up the show" and Moses referred to the Tuscaroras' blockade as "the braves who are whooping it up."

These words didn't seem strange to us as they were the same ones our heroes Cisco and Pancho used and we mimicked as we played cowboys and Indians. I loved being the Indian brave because I could be totally bad. I could go back on all of my promises and tie kids up in the fort and go away and forget about them for hours, or tie them to trees and go home for lunch. It gave me a break from the uphill battle of trying to be more civilized than I seemed capable of.

The Indians set up a barricade and refused to let Moses' surveyors on their land. Several of the tribe members wore their war-conference headdresses, a myriad of feathers reminiscent of the plumage worn by the Indian in the concentric circles on the old television test pattern. Capturing the national press, they smoked peace pipes and claimed they would never give up their land, reminding the rest of the United States that they were part of the landscape before Lewiston was even a thought and that no matter how powerful Robert Moses was he was still doing something illegal.

Finally the war party of two hundred, who stood at barricades on their land, were confronted by thirty-five Niagara County deputy sheriffs, fifty state troopers with riot equipment, tear-gas bombs, and submachine guns, and a number of plainclothes detectives. No non-Indian was allowed beyond the blockade unless they were from the press — the media-savvy natives knew that the national press was all they had going for them, especially since the *Niagara Falls Gazette* had already taken a stand against them. In April of 1957 Governor Averell Harriman approved expropriation. In response, the Indians toughened their barricades.

My mother was passionately interested in history to the exclusion of the present but came very much alive for the reservoir debate because it was history in the making. She dropped her usual acquiescent role and sprang to the fore, demanding a press pass for me, saying that I was entitled to one as much as any other newspaper employee, and *The Franciscan* was in fact the only *truly* local paper. Much to my father's shock, since Lewiston was now the enemy of the Tuscaroras, I was granted interview time with the chief for the next day. My mother remained nonplussed, but I was convinced I was living the life of glamorous journalist Brenda Starr, my cartoon heroine. I secretly hoped that Basil St. John, the mysterious orchid grower who was Brenda's secret lover in his spare time, would suddenly enter my life since I was now "trailing a lead."

My father disagreed with my going to the reservation, saying things had become dangerous as "tempers on both sides have flared" and it was nowhere for a girl to be. He didn't forbid it, saying he never knew my mother to make a mistake in judgement; however, he said his opinion was simply "for the record."

As we approached the reservation in our two-toned grey Plymouth with its gigantic fins, which still reeked of new-car smell, my mother was stopped by rifle-toting state troopers in front of a wooden blockade at the entrance to the reservation. She showed a pointed-lidded state trooper a press pass which stated I was the editor of *The Franciscan* and he laughed, saying that I was only a kid. Humiliated, I slumped in my passenger seat and wanted to go home immediately. My mother assumed an expression I had never seen before and said that she was unaware that freedom of speech was reserved for adults. The state trooper leaned in the car and asked my age and I said ten when I was really nine, actually believing it made a difference. He said that this was not a kid's game, and that we were in the middle of some pretty desperate characters who were refusing to obey the law. He made a circle with his arm, indicating that Mom had to turn around and leave. My mother said that she realized the gravity of the situation — she was surprised that state troopers would invade property owned by someone else. Then she, my mother, the same woman who made me call and make her hair appointments because she was afraid the hairdresser would bully her into a time slot that she didn't want, the same mother who never committed a fashion faux pas, gunned the motor, rammed right through the barricade, drove up to the longhouse, and slammed the car into park. As I looked in the rear-view mirror I saw the guards who fortunately hadn't followed us but only looked shocked and began talking on walkie-talkies. My mother never looked back and said she was waiting in the car and I would have to go the office of the chief immediately in order to be on time for my interview. I couldn't believe that my mother, who had acted so crazy, was now sitting in the car as though she were dropping me off at Girl Scouts and I was supposed to handle this on my own. To say nothing of the fact that I had been afraid of Indians as a little girl and now that rusty arrow of terror had re-entered my heart.

My mother's face had that same set look as when she drove through the barricade. (My first thought was how angry my father would be about the scratches on his new car.) Being a quick learner I knew there was no arguing with that look, so, no longer feeling like Brenda Starr, but like a nine-year-old with a crazy mother, I opened the car door and trudged shakily through the longhouse, which was full of Indian men lounging on card chairs and looking sullenly at me or tired white men with cameras from the *New York Times* and the Canadian *Telegram*.

I slunk along the hallway to the office that had "Chief" hand-written in Magic Marker on the door. I pulled down my black-watch-plaid uniform kilt, tucked in my oxford cloth shirt, pulled up my green knee socks, straightened my tie, pulled my hair apart, tightening my blond ponytail elastic, looked down at my Bass Weejuns with the Indian-head nickels in them, and knocked.

As the door opened, there he stood in a full Indian headdress. First I recognized the eyes, the cat's-eye marbles, the large ones, the size of the shooter marbles we called bloodies. The ducktail was gone and now he had the shiny braids I had when I last saw him. Now he was six-three and I was five-seven. He leaned on the door frame and nodded. Whether it was a nod of recognition I'll never know. Neither of us was the person the other had met so long ago. He didn't shake hands but said, "I'm Mad Bear," and I replied, "I'm Cathy McClure."

I had a terrified moment when I was sure he would mention the past or else say something like "How're things by the store?" or "Say hi to Roy," to let me know he knew the incident had really happened. I had never let that incident be real. I called it a bad dream in my head and I didn't want Mad Bear to mention it now. As I stood there I knew he felt the same way and we had agreed to never let that episode be real and for some reason which I can't explain, we shared the guilt and shame of it together. The moment ticked by.

He sat down and patted a chair for me to sit next to his desk. He treated me with respect and kindness. He spoke in a slow and concentrated way and answered my prepared questions, explaining carefully that although he agreed with Moses that the Tuscarora land was unused, he didn't believe that land had to be used in order to be important to the Indians. He said the Indian view was that they were only custodians of the earth, which is sacred to all man. Land is something that cannot be sold or bartered, being held in common by all, like the air we breathe or the water we drink. The fact that the land had not been used, as Moses' aerial photographs had so clearly illustrated, made it more, not less, sacred. He called me "Miss McClure" and said he would like me to meet Elton Greene, a name I had heard nightly on the news. At the door stood Elton, but I knew him as Black Cloud from Shim-Shacks.

As the three of us walked out to the swamp, we jumped over traplines near the beaver dam. The majority of the Tuscaroras still made their living from fishing, hunting, and farming the land. As we parted our way through the bulrushes, Mad Bear and Black Cloud knew exactly where to find the pike eggs nestled against cattails in the watery, embryonic bog. If the inlet was destroyed for the proposed reservoir, the eggs would dry up before they had a chance to hatch. Open water held too much current for the eggs, carrying and ultimately crushing them against the rocks while dry land fossilized them. The swamp was nature's incubator, giving the pike eggs the watery, warm, still protection they needed for a calm, healthy start in life. If the swamp was dammed, then the Tuscaroras' livelihood was equally damned. As we stood in our matching knee-high black boots, Mad Bear touched a tree and asked me to place my palm flat on its bark. As we caressed the tree, he told me it was alive and felt pain in the same way he and I felt pain, and when we were cut we ran blood while a tree ran sap. Without a touch of anger in his voice, speaking in a tone of patient concern, as though he were talking of the well-being of a beloved family, he explained that if the reservoir was built, all of this life teeming around us would be suffocated, as if a truck were to come along right now, dump a load of topsoil on the three of us, and bury us alive.

As they walked me to the car, I asked Mad Bear why *he* was the chosen leader of the protest. He said it was part of the Bear Clan's tradition to ward off evil spirits. His great-great-grandmother had warded off evil spirits that took the form of stone giants and flying heads with no bodies. These flying heads were terrifying the Indians until one night a head flew through the door of his ancestor when she was roasting chestnuts. His old gramma was fearless and pretended she hadn't seen the flying heads as she sat facing the fire. Every few minutes she pulled a charred chestnut out of the fire and ate it. The flying heads thought that she was eating hot coals, and assumed a woman who could do that and not flinch was not to be messed with. Therefore they hightailed it out of the tribe as quickly as they had arrived, never to be heard from again. Mad Bear concluded by saying that, in the tradition of the Bear Clan, he had to have the courage to eat hot coals, or the cunning not to, to ward off the evil spirits that this time took a different form but were no less treacherous to the Tuscarora way of life.

I wrote up my article for *The Franciscan* entitled "When a Tree Bleeds" and it caused quite an uproar as it got carried home and disseminated through everyone's lunch pails along with basketball scores, the altar-boy schedule, and the joke of the week. Many assumed I had been duped by the Indians, and Dolores, who always had "her ear to the ground," as my father described her folk wisdom, told me I'd had "too much of the peace pipe." Roy said nothing, but I noticed he'd cut out my article and tacked it up on the bulletin board above his desk in the storeroom.

Father Flanagan discussed the issue at Sunday mass, saying we had some decisions to make and he hoped we'd all come to the council meeting as the apostles came to the Last Supper. These decisions should be made with God as our leader, not by the likes of Huntley and Brinkley or any other godless boys of the eastern seaboard. It was Jesus Christ our Lord who said that we are one family under God the Father; therefore, progress should benefit us all within that family.

My father remained silent on the topic at home and worked on the night of the big meeting to vote on the fate of the reservoir. I waited up for my mother and when she came home she regaled me with who said what. Apparently she had stood up, reminding the group that Robert Moses was merely a state employee, not the ultimate spokesman for defining what was progress. He had a job to do and he wanted it done cheaply and he shut us up as opposition by pitting us against each other. She referred to this as a legal massacre of the Indians, saying that history would be the final judge.

Moses' men stood up and said that not only would 282 homes be relocated, but 2,726 men would be out of work and two cemeteries destroyed if the reservoir was in Lewiston. Niagara Falls and Lewiston took the side of the Power Authority and Moses offered to pay triple what he started out with to the Tuscaroras to placate liberal guilt. The Indians were not letting Moses off the hook that easily. They voted unanimously to reject the money, saying their land had nothing to do with money. Moses could quadruple the amount and it would make no difference. If someone offered you thousands of dollars for your family, would you take it or simply be insulted when the price was raised?

Finally the issue went to the Supreme Court and the vote was six to three against the Indians. The court pointed out that the tribe had not acquired their land by treaty but by gift and purchase from the Senecas. The three dissenting judges were Warren, Black, and Douglas. Black's dissenting words, "Great nations like great men should keep their word," were the title of "My Last Week In Review."

My mother crawled back into her Republican closet faster than the pike eggs could dry up from lack of swampland and the Tuscaroras turned to bingo. Father Flanagan drove to the golf course in a shiny new Cadillac with Robert Moses and the nuns suggested it was someone else's turn to learn about journalism. It was time to hand over the mantle of *The Franciscan*; however, no one wanted the job so my purple press was laid to rest.

I began to see that the nuns and priests could talk about being our brother's keeper and the good Samaritan; however, once someone like Moses divided the waters, the real instincts of human beings lay at the bottom of the exposed riverbed where most of us were bottom feeders at heart. The big fish ate the little and that was how it worked. To me that was a revelation. I had spent years of my life believing everything that everyone *said*, even the advertisers on television! I had spent untold hours berating myself for being unkind and not always thinking about others first. I wanted to be the type who could breeze into the role of the sister in *The Nun's Story*, never be tempted by worldly goods, care only for the lepers of the world. I thought that a good Catholic was supposed to hear how to be altruistic from God — have the calling — and then act on it. I blamed myself for God's silence. If only I wasn't packed with selfish thoughts and a soul besmirched with the dirt of greed, God could have found His way in.

It never occurred to me that advertisers only wanted to sell products, and nuns and priests and parents only gave the party line but grew up with the same prejudices and instincts that everyone else had. I had swallowed it all. I had been one of those baleen whales who cruise through the ocean depths with their mouths open, ingesting everything that came along. My stomach felt full of junk. I could no longer take it all in. You didn't have to read Marx to find out about power or Darwin to get how the fittest survived. You could live in Lewiston and figure it all out.

I was cast in the opposition where I emotionally remained, regurgitating my first ten years. The problem with a small town is that when you don't buy into the powers that be, there are very few other choices. It's like a play where there is only a "virtuous" lead, a villain, and bit players. Better to be the villain because you're not duped into believing you're in more than a play, and at least your name goes on the program.

CHAPTER 11

mother agnese

Mother Agnese still lives within me. She's been my most admirable role model and my most formidable foe. We saw each other through several stages. She was my school principal and my teacher from first grade on and off until puberty. We both gained power in our own ways. I met her as Sister Agnese, then she became Mother Agnese, then Mother Superior. As she crept up the ecclesiastical ladder, I passed from being a little girl to a teenager. I started as the good Catholic girl who wanted to be Mother Agnese for Halloween, trying desperately to emulate her holiness. (Fortunately my mother convinced me that Halloween was only *called* the eve of "All Saints' Day" at school by Mother Agnese. For the rest of Lewiston, it meant picking out a costume at Woolworth's, and that it was more normal to dress as Tinker Bell than as a Franciscan nun.) Next there was Cathy, the troubled child who stabbed her classmate, and finally there was Cathy, the angry teenager who went head-to-head with Mother Agnese, fighting for her emotional life.

She always had the advantage, yet I was never given a handicap. She had God on her side and I was still trying to slide in on the right side of eternity, where she held the tickets to most of the seats. She, unlike Father Flanagan with his Irish lilt and weakness for "a wee drop," was an ascetic. She never took off the psychological hair shirt in all the years she taught me nor in the many years she was my principal. Although I didn't always agree with her, she never spoke with what Cochise, another one of my heroes, called a "forked tongue."

Like most formidable opponents, she ultimately became one of my greatest influences. I learned that you can't punish the martyr, and you can't take from the ascetic. If you try, you're involved in a tug-of-war in which they let go of the rope. Her voice is one of the few I still hear in my head whenever I face a moral dilemma. I still see her starched wimple framing her brow furrowed in judgement. Yet her message — stand up and be counted — wasn't really a bad one. I always felt that we had a special bond. At some level I recognized that we had similar personalities, we just played for different teams.

It's no wonder we were at odds so early. My initiation into school was truly inauspicious. My father was right when he said that, after working in the store for years before I went to school, I had no idea I was *really* a five-year-old child. On the first day of school, I vainly circled the room looking for my desk. I was mortally offended when I found out all I was allotted was a *nap rug*. Clutching my new zippered briefcase to my chest, I had arrived armed for learning, with paper, retractable pencil, note-book, protractor, eraser, nail file for manicure emergencies, and restaurant lunch money. I, and apparently my mother, had no idea that school was *over* at lunchtime. By eleven the din of children crying for their mothers was so loud, I felt like Scarlett O'Hara trying to help the thousands of wounded Confederates in Atlanta.

Over the first few months they attempted to make me into a devout kindergartener who sat inert in a circle learning to count from one to ten, and singing "The Farmer and the Dell." When you were really lucky you had a turn to be the farmer and got to pick the mouse from one of the stunned faces in front of you. I felt I had bigger fish to fry than *that*! Our most active moment was when we lined up for the lavatory.

My mother, who enjoyed pedagogy, had spent hours at home teaching me to read, to add and subtract, and all about history and anthropology. I even had a Mau Mau skirt. In the long run she didn't do me any favours, for that's when my delusions of grandeur began. Actually I was no smarter than anyone else; however, based on what I knew compared to my classmates, I *believed* I was the next Madame Curie. Naturally I was insulted when Mother Agnese suggested I spend whole afternoons learning the colours and reading Dick and Jane books. Mother Agnese had two aspects to her career: one was teaching reading and mathematics, both of which I already knew and was therefore bored and disruptive; the second was her vocation to strengthen our faith in God. Unfortunately, I seem to have been born a rationalist and, unlike my parents or others around me, had dexterity for the high jump, but not for the leap of faith.

I never blamed her for her anger toward me. I was demanding of time and attention. I was a bratty only child who thought she was smarter than she actually was. Once Mother Agnese's favourite, I had ultimately disappointed her. When she saw that I had no faith, but only the energy that was turning in upon itself and coming out as aggression, she was right to cut her losses, freeze me out, and focus on those who were willing to listen to her message.

Although I feared, even loathed her at times, she never disappointed me. Mother Agnese is the only person I ever met who never once stepped out of character. She lived and died a martyr. In the end she dropped dead from liver cancer while still in her forties, while attempting to make it to the communion rail at morning mass. As she wasted away, it seems she simply donned more and more layers of underwear and never even saw a doctor, offering up her suffering for lost souls when most mortals would have opted for a morphine drip.

She disdained talk of the usual minutiae of a Catholic girlhood education, such as who cleans the altar, who walks first in the May Day Parade, what dress to wear to first communion, or how to set up a Catholic home. She always went right to life's marrow. In grade one she had a daily theme and she wrote it on the blackboard. One was "What are you doing, or what will you do today" — ("today" was in pink chalk) — "to convert souls in deepest, darkest Africa?" Then we would go around the room and say what we were going to sacrifice that day to help the missionaries. Anthony McDougall would agree to stay in his seat. Clyde Ayers would give up baseball in the playground. Linda Low always gave up her lunch. I never had a lunch, so Mother Agnese suggested that I "take the vow of silence," since that would be my greatest sacrifice. I usually lasted for about an hour and then toppled off the tower into babble and left the rest of the work up to the missionaries. Mother Agnese gave me a D on my report card under "Self-control." Who gets a D in grade one?

We spent a great deal of time talking about our souls and how to keep them in good working order so that in the event that we were killed our souls would have no trouble reaching Saint Peter, who held the keys to heaven's gates. I was concerned about the existence of my soul and on various occasions tried to find out where it was located. Was it part of my mind or my heart or some other organ? Mother Agnese told us that God, and on rare occasions certain humans, of which we were to assume that she was one, could see right through your body into your soul. God lived in our soul and if it was dirty or decayed or worm-infested, He was not going to stay long. After all, who wanted to live in a dirty house? Every morning we had to house-clean our souls and make sacrifices that would tidy up our Godly abodes. I became worried about my soul and was really attuned to everything that had to do with its existence. There was a shoe-repair man in Niagara Falls called the Sole Man and in grade one I insisted on going there to take my saddle shoes for repair. I carefully perused his shop and looked at him carefully when he spoke; however, he didn't seem to be different from any other man and offered me no inside track on salvation.

In grade two I remember being jolted when the radio announcer, who had the same accent as Roy's, said Ella Fitzgerald had *soul*. I was alarmed by this and told Roy we *all* had souls. Roy didn't seem to be as personally tortured about souls as I was and simply said that some singers had more soul than others. He said Billie Holiday was all about wounded *soul* and Bessie Smith was *soulful*. Although I listened carefully, I couldn't tell any difference between their souls and Perry Como's.

One day when discussing capital punishment in grade two, we were debating whether it was right for the state to execute a man if he killed another. This was the famous case of the man the press called Joe Smith, who was being sent to the electric chair. Linda Low said that only God could take a life, but that maybe the executioner was working for God just as the Pope was working for God. After all, if execution was wrong, the Pope would have said something on behalf of God. Then Anthony McDougall suggested they have a public execution with the victim's family "turning on the juice" since the man on death row had killed their son "in cold blood." He felt the family who suffered should have some retribution. Mother Agnese piped in that Joe Smith also had a soul that was no different in *kind* from the souls of each person in our class. She asked the class if Joe Smith beseeched God for forgiveness one minute before he was executed, would he go to heaven? Of course, since God was all-forgiving, the answer would be yes. Even Anthony McDougall got that one right.

I suddenly had what I thought was a flash of genius when Mother Agnese mentioned that Joe Smith had a soul. I stood up, saying that I had solved the problem of the soul. Mother Agnese said that I had to sit down and raise my hand. (I felt she was being rather pedestrian since I'd solved such a huge problem that plagued mankind.) Finally when called upon, I said that I had established a sure-fire experiment for confirming the existence of the soul. I saw myself as an ecclesiastical Madame Curie. Patrick Hyla, the boy who was good at math and destined to be head altar boy, spoke for the class when he asked what I meant by the *problem* of the soul. In my enthusiasm I bounded ahead, saying that all we had to do was weigh Joe Smith before he was executed and then one minute after. That way we could confirm the existence of the soul and even know how much it weighs as it leaves the body for heaven or hell. I said that I thought the governor, particularly if he were a Catholic, would understand this request since we were trying to establish valuable information about the soul.

The class was silent, slow on the uptake, but following a lull I noticed they were looking at me as though I were Count Dracula dripping blood. Mother Agnese looked appalled, shook her head, and asked me to come to the front of the room and stand under the crucifix. She then said that I was exactly like one of God's Apostles. Turning to the horrified class, she asked, "Which Apostle does Catherine resemble?" I smiled broadly, hoping it was Saint Peter because he held the keys to the church and was my favourite. No one knew who I was until one of the dimwits who sat in the back suggested Judas. Then Mother Agnese said I was like Thomas, one of Jesus' favourite Apostles. When you are one of God's favourites you can hurt Him more profoundly than any other mortal. Lucifer was God's right-hand man until he defected for the fires of hell.

I could tell things weren't going well, but I hadn't figured out exactly where they'd been derailed. "Catherine, do you know what Thomas said to the other Apostles when they told him that Jesus had been resurrected from the dead?" I didn't answer because Anthony McDougall was shooting rubber bands at me every time Mother Agnese turned her head and Clyde Ayers was firing moist spitballs out his lunch straw. She gave an exasperated sigh, and answered the question herself. "Thomas said that he wouldn't believe Jesus had arisen from the dead until he put his fingers into the nail wounds and put his hand into His side. Eight days later, after he checked the wounds of Jesus, he believed that Christ had arisen. Catherine, what is wrong with the doubts of Thomas?"

I thought for a minute. Still in grade two I hadn't yet realized that there was a perfect Mother Agnese Answer. I gave the answer I *felt*. "Well, I don't think there was anything wrong with it. After all, there could have been impersonators. I'm not criticizing God, you know." I really wanted her to get that part straight. "Sometimes in the drugstore people impersonate others to pick up their prescriptions or make up fake prescriptions by stealing a whole prescription pad from the doctor's office. You have to double-check if you don't know the customer and it's a narcotic. Maybe someone was imitating God, and Thomas wanted to be sure he had the right guy. You've heard of double-checking, haven't you?" Her face looked impassive, so I continued. "Better to be safe than sorry; that type of thing." There was a thick silence which I pushed through for one last kick at the can. "If someone rose from the dead, I'd want some proof that it was really the dead guy. After all," I added lamely, "if people as unimportant as Ed Sullivan and Jack Benny have impersonators, why wouldn't God?"

Mother Agnese just shook her head as though there was no hope for someone as truly evil as me. "Catherine, I used to think that your soul needed a spring cleaning, but I now realize its entire structure is in peril. Could you please step up on the pull-down-map ladder and locate the crucifix." I stood on my tiptoes on the ladder, touching the cold ceramic crucifix, awaiting more instructions. "Please place your fingers upon God's hand and side wounds and then tell us what it feels to be a doubting Thomas." As I climbed down the ladder with shaking legs that made the ladder jiggle, I tried to understand what I had done wrong.

"Now, Catherine, do you know what Jesus said in rebuke to Thomas when he felt his wounds?" I had *really* lost touch of this exercise. You could hear a pin drop in the room. She continued, "Because thou hast seen me, Thomas, thou hast believed; blessed are they that have not seen, and have believed.'"

Maureen Toohey raised her hand and said, "We have to believe in the soul. It doesn't matter how much it weighs."

"That's right, Maureen. We *believe* that Joe Smith has a soul. We accept that as an act of *faith*." I started to head back to my seat and Mother Agnese caught me by the back of my Peter Pan collar and said, "Catherine, you have my sympathy. It's a terrible burden to lack faith. You have been given many gifts — athleticism, leadership, intelligence, to name the most prominent. These gifts are only tools of the devil without the gift of faith. Each one of these traits makes you more appealing to Lucifer. You must pray for the gift of faith, pray harder than those whom you imagine to be more lacklustre. Remember, strong people have strong temptations."

I nodded, wanting to get back to my seat before I began the search for faith. Sighing with relief as I finally sank back into my desk chair without further humiliation, I found a crumpled note on my marred wooden desk which read, "You stink Mrs. doubting Thomas."

As I walked home from school that day, I realized that I was really a mess. I'd had to go to Dr. Laughton because I jumped around so much. He'd said maybe I had worms since I never sat down, and now Mother Agnese said I had worms in my soul. Maybe that was the problem. Maybe all the worms were connected. My faith had been eaten alive from within. Everyone else in my class got it but me. I was just stupid. After all, I got a D in self-control, and was going to hell if I didn't get hold of this faith thing. I prayed to God, asking Him to help me and to strengthen my worm-eaten faith. Then I thought that maybe I'd be like Saint Paul, who was struck off his horse by faith, or like Mary Magdalene, who was a penitent. I now realized that lots of people who knew me were aware that I didn't have faith, but they just didn't want to embarrass me by alluding to this obvious defect.

When I got home my mother noticed I was pensive so I told her what happened and she was madder than I'd ever seen her. She went right to the phone and made an appointment to see Mother Agnese the following day. I was shocked to see my mother galvanized into action. She said Mother Agnese was being medieval. (I assumed that was about the middle of evil.) My mother said you could still have faith and exhibit intellectual curiosity. She said that measuring the soul was slightly impractical, but overall not a bad idea. She gave the example of Charles Darwin, who questioned the universe. Although unfortunately not a Catholic, he *did* believe in God. In fact, he'd previously studied to be a minister. He was simply interested in figuring out the rules that God used to govern the universe. Because Darwin wrote *On the Origin of Species* did not mean he lacked faith. If Thomas Edison had waited for God to light the world, we'd still be in darkness. As far as my mother was concerned, there was nothing wrong with science, and blind faith was as ill-informed as atheism. These were new words to me but I recognized them as "fightin' words" and I was relieved that someone, somewhere, thought I might not burn in the fires of hell.

While hiding on the stair landing, I heard my mother telling my father that there was nothing more important than the Catholic faith. However, she was not going back to the Middle Ages to get it. Besides, it was mean to ostracize a little girl. What kind of way is that to treat an inquiring mind? My father said it was not good to undermine authority and he hoped they, as parents, wouldn't pay for it later. My mother said, "Well, do you want her to be like Irene?" My father asked what was wrong with Irene and my mother responded, "Nothing, I'm just using her as an example of an uninquiring mind. That's no way to go through life."

My father also seemed slightly taken aback by my mother's vehemence and spoke in measured tones, "I'm not saying I want her to be an unthinking dolt. It's just that she is quite wild and possibly Mother Agnese knows more than we do about how to inculcate faith in a child. Maybe the inquiring mind should come later. Clearly Mother Agnese feels the way to educate *young* girls is to instill faith in them and then *later* allow them to see the complexities of the world and to learn how to question authority, whether it's God, the Church, teachers, or plain adults. Questioning should come after a healthy respect is instilled in them. I'm only saying this because she has taught girls for many years and presumably she is the expert in the area. Cathy is already a spirited child and maybe Mother Agnese feels that she needs to be curbed."

My mother listened to my father and then said quietly, "I'm just wondering what she is expert at doing."

My father replied in a kind voice but one that said he knew from whence he spoke. "Don't forget, I work with Cathy all day. You have to sit on her way more than you think, especially if she gets a bee in her bonnet about something. Don't kid yourself. Roy keeps her in line far more than it appears. He has her respect."

"So what's the problem?"

"I've seen her rip Irene up one side and down the other if she thinks she is wrong or attacking Roy. Cathy is a great worker, she does the work of an adult, maybe two, and she is loyal with a great sense of justice; however, when she feels wronged she will attack, no holds barred, and unfortunately she seems to feel entitled to do so. I don't think that is good for a little girl. In fact, I sometimes worry that she doesn't know that she *is* a little girl. What will happen when she is older? Teenagers can get out of control if respect is not laid in a careful foundation. Look at what happened to Sarah Welch. Girls can go astray and they need a firm hand. . . . That's all I'm saying."

I listened to their breathing silence from the stairs. My mother always agreed with my father but now she was silent. I became frightened. Did this mean they were getting a divorce?

Finally my father said, "Naturally you have to do what you think is right and obviously you feel strongly about this and I agree with you. I'm just trying to look at it from all angles."

I felt much less as though my soul was besmirched. I did learn, however, that I had to put any religious questions on ice because I never wanted to go through that inquisition again. I learned that there were Mother Agnese Responses and then there was how I really felt. I also learned to differentiate between them and keep mine under lock and key if they didn't match.

About two weeks later, while I was perusing the biography shelf, searching for another book on Clara Barton in the children's section of the Lewiston Public Library, Mrs. Canavan, the librarian whose children attended my school, greeted me by sarcastically chuckling, "What can I get for you today, Little Miss Doubting Thomas?" I had gained back my equilibrium and told her in no uncertain terms that it was good to question things and it was not a sin to wonder about the soul, and I preferred to be called "Catherine" in all future library inquiries.

—

In 1952, at four, I believed that my opinions on the world, faith, and the soul were of value to myself and others and that television was designed to entertain and talk to me. By 1955 I'd learned that my views were not only uninteresting, they were heretical and if it had been another era I could have been burned at the stake. RCA Victor, someone who I had once thought of as a friend, who had tricked me into believing that he addressed only me, had now been turned into a country-wide phenomenon with TV dinners to match. In fact, by 1956 it was unusual *not* to have a television. Our home was no longer a mecca for the uninitiated. Those who wished to revel in the wit of Topo Gigio on Ed Sullivan could do so on their own time in their own living rooms. I had become completely blasé — even dismissive — about television except for the galvanizing moment when Elvis Presley appeared on *Ed*

Sullivan. That appearance rocked Lewiston to its very core and not a soul who watched it ever forgot it.

The week preceding the big appearance, Nee-Nee McGrath (her name was Denise but her baby sister could only say Nee-Nee), my teenage babysitter with the page-boy hairstyle and fringed bangs who carried around a transistor radio with rabbit ears, told me that this was the most exciting week of her life and in fact would make "human history," the week that Elvis Presley would be "on the air." The phrase bewildered me. I thought birds or the Holy Ghost were on the air — not Elvis.

Not wanting to be out of it, I charged to the dictionary to find out who Elvis Presley was. I found a Priestley who had in fact discovered oxygen. No wonder he was "on the air." In order to strut my knowledge of popular culture, I pointed out to Nee-Nee that Elvis Priestley was the great inventor of oxygen. In complete agreement, she said Elvis had invented every breath of air that she inhaled as well as having invented rock and roll. It was several years later in chemistry lab, when I saw a picture of Joseph Priestley, that I realized that although Joseph and Elvis breathed the same air, they were in fact not one and the same.

In order to be able to converse with Nee-Nee and be part of the electricity of the moment, I began to read all of the magazines in my father's store that had to do with Elvis. I read them aloud to Roy until he couldn't take it any longer. I had him over a barrel because he wanted me to read everything that had to do with Marilyn Monroe to him. Naturally I informed him that for each Marilyn article we read, he had to listen to one Elvis. I made him listen to Elvis on the radio; he paid me back by dragging me to endure dozens of screenings of *Niagara, Gentlemen Prefer Blondes,*

How to Marry a Millionaire, *The Seven Year Itch*, and his favourite, *Bus Stop*. (We could spend a whole day with me acting the role of Cherie to his Beau. In fact, we had been known to regale Shim-Shacks tavern on occasion with excerpts of our dramatic renditions from *Bus Stop*.) I spent a great deal of time trying to get why Elvis was so popular, or Marilyn Monroe for that matter. When I asked Roy, he said some things are understandable the first day you wear stockings and high heels. He promised if I still didn't get it by then, he would explain it all to me. So I decided to shelve it and live vicariously through Nee-Nee's enthusiasm.

Nee-Nee brought over a box full of Elvis Presley bubble-gum cards that she traded with her friends. She carried them around in a robin's-egg-blue plastic-covered box labelled *My Ponytail Treasures* that had ponytailed bobby soxers sketched on the cover. When she came to our house, she always brought her blue matching diary with a lock and key — *My Ponytail Diary*. That was not all. There was a blue plastic 45 RPM record carrier with folding handles — *My Ponytail Platter Tote*. She carried all of Elvis's latest hits in order of their popularity in the American Bandstand countdown top ten, from "Love Me Tender" to "Heartbreak Hotel." She danced with the fridge door to "Don't Be Cruel." She told me it would be embarrassing for me to wear ankle socks for Elvis's performance on *Ed Sullivan*. I had to wear popcorn bobby socks, which I immediately went out and bought, but my legs were so thin that they fell down around my ankles.

As we neared the performance date, there was a note on the blackboard in pink chalk under the area marked "Special Events." Coloured chalk was reserved for important SOS messages. (The last time pink chalk was used was when the Russians sent Sputnik into orbit and we all had to fall to our knees to pray that there would not be another war.) The notice read, "2:00 today — assembly meeting — speaker Principal Mother Agnese — addressing a delicate matter." Mother Agnese never called an assembly unless the topic concerned one of the seven deadly sins. . . . Sure enough, her mission on this occasion was about the sin of *lust*.

She told us that Elvis Presley was a Southerner who was a member of an "offshoot religion" (presumably from the Catholic trunk) that baptized people in rivers by dunking them underwater. I had to admit it did sound a bit primitive. She said if we watched Elvis on the *Ed Sullivan Show* the following week, we would be committing a venial sin. Linda Low, who loved to find the fly in any ointment, asked, "What if someone makes us watch against our will?" (As though someone is going to chain you to a television to watch Elvis Presley! Why she never got yelled at, as I always did, was beyond me.) Mother Agnese answered this question as though it were normal, that maybe there were actual kidnappers who would round up children for the sole purpose of forcing them to watch Elvis Presley against their wills. Mother Agnese suggested one should spend the time with their eyes closed whispering "ejaculations."

Mother Agnese said that in the event that we "forgot" to tell our parents about this, there would be an announcement on Sunday "from the pulpit," warning parishioners that they would be sinning if they watched the degrading, lascivious performance of Elvis Presley, who was no more than the devil's disciple. There was an audible moan in the audience as the older girls in grade eight sank into despair.

I really wasn't interested in watching Elvis Presley on television when Nee-Nee was making such a fuss about it. I was only going to do it so I wouldn't seem like an only-child freak, like Trent McMaster who was out of it — that is, until I heard that it would be a sin. Then I really wanted to see it with "every fibre of my being" (a phrase I got from Nee-Nee). What could he do that was *so* bad? Since I wanted to be perfectly clear as to what the sin was, so that when it happened I wouldn't miss it, I raised my hand in the assembly and asked, in front of the whole school, how you could hold a guitar, sing "Hound Dog," and be sinning at the same time? The older grades began tittering and I realized I'd asked something stupid, *more* stupid than Linda Low's idiotic question which I had previously not thought possible. Mother Agnese answered me in a tone that assured me the answer was obvious, "Catherine, it would clearly be the sin of lust."

Lust?

I sank into my seat, but fortunately the attention was taken off me as Anthony McDougall jumped into the aisle and began gyrating around with his heels in one spot, swinging his pelvis and howling. Presumably, although it was hard to guess what Anthony might be thinking, he was demonstrating Elvis's sin. Everyone knew Anthony because even the older classes had had him in their grade at some point or other. Mother Agnese charged over to him and smacked him with a yardstick, a yellow one that said "McClure's Drugstore — Inches Above Its Competitors," until it splintered at the twelve-inch mark and he flopped back into his seat laughing his head off, appearing impervious to pain. (I noted *she* didn't get sent off to Dr. Small for violence against Anthony McDougall.) Clearly Anthony, who couldn't add two numbers, knew something about the sin of lust that I didn't know. I was puzzled. I looked up *lust* in the *Oxford English Dictionary* on a stand in the front parlour. It said, "Pleasure, delight (sometimes coupled with liking)". . . . Big deal. What was the mystery of lust? As far as I was concerned, Anthony McDougall, with all his bullying antics, had done much worse things than shake his hips in the aisle. Others, however, seemed scandalized by his behaviour. Sister Immaculata told Anthony he was the scourge of grade three. The grade-six girls ignored Anthony and dabbed their teary eyes as they were still absorbing the Edict of Elvis.

Mother Agnese explained to the weeping crowd, who longed for Elvis more than the wedding guests at Cana longed for wine, that not only was it a sin to watch Elvis, but that she was involved in stopping the performance, or curbing it to remove the wanton aspect of his performance. She informed us that Ed Sullivan was not responsible for the moral development of America's youth, and he and CBS would not be the arbiter of our salvation, as long as she and other concerned Catholics had a breath left within them.

When I told my household about the Elvis assembly, my mother said, "No wonder she used pink chalk," and my father said Elvis had snowballed into big bucks and that Ed Sullivan took his cues from the Nielsen ratings and CBS, not from Mother Agnese, who was head of a parish school in a small border town. My father said that he didn't know whether that was a good or a bad thing, but it was nonetheless a fact. Dolores, who I had expected to say that Elvis was horrible since she thought most things were bad, surprised me. She pooh-poohed the whole thing and said that Elvis couldn't be more lustful than Frank

Sinatra was in his hot crooning youth. She said, "Given the choices in *this* town, a teenage girl's got to love *someone*."

Love.

I thought that was a strange context in which to use the word *love*. I wondered how *love* and *lust* were connected. I knew love was good and lust was very bad. I certainly hoped they didn't overlap. I wanted to love somebody sometime when I was grown up. Even Nancy Drew had Ned Nickerson as her boyfriend. Were they lustful? Could someone be lustful alone or did it take two people?

Finally at four o'clock on the fateful Friday before the concert there was a last-minute reprieve as the loudspeaker crackled to life. The triumphant voice of Mother Agnese, sounding as though it was submerged with Lloyd Bridges underwater, announced that due to pressure from God fearing Americans, Ed Sullivan, who obviously would sell his soul for the almighty dollar, had been forced to make a compromise surrounding the appearance and agreed to show Elvis's body only from the waist up. Therefore it would not be a sin, but only bad taste to watch Elvis Presley live on *Ed Sullivan*. Much to Mother Agnese's shocked dismay, there was a deafening ecstatic wail from the students of Hennepin Hall as we all prepared for our evening of bad taste.

Our living room was packed to capacity Sunday evening at eight to see *Ed Sullivan*. By this time many people had their own televisions, but they got together to watch history in the making. I guess in case something lustful happened and it was really scary they could turn to each other.

I was really embarrassed to watch Elvis with my parents, and our neighbours, the McMasters, the Millers, and the Schmidts. All of us, Dickie, Frank, and Trent, sat in the front on the floor and the Millers and their three boys sat in the back. What if Elvis did something lustful in front of everyone? This whole Elvis performance had actually made me nervous. I wouldn't have minded watching the lustful part *alone*, but all these boys and my parents all in the same room humiliated me. If I was going to learn about lust, I wanted to do it on my own. It was like having an audience watch you the first time you tried something. Was there no privacy in one's first experience of lust — one of the seven deadly sins? I wondered what was required of me. Deep down I was afraid that I might inadvertently humiliate myself and do something overtly lustful. After all, I didn't know that I was displaying my sinful and disgusting lack of faith in my doubting Thomas episode, yet I was forced to climb the ladder and repent in front of everyone in the class. I didn't want to be the only lustful person watching Elvis tonight, especially in front of all of these boys. I had learned there was something about me that told other people how I felt inside and, what's worse, it never seemed to be what other *normal* girls were thinking or feeling.

Another anxiety-provoking factor was that somehow I felt responsible for Elvis's behaviour. Was it because it was my TV? Who knows? Mrs. Schmidt embarrassed me in front of everyone by saying, "Well, I heard that Cathy was so nervous about seeing Elvis tonight, her mother told me she was up feeding her monarch butterflies this morning at 4:00 a.m." Everyone's laughter sent my fair skin into a rose shade of blush. I longed for a trap door to fall through so I could miss this whole lustful evening.

My father brought home Skippy strawberry ice cream from the store and handed everyone a cup with a matching plastic spoon, and we tuned in. While the jugglers were on, my father, who was going bald, said, "Well, I hope this Elvis hasn't stolen my haircut." Mr. Schmidt said, "Well, if I get corrupted, I'm a lost cause, but you Catholics can always go to confession." Not recognizing his jesting tone, I popped up and said that he needn't worry about going to hell since Mother Agnese was making sure that Elvis's lustful bottom half was cut off. Everyone started laughing and the Schmidt boys were rolling on the floor, poking each other and pointing at me. The ultra-sophisticated Presbyterian Miller boys, who went away to a prep school called Choate, were described by Trent's mother as fine young men who knew their manners and would make a mark in this world, only smiled politely. Jim, the eldest of the three, a teenager old enough to wear a herringbone suit jacket and read the paper, had adopted an accent sounding like Edward R. Murrow. "Cathy, I know your principal seems important to you, and in *your* world she is, but I frankly doubt that she will have the authority, nor will her cohorts have the power, to tell CBS what to do." He smiled at his brother Phillip. Then Mr. Schmidt piped in, "Why, the crooner has already been on *The Steve Allen Show* — top *and* bottom. I think you'd better tell your nun there that the horse is out of the barn."

I was horribly humiliated. Finally a chastened and more flummoxed than usual Ed Sullivan appeared on the screen, and said that they were going to have a "really big show, but due to some last-minute pressures from the powers that be," he had to make a slight change to his format. Elvis would appear, but he would be filmed only from the waist up. I turned and looked at everyone and lifted my eyebrows, waiting for an apology. Phillip Miller said, "You don't actually believe that pressure was from your principal, do you?" "No," I snapped, "I'm sure it was the principal of

Choate." Then I stomped in to get another Skippy cup and my mother said there wasn't enough for everyone to have two. To this I responded, "So what!" Mrs. Miller whispered just loud enough for me to hear, "Boys, Cathy is only a little girl, now be nice."

No one said any more and we all silently absorbed the performance. There wasn't one soul in Lewiston who didn't tune in to the face and shoulders of Elvis singing "Hound Dog" to a real live hound dog who was shown in a full-body shot. My father broke the ice by asking, "Which one is Elvis?" and my mother said that it was interesting that Topo Gigio called Ed Sullivan "Eddie" and Elvis Presley called him "Mr. Sullivan." My mother, I'd begun to notice, didn't seem to focus on the same issues as other people, or at least she didn't come at them from the same angle.

The next day at school I told Mother Agnese that some Presbyterians who were home from Choate boarding school were sceptical about her having so much influence on the networks and on Ed Sullivan, to say nothing of Elvis Presley's agreement to be a TV amputee. She looked quite calm, as though she knew all about Choate and was not the least bit impressed by it. She acted as though she completely understood, and even expected, the condescension of the Miller boys. She said, "Catherine, our fight is not always with the obvious tempter. Elvis Presley is no more responsible for his behaviour than Anthony McDougall." (I had no idea that Elvis was *that* stupid.) "We all have our own Sodom and Gomorrah. The powers of the eastern seaboard are the ones we must battle. They are the ones with little faith and deep pockets. I feel sorry for the Miller brothers as they are slowly being metamorphosed into pillars of salt."

Many years later the Amigone brothers said Mother Agnese's

four Choate-educated (Protestant) brothers had flown in on their private plane from Connecticut for the funeral, and had seemed uncertain as to whether the corpse they saw was that of their once-beautiful debutante sister.

—

Mother Agnese and I had an uneasy peace for a year or two while she soldiered on teaching our class. In many ways we were symbiotically attached. We were like the nursery rhyme "Jack Sprat." She needed to suffer and we needed to torture. Our class was the worst in the school and, as she frequently told us, we were her penance. If one is to offer up her sufferings for the poor souls in purgatory then one has to have sufferings. That's where I came in, with five boys. We, known as the Satan's Six, gave her all the raw material she needed.

Your name went on the board if you were not "an ambassador of the Catholic faith." My name was perpetually printed on the board for one thing or another. Usually around two in the afternoon my legs would get jittery and I would have an overwhelming desire to get up from my desk. I felt so trapped — being stretched on a rack would have been preferable to having my body folded under my tiny desk. In spite of our desperate desire to move around, we were supposed to work in our letter box. I hated that green three-by-five-inch box full of tiny cardboard letters no larger than a small fingernail. My letter box was like a Pandora's box which I dreaded opening. Within fifteen minutes of scrounging around in this tiny box in order to line up all the letters in alphabetical order, I would go berserk. I couldn't understand the principle. Why did we nose through these boxes every day looking for letters like animals looking for grubs? Since

I already knew the alphabet and I could spell whatever I needed, I didn't understand why my scholastic life had to be confined in a tiny cardboard box. Wasn't there something to learn outside of it? I'm sure part of my distaste for it was that I was really bad at it. It seemed as if only my letters blew off my desk whenever Mother Agnese rushed by with her ropes and rosary swaying.

Something always came over me about fifteen minutes into the exercise and I would start fights and take other people's letters if I couldn't find my own. Sometimes Anthony McDougall would blow on my letters and knock them off my desk. I would start poking at other people's letters or take their vowels just for a little fun. Every day I would swear that I wasn't going to disturb other's letters but I always fell short of the mark. By two-thirty I had usually stolen all of Linda Low's vowels, or I would have wild physical battles with the boys for their letters and it would all end in mayhem.

Then my name would go on the board and I'd be sent off to solitary confinement, kneeling alone at church and saying the stations of the cross for my penance. I was to ask God's forgiveness and to try and find a way to develop patience and rid myself of "sticky fingers." Actually, being in church was better than being in school. It was quiet and the stone floor felt cool, a relief after our boiling hot, stuffy, crowded classroom. I felt uplifted under the vaulted Gothic ceiling and inspired by the altar and the walls of the chancel, the colour of a blue Mediterranean night sky with glittering stars painted on. The stations of the cross were copies of the works of Fra Filippo Lippi, a Renaissance master. He perfectly represented the quiet agony on Mary's face in her beautiful cobalt-blue dress as she watched her Son hang upon the cross. The entire crucifixion came alive for me as I knelt in front of each station. When the strong afternoon sun shone through the window, the stained glass radiated and I actually felt for fleeting moments that I was in God's presence. Sometimes I lit all the candles in their cranberry glasses with the long sticks provided for all the poor people that didn't have enough money to pay for a votive candle. (Not that I ever paid for them, but I figured since God could make the world in seven days, He could spring for a few votive candles. Mother Agnese and Father Flanagan didn't share this view of God's generosity.)

On certain occasions I made up miracles or walked down the aisle as Joan of Arc or Maid Marian marrying Robin Hood. Once I was there with a girl from grade six who had to do the stations of the cross for combing her hair during geography. She made me pretend to be the priest presiding over her wedding. I got a real surge of power pretending to be Father Flanagan standing behind the communion rail marrying her to Elvis Presley: "Do you, Elvis, take this woman, Anne Marie Fassiano . . ."

There was one ground where Mother Agnese and I had a bond, a truce. It was over sports. She was the athletic director, as well as spiritual adviser and principal. Father Flanagan referred to himself as "men's athletic director" and taught the boys sports and formed the teams for competitions. Outfits were provided for the boys' baseball team sponsored by McDonald's Dairy. The girls had no equipment or teams, nor were we ever placed in any competitions with other schools. In fact, there was absolutely no athletic program for girls. In the fall we gathered chestnuts; in the winter we huddled in groups, hiding from the boys who threw snowballs; and in the spring we were the audience for the boys' baseball game. While the boys went on field trips to identify deciduous and non-deciduous trees, the girls were left in the school cafeteria to make belts decorated with tiny rice-sized beads that spelled out "Niagara Falls." All of these crafts were ultimately donated to the African missions. When I watched *Ramar of the Jungle* on Saturday mornings, I checked out the natives' costumes, but I never saw one of them in one of our beaded Niagara Falls belts.

Once a team of experts from the University of Buffalo, who were running a study funded by New York State, came in to test our reflexes and measure how well we did at certain gymnastics. The amazing part of this exercise was that in this case *our* meant boys *and* girls. The professors all wore matching tee-shirts and whistles around their necks woven in boondoggle. They carried clipboards and charts and wrote down all our dimensions and even wrote what we'd had for breakfast. They had stopwatches and made us go through a whole routine, including balance beams, high jumping, broad jumping, rings, the horse, the parallel bars, and the uneven parallel bars. We had to check in at each station and give them our name.

Mother Agnese gave the school a big lecture before they arrived about how the professor was not sure he wanted to come to Hennepin Hall because we had no formal athletics department. She said that we had to ask for God's help, so that these "so-called experts" could understand that Catholic faith was more integral to success than any planned athletic program. She pointed out that when Jesse Owens won at the Olympics, he thanked God first and then the United States. We all knelt on the hardwood floor and said the rosary in hopes that God would inspire us on the uneven parallel bars. She suggested we make the sign of the cross before our journey on the course started and again after it finished.

Men arrived with trucks and set up equipment in the lunch-room while the whole school ate lunch at their desks, except for those who went home for lunch, and for me, who went alone to Bradshaw's Restaurant.

Of course the boys went first. They all wore pants while we had to wear our kilted uniforms, not ideal for doing reverse parallel or an "upside-down parrot" on the rings. Finally it was the girls' turn. Now I understood why I had trouble sitting at my desk. I was born to run through this obstacle course. I whipped through it so fast the college-student aide couldn't keep up. He yelled to the director, "Hey, we got a live one here," after I'd finished the course and he checked my time. They raised everything and I tried the next level and the next, like a stairway to heaven, until it was only me and one other boy, Luther McCabe, from grade six. Luther was better at the rings than I because he had stronger arms and he could do a reverse faster than I could, but I beat him on every other thing — even the fifty-yard dash.

The physical education professors came back over weeks and taught me how to do the uneven parallel bars, use the blue chalk on my hands to absorb my sweat so I wouldn't slip, and how to bend my knees when I dismounted so I wouldn't hurt my back. On the balance bar I learned a routine of how to extend one leg in the front and one in the back and bend at the same time. My broad jump was something else again, and they had to take pictures to believe the distance at which I landed. However, the high jump was my speciality. I took to it as though I'd been a grasshopper in a previous life. Finally the whole school was watching as the professor raised the black-and-white-checkered pole higher and higher, and each time I cleared it, landing triumphantly in the sand pit.

"Well, Sister, I've got to hand it to you," remarked one of the professors, "you were certain they would perform well and they have. They are on average higher than the public school, and the McClure and the McCabe kids are amazing. McClure could have made it in the floor-exercise category but she is weak on the rings. She has strong long legs, and flexibility. My God, you don't even have a swing set." I, in fact, did have a swing set and a jungle gym in my yard at home.

"Yes," Mother Agnese said with her arms folded within the long drop sleeves of her uniform, simultaneously exhibiting a mysterious smile. "Well, we have our *own* ways of reaching for the best."

"Sister, I hope that you don't mind when I tell you that you look exactly like Ingrid Bergman in *The Bells of Saint Mary's*, especially in that outfit." Mother Agnese simply looked at him as though he were from another planet. Much to my horror, he continued as I practised. "I notice you don't have a western New York accent. Sounds East Coast to me." Mother Agnese dealt with this by completely ignoring it.

I told Roy that the athletic director told Mother Agnese that she looked like *Ingrid Bergman* and referred to her habit as an *outfit*. I was completely scandalized. I suggested to Roy that maybe the professor didn't understand how awful it was to refer to a nun's person. At least I'd never heard it done. Roy didn't seem to think the professor was as off-base as I thought. He reflected upon it for a full minute and said, "There's no denying Mother Agnese is one *fine* lady, but I wouldn't want to run into her in a dark alley, even if it was a shortcut to heaven."

Mother Agnese worked with me every day after school on the track-and-field equipment my father donated. We tried approaching the bar from every different angle to establish my optimal position. We worked on the straddle jump and developed an approach procedure which included the sign of the cross, taking off with my inside foot, planting, throwing my arms up. The most important bit was when to spring and when to lower my back leg from the straddle.

She and I went to Lewiston Porter High School and watched their team and listened to their coaches. I was so young that they found it amusing, and all the older boys and coaches helped me out and laughed and clapped when I vaulted over the bar. I followed our practised approach minus the sign of the cross since I didn't want to look like an apple polisher in front of all these big foreign Protestant creatures, some of whom even had whiskers. Mother Agnese put her entire body in front of me as I sprung forward and I fell to the ground in order to prevent bashing into her. Her starched habit was almost as wide as the twelve-foot bar. I could tell that the boys thought a nun was weird and they had never been in contact with one before. She made no effort to make them more comfortable. As I ground to a halt, she said, "Catherine, I believe that you forgot part of your takeoff procedure."

Although I knew what she meant, the boys looked puzzled. I knew what I had to do; yet I hesitated because I was totally embarrassed to do it. I was young, but not so young that I didn't know what was ridiculous to teenagers. After all, I had a teenage babysitter every week and I listened to her as she talked on the phone. Knowing what I had to do, I reluctantly returned to the starting block, hung my head, and quickly made the sign of the cross, and *then* planted my inside foot and ran at my usual forty-five-degree angle. The boys shook their heads in amazement at my height, patted my back, roughed up my hair, and made soothing sounds of approval, which were ambrosia to my ears; even Mother Agnese smiled.

On our way back to school, Mother Agnese asked me if I was embarrassed to be a Catholic. I'd been waiting for this. She told me I was a Catholic ambassador just as Jesse Owens was an ambassador for the black Americans and a foil for Hitler. I must always try and make converts and have exemplary behaviour in front of others. Did Joan of Arc deny her Catholicism? Did The Duke of Canterbury stand up to be counted when the king wanted to be divorced? She continued, "Catherine, it is easy to be a nation of sheep, but we must always stand up for Christ and His word. In every situation you're in, no matter how much you think you are alone, God is watching you. Stand up and be counted amongst His flock. Would you deny knowing your mother or father . . . or Roy?" I knew from that moment on, I would always make the sign of the cross before every approach.

The night before the Niagara Falls Junior Track and Field Meet, my mother and I were sitting in a booth at Schoonmaker's Restaurant with Mrs. McMaster and Trent, the class suck, who was basking in his recent glory after having won the diocesan science contest for his drippy display of osmosis, when Mrs. Schoonmaker came over and gave me a free Vernors and said, "Good luck tomorrow, Cath," and Mr. Schoonmaker and the other bartender held up their glasses in a toast and told me not to jump over the bar.

Trent piped up with "Cathy, you do realize that your father was

Buffalo high hurdle champion, and then regional champ. You simply have his genes for jumping. I'm afraid unless you plan to become a Mexican jumping bean in later life, this genetic advantage will be of little use. I have genes for *science*."

No one said anything, such as "Trent, how are you going to clean the test tubes — with your tongue?" Which is what we were all thinking as he gesticulated with his stubby frostbitten digits. Trent had a right to be bitter. My mother put her hand on mine at dinner, hoping I wouldn't retaliate. I think I remember this because my mother so rarely gave me any direction. She had never said one word about my involvement in the Trent river episode, but now I felt, as her shaking hand rested on my wrist, how hard the event must have been on her.

I came in number one in my age group at the Niagara Falls Track and Field Meet. Although I met the height requirement I was the youngest participant by far. I made the sign of the cross and flew over the pole. I was second in the hop, skip, and jump, and fifth in the broad jump. Clearly the high jump was my sport and I was ready to jump, leapfrogging from the district to the regional to the state championships to the Olympics. I'd begun to compose my acceptance speech for my gold medal.

In preparing for the regional event, my father worked with me every night and built a sandpit for my many tumbles. He also brought home packing material to absorb some of my falls. I was covered with black and blue marks, but the odd thing was I never felt any pain. My mother couldn't come to the meets or the practices because she said it made her too nervous. She was leaving it to my dad and Mother Agnese.

As we prepared for the regional meet, Mother Agnese told me

I had to visualize jumping over the pole with God's help. I had to reach toward heaven and picture Jesus reaching down and taking my uplifted hands, gently pulling me over the pole. She said that there would be lots of people at the regional meet in Rochester and what I needed to do was count on my guardian angel to help me stay focused. At the exact moment before I threw my outside leg over the bar, I should simply let God lead the spring. If I had faith, He would lift me over the bar.

Mother Agnese never missed a meet and she always reminded me of God, but also she had kept a careful log of all my best jumps and what angle I was from the pole. She stood at the edge of the track and watched all the warm-ups that the high school girls did and had me do the same. We worked on warming up and trained with a fifty-yard dash, then a one hundred, and so on until we found the exact warm-up that was energizing but not tiring. I pictured God's pull and He in fact *did* lift me over the pole.

At the regional championship it was raining cats and dogs. Mother Agnese labelled this weather glitch "God's challenge." She said it was good it was raining because a lot of people would slip or be distracted but we knew the purpose of the rain. The high jumping had become something Mother Agnese and I now did together. She referred to *our* wins and *our* practices. We were the team. As bad as I was at sitting in my chair and speaking out of turn in school, I was controlled and dedicated when it came to high jumping. I would practise until my calf muscles seized up, or until it got dark, whichever came first.

I lined up in the torrent of rain and the wind was making me shiver, but I counted on my guardian angel to block out the spring chill. I made it to the finals. There were ten of us. Some of the contestants looked more like strong boys than muscly girls. One even had a moustache. Mother Agnese read my mind: "Catherine, correct me if I'm wrong, but have any of these Amazon athletes made the sign of the cross before their three preliminary jumps?" I shrugged. "Well then, I can tell you right now that no matter how strong they look they will not touch your speed or height."

I felt dubious. I saw a girl in the pit bend her tree-trunk legs and lift a giant weight over her head, and another did the splits like a ballerina on the muddy grass inside the track. She had her own personal coach whose uniform matched hers, and he wore a whistle. Hoping to bring Mother Agnese back to earth, I said, "Look at that coach's whistle."

"Plastic doo-dads are available at Woolworth's," she said in disgust. "Whistles do not lift large women over poles, God does. Also remember that she has to carry all that weight over the pole and you are as light as a feather. God may need the help of the archangels to get *her* over the pole." That was the first and last joke I ever heard from Mother Agnese; however, I was thrilled to have shared a laugh with her.

There were three of us left: me, one from Rochester, and the last from Syracuse. One girl was what Roy would have called a big bruiser and the other looked like she was the daughter of Frankenstein, so tall she could have been Jack and the Beanstalk's progeny, had he had any. Then there was me. They raised the pole higher than it had ever been elevated, in practice or even when we "tested the limits," as Mother Agnese called it. I counted on God, made the sign of the cross, and said an "Our Father." I didn't care if the judges were waiting.

A staccato blast emerged from the heavens: *"On the field we have an up-and-comer named Cathy McClure. Don't let her delicate build fool you. She's a contender, there's no doubt of that."* I felt the eyes of the masses in the stands. *"This young girl attends all the meets with a nun and both of them pray. Seems to have worked so far."*

I ran and made it all three times. The girl from Syracuse only made it once. I won the Western New York Regional High Jump Championship and placed third in the broad jump. When they gave me my cup, they asked me to say a few words. I thanked God for lifting me over the bar, Mother Agnese for training me, my father for the equipment and uniform, and the New York fitness program for discovering me. As we walked out of the stadium, Mother Agnese said her eyes were watering because the runners had kicked up so much dust.

When we got back to school with the huge trophy, Mother Agnese volunteered one of the fathers to make a cabinet. When he balked about doing it immediately, she pointed out that he did the holy work of Saint Joseph the carpenter and would receive his heavenly reward, so he snapped to. When we had the school athletic award ceremony, Anthony McDougall screamed that I had won the broad jump because I was a broad. Mother Agnese locked him outside without his coat until his lips were blue when he pressed them against the window, pleading to return.

I never worked so hard as I did for the New York State Championships. Day and night for months. One of the by-products of this work was that I was actually better behaved in school, not because I was trying, but because I was sufficiently tired to stay in my chair. They prayed for me at the Sunday mass before I was to fly to New York.

I was to be billeted at the Harlem apartment of the New York City champion. Harriet Jackman was two years older than I, the top high jumper in my age group in all five boroughs. (I had no idea how many people lived in New York until I saw the city phone book.) The letter we received from Harriet's gym teacher/coach said that he would pick me up at La Guardia Airport. Roy had made me see *The Seven Year Itch* so many times that I was excited to see an apartment in New York, complete with doorman and awning. The coach wrote that on the day of the meet Harriet would take me on the subway and he would pick us up somewhere in Brooklyn near a bridge.

When I told Roy I was going to Harlem, he said it was no wonder the gym teacher was picking us up so far away. Realizing that I had no idea that Harlem was not Park Avenue, Roy lightened up and said that I might run into Louis Armstrong or some of the greats we listened to on his special radio down at the Apollo. He suggested if I ran into trouble I should say I was Adam Clayton Powell's niece. "Seriously though," he concluded, "don't go around there profiling by everyone, like you own the place. You best to shadow the girl you stayin' with. Bigger cats than you been skinned in that place."

My mother made sure I had a new dress for the awards ceremony, which Mayor Robert Wagner was going to attend. Mother took the most expensive heart-shaped box of Fanny Farmer candy from the store, and told me to give it to my hostess. She reminded me that the hostess was Harriet's mother, not Harriet. She said to be sure to wear my white gloves to the awards ceremony, and not to start eating before everyone was served at the dinner. She doubted that we would eat in restaurants, so she gave me money to treat Harriet to lunch at a deli of Harriet's choice, and said I was to help with the dishes at Harriet's house. When I asked which day they did the dishes, my mother must have realized that I wasn't conversant with kitchen management. She explained that there would be dishes after every meal — most people did the dishes after they ate. I really couldn't fathom how people had time to get anything done when they had to shop, cook, eat, and then do the dishes at home three times a day, but I guessed I'd see it all first-hand.

My mother waved from the Niagara Falls Airport and her final words to her nine-year-old daughter heading off to Harlem alone were, "Say please and thank you and don't be bossy. This is your chance to see the world."

I resented the giant cardboard name tag the airlines made me wear. I looked like the retarded kids who wore name tags home for lunch in case they forgot how to get back. When I got off the plane there was Mr. Colderos, with Harriet, who was black, like Roy. Mr. Colderos showed me his letter with my name on it, something my father told me to ask for before we left the airport. They gave me a fun tour of New York. We drove through all the different districts, where the traffic was so slow that I really got to see everything. There were people crammed on every sidewalk, and in the financial district, when it was quitting time, the crowds were so large that they spilled over into the roadway. The horns were beeping so loudly I thought there had been a wedding, but Harriet assured me it was just the din of the taxis at theatre time.

Both Harriet and Mr. Colderos had speech impediments. Neither of them could pronounce their R's and the way they pronounced their A's was all wrong. Even the phone operator had the same speech impediment when I called Lewiston. Instead of saying "long distance," she said "looong distance." Everyone spoke in a grouchy voice. For example, when I paused for a moment to look at my parents' area code, she said, "Looong distance, who ya *trying* to caul?" My father would fire someone who spoke that impolitely.

Harriet's apartment building was right out on the street, with no lawn in front, just like the ones in *Singin' in the Rain*. I kept looking for movie stars but I didn't see any. When we walked into the lobby, which was really only a stairwell, I saw mailboxes with padlocks on them. Some of the boxes had no door at all, and one was all bent out of shape. Harriet whipped up the stairs, jumping three at a time at lightning pace until we had leapt nine flights. As we rose, it got hotter and hotter, and cooking smells assaulted me as they mixed together with the stagnant air. Harriet simply high jumped over a sweating man in a full-length overcoat crouching on the narrow cement stairs, smoking, surrounded by ground-out cigarette butts. He looked up to us with red eyes, one of which was clouded over, and mumbled something. She completely ignored him, and when I bent down to decipher his request, she turned around and said sharply, "Pay him no mind."

As we jumped the stairs she talked about her straddle position and her workout schedule, which was about half of mine. We had lots to discuss since we had both been doing the same thing day after day. By the time we got to her floor, I was out of breath and had a pain in my side. Inside the apartment, the first thing I saw was a man about my dad's age on the couch in the small living room. He didn't look up. Harriet just walked by him, so I followed suit. She said her mother worked the elevators at Lord and Taylor, so she had to make dinner. I was surprised that anyone would make dinner, let alone a kid. Her mother had left a note telling her what to do and Harriet slammed things around quickly — put the meat in the oven and peeled potatoes. She used an interesting phrase for the potatoes, saying, "Skin these." I had been unaware that potatoes had any outer coverings. I thought they came from France in long strips. I lined them up on the counter after skinning them and they looked like brave naked soldiers ready to burn at the stake. She even made dinner rolls — not the Pillsbury Dough Boys from the package that you could unroll like my grandmother had, but she made them from different white powders and only added water. They were delicious. She called them "bakes."

Her mother came in about an hour later in a starched uniform that said "Lord and Taylor" on the pocket. She looked at the man on the couch who just sat there staring and asked, "Who let him in?" Harriet said, "He was in when I got home from picking up the billet so I didn't want to take him on." Harriet's mother then realized I was there, and smiled. I shook hands with her and gave her the candy. A college-aged brother named Lamont came home. As soon as he opened the door, he said, "Who let him in? I'm not having no trouble from him. I'm too tired." He also had a Lord and Taylor jumpsuit on.

The dinner was the best I'd ever eaten. We had a cut of meat that looked a bit like knuckles, where you ate chunks of meat and then took the bones out of your mouth and put them on your plate. We had a kind of orange potato and some yellow vegetable that looked like long tapered snouts. The rolls were so hot the butter melted on them. Lamont was going to go to college in the fall on a track-and-field scholarship. He asked all about the pole vaulters in Western New York and what their technique was. Then he said to Harriet, "You better do good tomorrow, girl, if you want a one-way ticket outta here." That was really the first time I realized Harriet and I were competitors. The thought crept in that maybe she needed this win more than I did. The man on the couch never said a word, looked at us, or moved. Now he seemed to be sleeping sitting up. No one offered him a morsel of food, nor did he ask for any.

After dinner Harriet and I did the dishes. Actually she did them and I talked. The mother said she would do them, but I insisted, as my mother had suggested. She finally sank into a chair and said she'd been on her feet for nine hours and it felt good to sit. She really looked bone weary. She put her swollen feet in a footbath, saying she was puffed up like an adder, and promptly fell sleep. Lamont had another job as a night watchman so he hurried away after Harriet made him a lunch.

I told Harriet I had money for a treat, and she said we could go to the corner store, but only if it wasn't dark. Since dusk had already set in she seemed worried and said we had to hurry. I wondered what the problem was. She seemed the type to know her way home even in the dark.

After dividing our M&M's on the curb in front of the store, we were strolling home licking our popsicles, when a boy who looked even older than Harriet's brother blocked our way on the sidewalk, smiling broadly, and said in a kind of singsong voice I'd never heard before, "Hey, Harriet, what's ya got there?"

She turned on him viciously and screamed, "Get out a my way, you sorry ol' thing — *hear me now!*"

He didn't seem offended but just moved to the side. "Emm, emm," he said in a mocking tone and laughed, clearing the sidewalk with alacrity. I was shocked that Harriet could scream like that. I had goosebumps from the whole episode.

She went right back to discussing the meet and how we could go for our deli sandwiches afterward. She wondered if we were too young to dine out alone. She thought maybe no one would wait on us. I assured her I'd been dining out for years and I was sure anyone would wait on you if you could order and pay the check. That is, unless they had different rules in New York. I informed her that in Lewiston they seemed happy to take your money for services rendered, no matter what your age. She remained dubious for some reason, so I suggested we take Mr. Colderos with us and she seemed much relieved. As we changed for bed, Harriet locked her room door and left it locked all night.

When we got up, Harriet's mother had gone to a job cleaning houses on Fifth Avenue and the man on the couch must have silently slipped away. We made our own breakfast, which was kind of exciting, and then we headed out for the subway.

Harriet knew every turn of that subway and she had a shopping list from her mother as well. I was amazed at this catacomb for commuters under the earth. I felt like a Christian hiding from Nero and was amazed when we rose above the ground and found Mr. Colderos standing at the top of the subway steps. We were in a suburb with trees!

We drove to a huge stadium where there were announcers overhead in a little lean-to on the top of the bleachers, and people had to pay admission just to see us. I was flabbergasted to see the hundreds of spectators. As Harriet and I stretched on the lawn, I noticed the majority of the athletes were black. I thought this was odd as I hadn't seen any in Lewiston, and only one or two at the regional event. Harriet knew some of the people and she immediately told them we were going out to lunch at the Carnegie Deli, which seemed to her to be a bigger deal than the meet. With my blond hair and pale skin I never did well in the sun and Roy had reminded me to wear my hat right up until my jump, since he'd seen me get sunstroke on a few occasions when we took out my mother's convertible. Unfortunately I'd left it on the plane in the overhead luggage rack, but I figured that God would help me out. Most of the black kids looked sort of scrawny, nothing like the intimidating German girls from Syracuse. They were laughing and chatting and didn't seem very focused on the event, so I allowed myself to fantasize about walking away with the state championship. I mentally prepared my speech, thanking Mother Agnese, McClure's Drugstore for the sponsorship, and the kind hospitality of Mayor Wagner.

They called our age group first since we were the youngest. I was amazed to see there were dozens of us and mine was the only white face in the crowd. I suddenly realized how Roy must have felt in Niagara Falls. The New Yorkers outnumbered everyone in the high jump, the only event that I was competing in. The field had a track around it with people running races, bright colours were flashing by in my peripheral vision, contestants were laughing, slapping each other's hands, start guns were firing every few minutes, and finally the sun was making me see spots in front of my eyes. There was no respite from the noon-day sun when I stood awaiting my turn in the middle of the track. These athletic events happened simultaneously, cameras flashing at each one, especially when Mayor Wagner approached our area. Bulbs flashed everywhere, contributing to the spots before my eyes. It was like a three-ring circus with a ring for the broad jump with its sand pit, one for hop, skip, and jump, and one for the most popular event — the high jump. The runners circled the three rings on a peripheral oval track. This area was teeming with officials trying to keep out the crowds and other officials.

First there would be preliminaries and then there would be twelve finalists. I watched and noticed that no one made the sign of the cross, so I was in like Flynn with God on my side. I told myself the things that Mother Agnese always said, like count on your guardian angel for the lead up and then switch to the Holy Ghost for the spring — after all, He had the wings, and He was in the sky.

Finally it was my turn. I had three trial jumps. I told myself not to worry, after all this was only the preliminaries. I thought the pole looked higher than usual. I followed a girl from Brooklyn who had a real fan club in the audience. She went over the pole in the strangest way I'd ever seen. I noticed between sets, while I sat at the sandpit, that some other girls were going over the pole in this same kind of flop. They began their approach straight toward the bar. Then they arched their backs over the bar and kicked their legs out to clear it, landing on their shoulders and back. As they arched over the bar they were clearing it by inches while I was clearing it by a hair.

I missed the first time and the pole fell over. I was jumping the gun and sprang too early to clear both feet. The second time I made it, but the pole just caught on the back of my foot. I was shaken by the third time and nauseous from the sun. But I told myself that I really had to stop quivering and jumping too early. My legs were wobbly and I suddenly realized I was in the middle of New York, Mother Agnese was not here to guide me, there was no one in the audience who cared, and that I really had to pray and offer up all my sins. In those two seconds I thought of more sins than I ever remember reciting in the confessional. I took deep breaths. The crackly voice on the microphone told me impatiently again and again to go ahead. I called out all the armies in the heavens. I made the sign of the cross and called upon my guardian angel, my patron saint, my namesake, Saint Catherine of Aragon, and God, the Father. I decided to call on the big gun, forget Jesus and the Holy Ghost. I told God how sorry I was for all my doubting Thomas behaviour. I told Him Mother Agnese was right that it had hurt Him more than Judas, who betrayed Him for thirty pieces of silver. I also knew I made fun of people and imitated them just to get laughs from the other workers at the store. I winced when I pictured how I made fun of Crazy Eddie by turning my baseball hat sideways and crossing my eyes and speaking with rapid-fire urgency the way he chattered about the Dodgers. I would never again, as Mother Agnese said, make fun at the expense of others. I promised God that I would become a nun in the Belgian Congo and never try to be the centre of attention again.

I came to the horrible realization, as I stood with hundreds of people looking at me, that I was really a bad person and that God was allowing me to get to New York to show me how pathetic I was. After all, you can only fall from a height. I had to realize, to have my nose rubbed in it. . . . I was a big fish in a small sea. It was all a plan, an elaborate plot on the part of God for me to confess all my sins, not just the I-disobeyed-my-mother-five-times-this-week kind of confession, but the gut-wrenching I'm-really-a-person-who-hogs-the-limelight-at-the-expense-of-everyone-else's-needs-and-I-am-truly-in-the-marrow-of-my-bones-a-bad-person kind of confession. Mother Agnese's lines of censure ripped into my brain, sounding like a distorted voice reverberating within an echo chamber, closing in on me. "Catherine, I hope they have a vaudeville show in the burning fires of hell, so you may be gainfully employed" took on new meaning for me. On top of the realization that my antics were hell-bent, I also had to face that my previously touted wildly athletic body was really not able to make it out of the preliminaries in Harlem. To say nothing of the fact that everyone who made it out of the preliminaries flopped over the pole and arched their backs giving them inches more space while I still used the antiquated straddle.

I had been flying too close to the sun and now God wanted to singe my wings permanently. He wanted me to feel the burn. I had to see it, feel it, ask for forgiveness, and *then* fail. That was the humbling plan so I could still have the opportunity to save my soul through humility as Mary Magdalene had washed Christ's feet with her hair and been redeemed. I had to become the penitent and how could that happen if I was determined to entertain? It *is* the meek that shall inherit the earth, the world of eternity.

All this went through my mind as I stood there, maybe in two seconds. I came to the horrible realization that this was my moment in the blistering sun. If I didn't make it through the preliminaries, I would not have a second kick at the can. I would have to see all the expectant faces at the airport. My father and

Mother Agnese would be most disappointed. My father would put on that brave smile and tell me I'd done my best. He was a great believer that hard work reaps rewards. I knew these kids hadn't practised as hard as I had. Some of their approaches were messy and inconsistent, yet they soared over the pole effortlessly, as though gravity only affected those from Western New York and ran out of steam once it came to Harlem. I guess all kids have a point in their lives when they realize their fathers don't know everything. It sure is a painful moment. I believed my father when he said I could win if I worked hard enough. He never told me that talent sometimes wins out and that's just a God-given endowment. I think I could have accepted that if only I'd known it ahead of time.

Mother Agnese now lived inside me and I knew her take on this would be to try and offer up my disappointment to Christ for the souls in purgatory. The whole thing came crashing down upon me as the loudspeaker bellowed, "Number 63, number 63, Western New York, begin now or claim disqualification." I ran at the right angle and straddled perfectly, but the pole was simply too high for me and it clattered to the ground. I was out. My high-jumping career was dead, never to be resuscitated.

My years droned on at Hennepin Hall School. As far as I could see I'd peaked at nine and was now on my way down the mountain. I was just putting in time waiting for something to happen, and what that would be I had no idea. After all, Saint Paul was stricken on the road to Damascus and he hadn't known it was going to happen. I'd ceased even to attempt to be a shining light since I'd bombed in both the athletic and ecclesiastical departments. I was no more than a lightning rod of discontent in the eyes of Mother Agnese, who had been promoted to Mother Superior, a title she took in stride. I made sure that I kept all my questions and doubts to myself, but with each passing year I felt more and more isolated, different from those around me. I put on a good cover, still captain of the teams, but I kept a different heartbeat, an arrhythmia that only I heard.

One day Father Flanagan walked into our classroom, accompanied by another priest who wore red satin and a matching little red beanie. Mother Superior fell to her knees and kissed the ring on his grandly extended hand. He was a cardinal who had come from the Vatican to see Niagara Falls and to attend an ecumenical conference. He said, in a thick dialect which I had by now learned was not a speech impediment but in fact a New York accent, that he had an announcement from Pope Pius XII for all of the United States. I guess he hoped that we in grade five in Lewiston would spread the word. He said he was sent with our Holy Father's message which would be fully explained in a film strip. He had a tape recorder and a projector. This was amazing to us since our only visual aid thus far had been chalk. Father Flanagan set up the projector, which he referred to as "Mr. Disney's Miracle," and the cardinal provided the vocal backup. First of all he wanted to show us the Vatican and the Sistine Chapel and the work of Michelangelo. Since I knew most of the biblical characters, at least through the eyes of Mother Superior, I was entranced by Michelangelo's version of their stories. All of the stations of the cross that I had spent so much time looking at suddenly came to life before my eyes as the images were thrown up on our wall in the dark room filled with Gregorian chant.

He showed us a slide of a girl who received a free three-week trip to Rome and got to stay at the Vatican and have a visitation with the pope. A written message flashed across the screen. *"Why, you might ask, was this girl from Wichita, Kansas, chosen to go to Rome?"* The next frame gave us the answer. *"She won an essay contest and became the U.S. emissary for the World Reading Foundation of Catholic Schools."* The next frame told us who could enter. *"Why, last year, the first year of the contest, we had over 3,000 applicants from Los Angeles alone. If you are enrolled in an American Catholic School and are under twelve years of age, you may enter!"*

The cardinal then handed out applications that were to be judged by a panel of archbishops across the U.S. The best twenty would be sent to Rome to be judged by a coterie of cardinals. The application only had a number on it and we were each given a ticket. At the top of the page it said to fill in only one side. He turned off his slide projector and then we were all given thirty minutes to complete our forms. When I looked at mine it read, "Complete this line and expand in no less than 25 and no more than 100 words; READING IS FUN BECAUSE . . ."

I was the first one finished and handed mine in. As usual I was sure I'd won. I could smell victory. Los Angeles! Who lived out there! Zorro and Sergeant Garcia, *please*. I began planning my trip to Italy. Of course I'd go alone. After all, I went to Harlem alone for high jumping.

I became obsessed with Italy and the Vatican. This obsession mostly took the form of adoring Michelangelo and the painting of the Sistine Chapel. My mother bought me a huge book of Michelangelo's work with a foldout of the Sistine Chapel, which I pored over daily, planning what I should see first. I got every book in the library on the art of the Renaissance, which became my passion. Mother Superior thought my interest odd since I was not at all artistic. My drawings were never chosen to go on the bulletin board for parents' night. My pink-and-green Easter basket made of construction paper was always a mess and looked as if it had been made in kindergarten, while the other girls' glue never showed. I loved the expressions on the faces in the paintings which gave me alternative interpretations of the bible stories. To me they were like amazing storyboards. I could tell by the expressions that Michelangelo had his own interpretation of some of the stories that I'd heard told in one definitive version for so many years. My favourites were the depiction of original sin and the expulsion from Eden as well as the last judgement. The work of Salvador Dali looked tame compared to Michelangelo's depiction of Charon's boat to hell. The faces of the passengers showed the sudden and horrible realization that they were heading on a one-way trip to eternal damnation as the fires of hell licked at their heels. For Christmas that year I got books on Giotto, Fra Filippo Lippi, Botticelli, and Fra Angelico and read them until they fell apart.

After about six months I learned that I had made the top twenty out of all of the Catholic schools. I was thrilled, although Mother Superior managed to contain whatever enthusiasm she may have experienced. Maybe she felt she'd been there before. My mother was not the least bit surprised that I was a finalist. I overheard my parents' conversation that night as I hid on the landing of the stairs. My mother said, "I think they believe she is just average, and they are begrudging her success with this contest. She has established a reputation as difficult and I believe they have slotted her to be a checkout girl at Helms's Dry Goods. She got a C in English on her report card, yet she wins an international prize. Does that seem strange to you?" My father's only response was "She hasn't quite won yet."

I was convinced that everyone in Italy either dressed as the cardinal did or wore togas, like in the paintings. On the wall of The Horseshoe restaurant there was a picture of a gondolier with a red-striped tee-shirt and pedal pushers. Finally I realized I had been living in the past when my mother and I, in preparation for the trip, went to see *Three Coins in the Fountain*. This splashy drama took place in Rome and featured the Trevi fountain. I had alternating fantasies: in one, I was sitting on the pope's balcony, giving him a few tips as we waved to the square full of admirers; in the other, literally more racy fantasy I wore a wide cinch waist dress, like the girls in the movie, and sat in the sidecar of a motorcycle, scarf blowing freely, as Rossano Brazzi drove me all over Rome, showing me the sights. All of this seemed a tad more interesting than the highlight of my summer, which was going to the Firemen's Field Day and playing fish with Trent McMaster.

By May Day the list had dropped to the top five in the U.S. and I was on it. There was a column about my possible literary triumph in *The Catholic Union and Echo*, saying that they only hoped they could say *arrivederci* to a certain girl from Hennepin Hall. The winner was to be announced by June first. Mother and I didn't buy any summer short sets in case I was going to be "abroad."

Finally June first arrived, and I tore off to school early and told my mother I'd meet her at Schneider's Restaurant for lunch with the news. I ran into the principal's office and asked Mother Superior if she had the announcement from Rome. She continued doing paperwork at her desk and said that she did indeed have the results and pointed to an envelope with a foreign stamp and weird fountain-pen writing that said, "Please post." She continued writing and I finally said, *"Well?"* She said she clearly didn't have the trouble that I had with the English language. She would pin the paper to the bulletin board in the school vestibule because that, as far as she was concerned, was the meaning of the word *post* and she believed in following holy orders. I felt like screaming, "To the moon, Alice!" but knew that she wanted me to offer up my impatient curiosity for the poor souls in purgatory. I went to my classroom and waited for her to unlock the door. Finally, at eleven, all the girls lined up in the hallway and we were to say our ejaculations of Jesus, Mary, and Joseph. As we passed the bulletin board, out of the corner of my eye I caught the stationery with the cardinal-red edges. Everyone continued toward the washroom but I stopped and read the letter.

A boy from Providence, Rhode Island, had won. I was first runner-up. Mother Agnese was behind me. She handed me an envelope that had my name on it, c/o Hennepin Hall. It said it was their honour to give me, as runner-up, an autographed holy picture blessed by the pope. I was told the Holy Father had written a few words specifically to me on the back of his picture. I had gone from a trip to Italy to a holy picture, of which my mother had drawerfuls at home.

I was enraged. I didn't want this holy picture. "You can have it," I said and gave it to her. She looked mad, not her usual controlled inscrutable martyred look, but that kind of slant-eyed mad she got when her words had been divinely inspired. She held out the picture to return it to me, but I was way beyond putting up with her religious jag at that moment. I screamed, "Maybe *you* don't understand the language. 'I don't want it' means *I'm not taking it*." The other kids down the hall were looking. No one ever raised their voice in the hall and never to her.

She remained very calm and spoke in a lower than normal tone. "Clearly you are disappointed, Catherine. I have only one thing to say to you and I hope that you listen well, as your faith is at stake. You may get a chance to see more than Michelangelo's version of the demons who are dragged to the inferno on the Judgement Day if you do not take heed. Catherine, you suffer the sin of pride and that is one of the seven most deadly. May I suggest something to you? If you are not as pleased with this picture of our Holy Father that he has autographed for you as you would be with the three-week trip to Rome, then you are not really a Catholic. There is little hope of working on your faith when you are not of the fold. I'll leave that with you. I'd like you to walk over to church now and light a candle and make your decision, one you can live with. You may leave early and then go straight home for lunch."

I walked over to the church, pushed open the heavy doors, and sat in a pew, the one that said "McClure" on it. I knew that it was time to feel really terrible — but I didn't. I felt free. I put my feet up on the bench and kicked back my kneeler. This church was just a building. There was nothing more for me here. I wasn't going to pretend any more. I couldn't take the subterfuge any longer. I was just covering bad plaster with wallpaper. It worked, but it was a cheap job. I didn't care about this holy picture and I'd wanted the trip. Finally the proof was in black and white. It was as obvious as the nose on my face. I didn't have faith nor was I going to heaven.

I decided then and there to stop worrying about it. After all, if hell was eternity I'd have plenty of time to worry then.

As I slowly walked back to the vestibule of the church, I realized I could stop trying to wear the straitjacket of meekness, silence, pridelessness, and every other virtue I had failed at on a daily basis. I'd start out every morning as a selfless junior Carmelite on a silent mission of penance in order to succeed in Mother Superior's eyes, which I saw as no different from God's, but would lapse into speech by the time we had finished the Pledge of Allegiance.

I'd even tried obsessive rituals to be a more selfless and deserving person. Since I couldn't make — or will — myself into a successful vessel or a "daughter of Mary" knock-off, I opted for anything that could give my life order. I opted for magical or obsessive thinking. I actually thought, or hoped, that if I drove my bike around the block three times and pulled into the driveway and did a fishtail on the gravel, then God might make me a good Catholic girl. Now I was finished with all these vain efforts. I could give it up, take off the mantle, the hair shirt of passivity, and breathe. I knew that I couldn't like myself and I should blame myself or kick myself in the head because life was so short compared to eternity, but that's not how I *really* felt. It actually occurred to me for the first time at that moment when I looked at the annunciation picture in the sacristy that no matter how bad hell was, I had a reprieve. I could be myself in this life.

What if I was flagellating myself for nothing? Why was I rubbing religion on my brain like a pumice stone? Did I really *want* to emulate Linda Low? I let myself say for the first time something that had been nagging me for a while — what if there was no heaven or hell? I let myself think it and for the first time I didn't let that thought scare the bejesus out of me. If I'm not so thrilled to see the pope, maybe he isn't so thrilling. Maybe he is just a guy from Palermo, the way the cardinal is really just a fat man from Brooklyn in a red satin dress with a matching beanie.

Mother Superior had gone over the edge and I was in free fall. She actually released me from her grasp. She had all the tickets to the merry-go-round and I had been grabbing at the ring for too long. She didn't know it yet, but I wasn't interested in the ride any longer.

I left the dark church and was blinded by the spring light and the cherry blossoms that were late this year. It had been a cold 1958, but it had suddenly heated up and the buds went to blossoms in a few days. The sky was blue and the clouds were light and fluffy and festive like white cotton candy. I strolled over to meet my mother for a burger and a Coke.

I skipped school that afternoon and went into Niagara Falls. When bad things happened, Roy was always the person I wanted to be with. He never said much, but what he said was always a comfort. I needed to tell him about the contest bust and my new decision to drop the Catholic faith. I didn't think my mother was ready for that. One thing I'd never told him was that the topic of the "Reading is fun because . . ." essay had been him. I'd been able to give him the gift of what I read and he gave me everything else.

When I went to his subterranean office under the grate, he was gone. He'd picked up stakes in the night, leaving only a picture of Louis Armstrong waving and smiling goodbye from a Cadillac. That day marked the end of my first decade, and I was never to see Roy or God again.

CHAPTER 12

father flanagan

It had been two years since I retired from the uphill battle of attaining eternal life. Now I was close to becoming a teenager and did just as I pleased — easier said than done. I had very little opportunity to express my devil-may-care attitude, mostly because there was no one to listen. Roy had moved on. And working at the store didn't seem to be part of my soul any more. It was just a job.

I was now at an age when boys no longer played with girls at home or at school, so the Bloods bled to death. Those glory days were gone. Now even talking to a boy seemed to mean something ominous. I wasn't sure what, but the boy-girl thing was a quagmire and I wasn't wearing the right boots for the terrain. Most dangerous things interested me, but for some reason, this one seemed very dangerous and very uninteresting. I didn't mind heading over a precipice, as long as I could steel myself. I just didn't want to be led there blindfolded. It wasn't the danger or being ostracized that made me back off the girl-boy thing, but I couldn't figure out what the goal was supposed to be. There had to be something in it for me. If I skipped school, I got a day off; if I sledded in dangerous areas, the thrill was in making it in one piece; if I was rude to someone, it was because they bugged me and I got it off my chest. Talking to boys offered no reward that I could fathom. It seemed of interest to other girls, so I guess I just didn't get it.

By process of elimination, all that was left was girls. The Baker sisters had transferred from paper dolls to junior golf. *Yawn.* Linda Low and her apostles were thrilled to run the Guardians of Mary Club, which was unspeakably boring. It made Trent McMaster's Blue Army look like the Green Berets. Then there were the other girls who came in from farms or somewhere who put their tongues on the frozen school-bus windows and seemed pleased to have managed toilet training. They were obviously out.

Then there were the *bad* girls. They were still too young to be really wayward since really bad girls talked to boys outside the post office or got into trouble of an unmentionable kind. I wasn't ready for *that* sort of bad. There was little left for me in Lewiston except for the up-and-coming bad girls. The ones who were late for school, who didn't pay attention, the ones who Dolores said were "sassy" and whose future she referred to as "diggin' their own graves." Miranda Doyle was one of those. She was two years older and one year ahead in school. I moved my chair to her grade for English and reading in the afternoon, and she and I often made fun of the characters in the books. She was a bad reader but she could be very funny about the characters and the situations in the earnest Catholic stories. I could tell that Mother Superior really disliked her and Miranda couldn't care less. That in itself was unusual and something I was beginning to admire.

I couldn't help but think that Mother Superior held it against her when Miranda showed up in an angel costume supposedly made by her mother for the Christmas play, an old white satin evening gown which said "Angel" in laundry marker across the front. Some of the other mothers were scandalized. I heard them talking about it as I helped my mother's Altar and Rosary Society put together the manger outside the church. Dolores got on the bandwagon saying there was no excuse for such behaviour. After all, the Doyles weren't poor. In fact they lived in one of Lewiston's larger homes. Instead of setting a good Catholic example to counteract her Protestant husband, Mrs. Doyle did things like put a Kleenex on her head when she couldn't be bothered to wear a hat to mass. My mother agreed with Dolores that these snubs in piety or "mere flippancy" were not good examples for her four daughters. *Flippancy* was a word I hadn't heard before; however, I liked the sound of it so I looked it up. "Treating serious things lightly." Now, this word certainly reflected my new philosophy and Miranda perfectly personified it.

Miranda was a beautiful girl who had black Rapunzel hair. When our whole school went to Frank Sturski's farm to learn about animal husbandry, we travelled in crowded car pools. Mother Superior made the girls place a phone book between ourselves and boys if we sat next to them or if we had to sit on a boy's lap in the car. I noticed the older boys from grade seven and eight pushed each other aside to get into Miranda's car pool and sit next to her.

She was flippant about Mother Superior's decrees and even the Ten Commandments. She asked strange questions that managed to upset Mother Superior. We read a short story about a boy whose father was a barnburner and Miranda said, "Thank God he didn't obey the 'honour thy father and thy mother' commandment or we'd all live in ashes." Mother Agnese couldn't get to her the way she had to me because Miranda had never really bought in. On top of her freedom from dogma, she could spot a human foible a mile away when, for most other people, it would only look like an irrelevant speck. How Miranda knew what made people tick, I had no idea; however, a friend who knew everyone's Achilles heel was an important ally.

Once, on our way home, we stopped into Reggie's Torpedo Submarine and Variety Store for wax fingernails filled with cherry Kool-Aid, and who was there buying bitters but Father Flanagan. Reggie, the proprietor, said to Father, "Oh, here is Elizabeth Taylor from *A Place in the Sun*," obviously referring to Miranda. Father Flanagan put one arm on each of our shoulders and chimed in, "A-ha, here we have beauty and brains walking abreast." I was thunderstruck with horror. My humiliation made me more stock-still than a snake that plays dead. After all, no one cared about being smart. No one said, "Oh, isn't Elizabeth Taylor *smart*." Stores sold makeup, not IQ points. To make this ignominy worse, there were older boys from the public school buying baseball bubble gum next to us and they laughed, obviously knowing who the pretty one was. I decided at that moment Father Flanagan would pay for that remark if it was the last thing I did, before departing for my eternity in hell. The upside of eternal damnation was that it made very little difference what you did wrong in *this* world.

As we walked home we donned our wax lips and fingernails and tried to convince Lloyd, the traffic guard who Roy had said wasn't "the sharpest tool in the shed," that they were real nails and we had just been for a manicure. Miranda, obviously mulling over what had happened in Reggie's, suddenly got angry, saying that Father Flanagan had no right to say she was stupid. "I was waiting for him to tell those grade-eight boys that I'd failed grade four. Why doesn't he just give us a hair shirt and some ashes?" As we took off our fingernails, bit into the wax, and drained the Kool-Aid, she added as an afterthought, "Anyway, who cares? He's a drunk." I assured her that he wasn't a drunk. The only drunk in our town was ol' Jim and even his son, young Jim, didn't speak to him. Neither did his wife, Marie, the retired madam who lived above the Buena Vista Motel. "You know, for being smart you're awfully stupid. I've noticed that about you before. This town is crawling with drunks. You don't have to be legless and sell pencils and wind-up frogs to be a drunk. You can even have a job, be a mother, be a priest, or even be the mayor. You know how many housewives souse it up while we're parsing sentences? What do you think Father Flanagan was buying bitters for — his personality?" I had no idea what bitters were. Instantly reading my confusion, Miranda rolled her eyes back into her head. "God, what do I have here — a kindergarten? What! You think Father Flanagan can help himself?" I knew there was something to this because my mother had referred to his "affliction" as "a weakness for the sacramental spirits." Miranda continued in exasperation, "If we spiked his holy water on a Sunday morning, he'd be feeling no pain by noon." We exchanged glances. The deed was done. All that was left was to work out the details.

Actually, quite a bit of planning went into the plot, and unfortunately it took a week of daily mass to achieve perfect timing. We had to know which holy-water font he used when he blessed himself. Finally we established his pattern of always using the one below the sign that read, "Wash not only thy face but thy iniquities." We worked out his movements: one, in the front door; two, dip into the right font with its swollen flaccid sponge soaking up the stagnant holy water and then bless himself — Father, Son, and Holy Ghost; three, kiss his crucifix. Aah — the taste of vodka. He was dead in the water, and ultimately pickled in alcohol.

Miranda called me late Saturday. She'd gone to confession, making sure she was the last in line, drained the holy water into a milk bottle, substituted the vodka, and scuttled home.

I had agreed to this plan with a great deal of bravado since I couldn't imagine that it would go anywhere. After all, why would a man make a fool of himself in front of all his parishioners because he tasted vodka on his crucifix? What would then "force" him to drink more? As far as I was concerned it didn't add up. Besides, Miranda talked a good line, but the fact remained she was in the sparrow reading group while I was in the cardinals.

By Saturday night I realized the plan was executed, which was farther than I thought the whole thing was going to go. In case the deed came off as Miranda had planned, we needed an iron-clad alibi if we were ever suspected. I called Miranda, who said we didn't even need an alibi. As proof of this she drew upon Perry Mason. If there is no proof that you did it or there wasn't a confession, they can suspect all they want. They can't prove a thing. We went through elaborate promises to one another that no matter how they tortured us we would never confess. Miranda seemed to understand a lot about interrogation. She said they would separate us and say that one of us had confessed. Even if we were interrogated separately we should never believe the interrogator.

I said, "Well, they wouldn't lie."

She said, "Of course they would. After all, we're lying."

That really scared me. I felt as though the whole plot had grown beyond me and was still multiplying like a virus. Anyway, I assured myself that it would never succeed, and if by some fluke it did, they would suspect boys, probably the older boys or even Protestants, who had vandalized the church.

My family filed into our regular pew in our usual iron-clad order. The parishioners' names were typed and slotted in shiny brass rectangle frames on the end of the pew. I grew up in the third row on the right side. Miranda's family — well, her sisters and mother — were farther back from the altar on the left. I insisted on going to twelve o'clock mass, assuming Father Flanagan had blessed himself plenty by then.

The gospel all went without a hitch. I shot Miranda an I-told-you-so look over my shoulder. She shot back the contented smile of the Cheshire cat. Then Father Flanagan got to the sermon.

He started out talking about using the bingo money for an air conditioner — uninspiring, but not unusual; he then began meandering until fifteen minutes later he was red-faced, banging the pulpit, rocking the goose-necked lamp, shouting in full Irish lilt, ". . . the church bulletin doesn't tell you, does it . . . No! no! it doesn't." Bang! "Is it better to reign in hell than rule in heaven? The bloody Limeys have reigned over the Irish for how long, *how long*?" He was screaming now, looking at all the terrified faces in the pews lined up like rows of potatoes in a field. He continued, "I'm no jejune Jesuit, all thought and no grounding. I'm a man, a man with roots in the Irish turf — a simple parish priest — but what am I made of? Irish soil. Irish blood and toil, *that's* what." My mother whispered "for heaven's sake" to my father, who simply patted her hand.

Mother Superior took this opportunity to scuttle into the sacristy and signal to the bewildered altar boys to ring the communion bells, jarring our chief potato-head into Pavlovian action. The second he heard the tinkle, he dutifully tottered down from the pulpit and returned to the altar to serve communion, not without shouting over his shoulder, "Remember the bell tolls for thee." The altar boys nodded in cajoling silence.

The phone call came within hours of the holy water episode, which would soon enter Lewiston folklore, and I was the one to take a bath. Was it our sudden devotion at daily mass that was the tipoff to Mother Superior, or divine inspiration? We'll never know. As we pulled up in front of the rectory, my father slammed the car into park before coming to a complete stop, jolting us both forward. Ashes fell on his shirt and he said between a bitten cigar end, "This is worse trouble than I've ever been in my entire life and you're only a girl and not yet old enough to babysit."

I didn't think the whole incident warranted such a rumpus, but as Mother Superior and Father Flanagan stood in the cold hallway that smelled like old cabbage, I had the distinct feeling I was in a minority. Father Flanagan patted my father's back as if to say, "Don't worry, Jim McClure, she's only a bad seed — you'll still get to heaven." When we hit the front parlour, Miranda, my partner in crime, was slouching on a couch. She always lucked out — I knew her parents wouldn't show up. She smiled at me as if to say, "This is big trouble, but when you get right down to it, who cares?"

Once we were all seated, and Father Flanagan asked Mrs. Skelly, his club-footed housekeeper, for some "liquid refreshment," he began droning something along the line that this latest incident was only the tip of the iceberg. I took this opportunity to survey the room for damage control. Mother Superior looked the most outraged. While Father Flanagan ran off at the mouth, she only looked straight ahead. The corners of her starched wimple never moved. She was saying the rosary. Bead after treacherous bead moved through her fingers at exactly the same rate. She was definitely the wild card here. After all, she had to sober him up and cover for him — not an easy task, given the circumstances. Now she wasn't even listening to him.

I have laughed hard in my life but never as hard as Miranda and I laughed when we had gotten together at Reggie's after the drunken sermon. I had laughed so hard I swaggered into the Wonder Bread, permanently denting it. We were both crying and breathless when we agreed the best part was when he said he was *soil*. Miranda, an actress at heart, beat her chest the way Father had and adopted the perfect Cork accent, which was much more pronounced when "under the influence." Instead of yelling at me about the flat Wonder Bread, Reggie got caught up in the fun, saying his favourite part was the slight to the Jesuits.

My triumphant reverie was broken by Father Flanagan saying, "Kate, this is your last chance. Now, with God as your witness, do you understand your transgression and can you ask God's forgiveness?"

"Yes." That was easy.

Mother Superior began in a bloodless tone, the kind she used when speaking for God and going for the jugular. She spat out each word just as each rosary bead had been left behind. Even Father Flanagan looked a bit sheepish.

"Since God is our witness, we must act as His holy orders command," she said, addressing Father Flanagan. "I have devoted my life to God and the Catholic Church. I am in charge of hundreds of souls that are awaiting God's message. Catherine McClure and Miranda Doyle have thwarted my vocation and I won't have it." She whispered as though it was too awful to enunciate, "What shame your guardian angels must feel at this moment." Back to her regular voice, she said, "This is not our first conversation of this sordid nature, is it Father Flanagan?" Father sat there looking like a stunned bird. "I run a Catholic school, a temple for young souls, and just as Jesus expelled the merchants from his temple in justified anger, so must I expel Catherine and Miranda."

Expel?

"It is far better that they atone for their sins on earth than in hell. It is far better that they realize the gravity of their behaviour now."

Miranda said in a tone sounding honestly confused, "Sister, I have no idea why you think this liquor thing was us. I mean . . ."

Mother Superior interrupted her, not willing to listen to her explanation for one moment. "I take my directions from the Almighty and He has informed me who committed this sin. Not only have you committed a mortal sin on your own soul, but you have deprived every other well-intentioned Catholic of Sunday mass."

Miranda asked in a convincingly indignant tone, "Have you any proof?"

Mother Superior wheeled around and faced her. "Miranda, do not blaspheme. You have understood a Godless world very early in your life and I suspect you will do very well in it." (Mother Agnese was the only one in Lewiston to predict Miranda's success. She became an international headhunter, never married, and lives in a penthouse in Chicago.)

She turned to me, and her hatred bore a hole through my chest. I felt as though I were breathing through a reed. "Catherine, you think you are special. I was once taken in by the myth of strength that you perpetuate. You are no longer worthy of my attention. Strong people build on their strengths, they do not capitalize on other's weaknesses; that is easy. What I once thought was a boundless spirit that could have been offered to God, if that were to be your vocation, is really no more than a weak spirit, one that could not handle the rigours put before it. These rigours were not tests of huge proportions but were the normal self-control expected of a Catholic schoolgirl. Yet you speak of Joan of Arc and believe that *you* should have played her in our pageant? In your weakness you have been swayed by someone who knows no better. To work as Satan's disciple gives illusory moments of pleasure, but they are bought at a dear price."

No one said a word. Mother Superior stood up, forcing a

shocked Father Flanagan to his feet. She said, "Goodnight, and may the Holy Spirit be with you," to no one in particular, backed out of the double doors, black veil flying, and was gone. Since there was no point pleading with someone who wasn't there, we all shuffled out silently, passing Mrs. Skelly as she was clumping in with the tea.

I walked on the ribbed rubber runners down the cold rectory corridor to the vestibule, where my boots were thoroughly chilled. I wondered if I really was going to the public school with the other Catholic children whose parents cared so little about their souls they couldn't pay the few dollars a year it cost to send them to Catholic school. They were the children who didn't know any of the prayers for their first communion, who had seemed tough, hard, and so lost. Were we to have no uniforms and trundle back to Catholic school once a week for religious instructions given by the priests and nuns out of charity?

As I staggered from the dark hallway into the darker night, waiting for my silent father to relight his cigar, I pictured the Masaccio painting of Adam and Eve expelled from Paradise. I thought of all of those Renaissance pictures of the expulsion from Eden, of Michelangelo's snake wrapped around a tree and handing Eve the apple. I knew at that moment that my expulsion from Catholicism was complete. I was shocked that God, if He was there, chose to remain silent, as silent as my father, at this time when I last called upon Him.

CHAPTER 13

father rodwick

Shunned from the fold, Miranda and I slunk off to public school.

The term "trial by fire" leaps to mind when describing our brief

foray into public life. It was the end of the first week of junior

high school and I still couldn't find my locker. After getting uncer-

emoniously booted out of Catholic school, I felt like Dr. Manette in *A Tale of Two Cities*, who had been locked in the Bastille for so many years he was unable to cope with the light when he got out. We were no longer cloistered and the open spaces were giving me the bends. No one took the least bit of interest in our attire, our makeup, or our souls.

Miranda and I picked up our book bags for the pilgrimage back to Hennepin Hall for our weekly religious instruction class. We had to make the trek as the "prodigal daughters" of humiliated parents. Like the other poor souls who were deprived of a full-time spiritual education, we swarmed out of the public school exits like locusts before a storm, ready to devour any salvation in our paths.

To be prepared for such an auspicious occasion of enlighten-ment, we needed to fortify ourselves with nourishment, so we stopped into Reggie's sub shop. Although we knew that food was forbidden in class, we reasoned that if Christ's disciples needed loaves and fishes we needed the 1950s equivalent: a hoagie, wax lips, and Dubble Bubble.

"*Jesus H. Christ*, it must be ninety-five damn degrees." (Now that we were in public school we swore like sailors and no one even raised an eyebrow.) "They said on the radio it's the hottest day in forty years." Since no one was answering me, I continued wondering aloud, "Why did I believe I should wear my back-to-school outfit — just because I was going back to goddamn school?" I was dragging along in my kilt, oxford cloth shirt that hung out the back, slipping knee socks that were giving me a prickly heat rash, and Bass Weejun loafers. We looked like a bedraggled *Brigadoon* road company.

Miranda had a flair as a Father Flanagan mimic, among other

things. She spoke with only a trace of an Irish accent and craned her neck at exactly the angle he used when he wanted to disseminate the word of the Lord: "Saint Valentine wore a hair shirt all year and offered up his suffering for lost souls — can you not offer up your suffering for the souls who languish in purgatory?"

Reggie, who referred to himself as "a submarine architect," was thoroughly impressed with Miranda's pious imitation because he, too, knew Father Flanagan. He even gave her the hot peppers for free. We always got hot peppers so we wouldn't have to share with others, but took them out of our subs before they burned our lips.

I never understood what caused Miranda to have such an effect on men. I knew she was beautiful, but it was more than that. I looked at her in the window of the sub shop. My father once said she had "alarming beauty with disarming charm." I remembered that line because I had never heard him say anything like that about any woman before or after — let alone about a fifteen-year-old.

Miranda's thick hair was so purely black it looked dyed. My own hair was fine and pale blond, and I always marvelled at how Miranda had only to wrap the rubber band around her ponytail once while I had to twist it three times. She had porcelain-white skin. Her eyes were large and blue and her eyelashes so long that they brushed her sunglass lenses. Her eyes turned up slightly at the corners.

"Don't turn those electric eyes on me," Reggie said. "There's no free candy here. Remember you're not the star of *Black Beauty* here, Little Miss Elizabeth Taylor." He scooped extra penny candy into her small brown bag and said she could pick a "bonus item." She smiled and chose a "Daddy Long Legs" Turkish taffy sucker.

At the breakfast table I told my mother that Reggie said

Miranda looked like Elizabeth Taylor, the infamous *divorced* actress whose picture was splashed on the cover of *Photoplay*. I wondered if it was a compliment. I thought the way that Reggie said it, it was more of an accusation; however, underneath it must have been a compliment because she got extra candy.

My mother looked disgusted. She turned to my father and said, "Filling girls' heads with that kind of nonsense at this age is dangerous."

My father said, *"Dangerous?"* as though my mother were exaggerating. They very rarely disagreed and my mother never exaggerated; that was my department. My father realized they had "had words" and he went over to her chair, rested his hand on her shoulder, and said, "Well, I think that you look like Grace Kelly and I never told you before because I thought it might be *dangerous* for you to know that."

They both laughed and my mother said, "I guess I'm lucky that you kept it to yourself."

As he left for his store, my father said over his shoulder, "I just wanted to tell you before Reggie did."

I had no idea what that interchange was about, but I was aware it took place in the physical realm, a place I'd never seen or heard either of them visit in the past. As far as I could figure out, there was a big fuss being made over next to nothing.

Our next stop was Woolworth's. We had infinite admiration for the cosmetician, as she insisted on being called. Even when we saw her in church on Sunday we referred to her as the cosmetician. There was something terribly official about her salmon-coloured smock with the Woolworth crest on it. She was the one who said Miranda's eyes were almond-shaped and all her features were so perfect they only needed "accenting." She said, while applying "coral reef" lipstick, that my face needed "contrast" and that I looked like a "faded blond." Who wants to fade before fifteen? On the other hand the cosmetician called me "delicate" and "leggy."

"She is Western New York's high-jump champion. Delicate, huh?" Miranda said with disdain.

"I guess that's the leggy part," I added lamely. I had white-blond hair which wasn't bad, but I also had a blond face. The more makeup Miranda applied, the more exotic she would look, and the more I slapped on, the more I looked like a kewpie doll. What was amazing about Miranda was that she woke up one day looking "womanly" without any awkward stages. She had one of those hourglass figures with full breasts which looked great under twin sweater sets. I must have been in the washroom when God was handing those out.

We bought tons of makeup because there were two rules on makeup that I had figured out. First, for everything you bought, you needed its opposite: day cream/night cream; moisturizer/astringent; lip powder/lip gloss. Second, you needed to carry all makeup with you at all times in a special zipped bag. You never know when you might need an astringent. So off we lumbered on our pilgrimage, loaded down with food and makeup, knowing full well that the only forbidden items in the eyes of Father Flanagan were food and makeup.

Father Flanagan was waiting for us, his red nose beaming a welcome. We flopped down in our chairs, makeup screaming and red-and-white submarine bags signalling our defiance. He had a bemused expression on his face and began in his Irish lilt. "Well, ladies, welcome to religious instruction for our first September class as we are about to usher in a new decade. We have a few surprises in store for you this year. I'm back by popular demand." Miranda and I began choking and rolling our eyes. Some of the more religious girls, like Linda Low, scowled at us. Linda's mother ran a beauty parlour off the back of her house and Linda always had perfect hair, with roller marks and one or two hair clips left in to assure symmetry. Linda was still president of the Guardians of Mary Club. I was never quite sure what we were guarding since I thought Mary was guarding us. Although disgustingly boring, Linda did have a real following among those girls who wanted a fast track to the hereafter. Miranda and I had no following what-soever, but I firmly believed we were silently admired for our rebelliousness. We were also convinced Father Flanagan had finally turned tail after we vociferously spread the news of what we believed to be his ecclesiastical shortcomings. I was later to find out how wrong I had been on both counts and that the real foundation of my delusion was based on these two false assumptions. Christ said to Saint Peter, "On this rock build my church." I said, "On these foundations, I build my delusion of a Catholic girlhood."

Father turned to me, smiling, with his hands neatly tucked into the breast pockets of his cassock. "Catherine McClure, our most punctilious, often pugnacious parishioner, has raised several points of interest, as has our bevelled beauty, the insouciant Miranda Doyle. They have suggested, in ever so 'umble a tone, that I am preparing them for only one thing in life — the holiest of vocations — motherhood."

"Hear, hear," Miranda muttered between mouthfuls.

"Since Miranda Doyle is not at her most eloquent when masticating, perhaps we will let Catherine, one of our most loquacious repentants, express her sentiments."

As I unpacked my submarine, I said, "Gladly. We objected to the fact — I repeat, *fact* — that the boys learn philosophy and we learn how to build 'holy tabernacles' — the Catholic home." I said this with dripping sarcasm and heard a few titters from the rebellious wannabees in the back of the room, which served to boost my oratory. "The magazine *We Willing Workers* should be used to wrap submarines and not to 'teach girls.' I don't need to travel three miles to find out how to change the flowers on the altar."

"Thank you, Catherine. Your pearls of wisdom never cease to enlighten us."

"I'm not finished," I said, getting more angry by the second. "Speaking of flowers, I also object to the *fact* that you had a flower arranging expert — Mrs. Low, a beautician who moonlights as a florist — talk to us about altar arrangements for two weeks while you listened to the World Series on the radio in the back of the room." I felt quite pleased. He hadn't expected that zinger.

"Ah-hah, well, that makes this occasion all the more auspicious," he said, beaming. I began to wonder if he had had a few — his "bevelled beauty" line was somewhat of a tipoff. "For with us today we have Father Daniel Rodwick. He recently received a Ph.D. in philosophy at the Pontifical Institute after attending Notre Dame, and will be leaving for the missions in Africa when he is ordained. He has, in the interim, generously agreed to donate his time to us and has undertaken to teach philosophy to the entire gaggle of girls who have seen it in their hearts to attend our class of the enlightenment." Turning to me, he added, "Catherine McClure, I only hope that he can meet your stringent requirements."

Father Flanagan looked to the back of the class and we all turned around to see who had entered through the coatroom door. "Father Rodwick," he said, waving his hand toward us with the flourish that only a wee drop of the sacramental cups can enhance, "I present you with your ultimate test." Raising his arm and bowing, Father Flanagan announced in his gospel-giving tone, "Job had floods and famine, and you, Father Rodwick, as Almighty God's servant, have Miranda Doyle and Catherine McClure, a species Noah left off the ark."

The class was shocked into silence. A man, *here* — what's more, a *Jesuit* at Hennepin Hall! As twenty-eight dumbfounded heads swivelled around, we saw a young man in a black cassock and clerical collar walking up the aisle. He was tall, thin, blond, broad-shouldered, the most handsome man I had ever seen in my life. In fact he was the only man I had ever seen who was handsome. His smile was genuinely happy, his green eyes had never been bored. For a minute I wondered if Father Flanagan had gone to get an actor to put on this robe — I knew he was out to get us — but I doubted he'd go to all this trouble. He, like Miranda, wasn't one for going to extraordinary lengths. This Father Rodwick character had to be the real enchilada, otherwise it would be a sacrilege. Impersonating a priest was like playing God.

I didn't dare look at Miranda for fear I would have a giggling attack that would get out of control. When I finally sneaked a glance at her, she cocked her head and raised one eyebrow at me, as if to say she was definitely up to the challenge; and if this guy thought he was going to face lepers in a few months, he had no idea what he had in store for him right here in the tiny town of leprous Lewiston. I lifted my eyebrow in agreement. Even Linda Low took out her extra hair clips.

Father Flanagan continued, "Ladies, although the intellectual calibre will be uplifted by God's young proxy, the canons remain the same. No eating or makeup applications, girls to the washroom one at a time. May God be with you." At this point he bowed dramatically to Father Rodwick and left. Linda Low led the correct response of "And with your spirit."

"Well . . ." Father Rodwick smiled again. He had one of those Dr. Kildare smiles, the kind Richard Chamberlain used when he smiled at a patient who'd finally regained her sight after an operation. "I've never taught this age group or girls before." He swallowed, and I noticed he had a prominent Adam's apple and large veins pulsating in his neck. "You've never been taught philosophy, so I hope that we'll be able to help each other out. Stop me if I'm speaking over your head or in a condescending way."

While I was contemplating the meaning of the word *condescending*, Miranda was wasting no time. She opened her Daddy Long Legs sucker, the long thin taffy kind, and began licking it from bottom to top. Then she began pulling it and making it longer and snapping off the top. The whole class was looking from Miranda to Father Rodwick to see what he was going to do about it. He ignored it. Then she began leaning back in her chair, tilting her head backwards and making noises with her tongue on the taffy.

Finally he said in a friendly enough tone, "Miranda, there is no eating in here."

"Why?" she asked in an innocent and wide-eyed tone. "What about the loaves and fishes — didn't God distribute them while He was preaching? He didn't mind a few munchies here and there."

"Unfortunately there were two differences. One, Jesus Christ did not have to answer to Father Flanagan, and I do. Two, the loaves and fishes were consumed after several hours of hunger and thirst. I assure you, if we are ever together for over twelve hours I will serve you both loaves and fishes."

Together for over twelve hours? What was he going on about? He didn't know Miranda very well if he thought that lame cocktail chatter was going to swing her into line. Sure enough, her behaviour became more and more outrageous. She began making loud, smacking, slurping sounds when she licked.

Finally he said, "Miranda, I don't think that is very ladylike behaviour." He had no idea what impact the word *ladylike* had on all of us. No one, not Father Flanagan, nor Mother Superior, would have ever referred to our behaviour as *unladylike*. They would use the words *un-Catholic*, *heathen*, *unsanctified,* even *idolatrous*, but they never made any mention that we were females. He had no idea what a can of worms he was opening, nor how quickly Miranda could inch in.

"We had no idea that you knew the ins and outs of ladylike behaviour. Why don't you tell us a bit about your experience along those lines?" Miranda inquired.

"Miranda, throw it out," he said in a less affable tone. I could see that was his second mistake.

"If you want it, take it." She was still licking the Daddy Long Legs as she held it between her teeth. He took one step toward her, then two — his face became red and he stood frozen very close to her. She taunted him with the sucker in his face by tilting her head back. Everyone watched in silence, even the *We Willing Workers* crowd.

He didn't take it. I had no idea why. Father Flanagan would have pulled it out of her mouth at the risk of rattling her teeth, and told her to sit up straight and that she would have to clean the gum off the lunchroom tables after school and then maybe sticky taffy wouldn't look so appealing. Father Rodwick, obviously another story, looked bewildered, as though he'd been running somewhere and someone had removed his final destination. Once we all saw that he couldn't deal with Miranda, we knew it was game over for "The Rod," as she was soon to christen him.

—

As the weeks tumbled on, everyone, minus the inner sanctum, began to bring food and put on makeup. Sometimes when he would call on Miranda, she would say, "Just a sec," then pull out a lipstick, roll it up, and put it on slowly. After everyone watched this display, she'd say, "*Now*, what's the question?" He would look out the window at the distant church spire and again get that confused, fogged-over look.

Nearly everyone contributed to the mayhem. Although both Miranda and I were the hard-core heretics, the number of other occasional offenders was increasing as the weeks and months slid by. When we were discussing the Reformation and Martin Luther's concerns, I questioned everything he said on the issues of transubstantiation. I even read all of the dittoed sheets that Father Rodwick sent home — *nobody* did that. I tried to find holes in the logic and then confront him about them before he even had a chance to start the class. The strange thing about all this questioning was that he actually seemed to *enjoy* these arguments. He would throw the chalk up, catch it, and say, "Catherine, you're not the first to have thought of that. However, you're in good company, since Thomas Aquinas asked the same questions."

These were the same questions that infuriated Mother Superior and made her call me a "doubting Thomas" and Father Flanagan address me as "oh ye of little faith." They would ask if I had *forgotten* that Christ died on the cross for me, or had it slipped my mind that He gave His last drop of blood to redeem our lost souls. Did I need to stab His side to see only water issue forth, before I would believe He gave His body and blood for us, or could I *possibly* accept this on faith. Father Flanagan asked if I, like Pontius Pilate, was washing my hands of the Lord's persecution? After this barrage, I would then have to kneel and recite all of the stations of the cross. Maybe then I would think twice before doubting the Almighty.

The Rod brought in books for me to read and I began to feel that school was not the hellhole I had believed it to be since kindergarten. I read Descartes, Aquinas, More, Plato, and others, and was amazed to find answers to questions that I brought up in class. I felt less in the opposition. I realized there were other people like me who asked the same questions and someone liked their ideas enough to let them publish a book. From what I could gather, these people were all dead men and they were called philosophers. Everything I ever asked was answered in these books. The Rod and I began having long, convoluted debates in class and even Linda Low stopped listening.

This was the most intellectually fruitful time of my life. I devoured all the books and for the first time felt, or realized, that there was more to the world than the circumscribed town of Lewiston. Rebelling against my tawdry small-town life didn't seem to pack such a wallop of excitement any more. I felt as though I had been a person alone in the world who collected stamps and everyone thought it was annoying at best, and evil at worst, and then one day someone said, "I collect stamps too, isn't it the greatest thing to do? And many great people in the world who lived hundreds of years ago also collected stamps." I wasn't crazy! Or if I was crazy, at least I had some ancient company. I went to the library and looked at pictures of Descartes and St. Thomas Aquinas and, believe it or not, they looked exactly as I pictured them. I felt as if I had found a lost relative after being an orphan for all of these years. I even looked for family resemblance in Plato's face.

I still felt obliged to be in the opposition, but it was in form only now. Although I asked several questions and tried to be as inflammatory as possible, only Miranda really knew how to rattle The Rod's cage. One day, in an effort to uphold my rebellious front, I went on the attack over the Church's corruption at the time of Martin Luther. I even said that if I had been Martin Luther, I, too, would have complained about plenary indulgences.

Miranda picked up on this and added, "You think Martin Luther left the Church over philosophical differences, but you don't really know that — after all, it was hundreds of years ago!" The Rod hesitantly nodded in agreement, which encouraged her to go on. "Maybe he left because Catholic priests couldn't marry or . . ." her voice trailed off.

Sticking to the facts, he replied, "He was excommunicated. He didn't leave voluntarily."

"Yeah, well maybe he had himself excommunicated because he knew he couldn't hack celibacy — *you* know, abstinence — in the physical way."

He broke in, "I am familiar with the term *celibacy*, Miranda. What you're saying is, of course, possible. However, we are here to discuss the *philosophical* differences between the Catholic Church and Martin Luther. We are not here to discuss Luther's *personal* weaknesses."

"Well, I'm just trying to get to the bottom of this guy, OK? If you couldn't be celibate, would that be a 'personal weakness' or just a fact — like — well, you know, if you kissed Mary Magdalene while she was washing your feet and drying them with her hair —" Miranda flung her long dark hair behind her "— you know, you just couldn't help yourself."

"Yes, I believe that would be a personal weakness if you made a promise of celibacy."

"Don't all priests suffer from earthly passions?" She asked this while eating a cherry icicle, which was melting quickly.

He looked at a spot on the wall and replied, "All people suffer from earthly passions. It is a question of how they are directed."

Earthly passions? What was Miranda getting into?

The Rod said, "Miranda, we are diverging from the topic."

I felt that I could jump in at this point. "You said divergence is part of discourse as long as we can say in what way we are diverging. What's wrong with Luther's passionate anger? Jesus was angry at the temple when the merchants sold their wares there. What's the problem with earthly passion?"

The Rod looked at Miranda and she looked at me with complete disgust, the kind she reserved for Linda Low, the lowest of low. What had I done? I had said something stupid that had no bearing on what was going on, but what *was* going on? I tried to make him angry but I had somehow relieved the tension.

She continued her onslaught. By this time there was complete silence in the class, even I had bowed out. "Isn't it true that Lutheran ministers can marry?"

"Yes."

"Then I guess that's one of the things Martin Luther wanted to do." He didn't answer or look at any of us. She forged ahead. "Well, let's face it, those corrupt popes were doing the big 'it,' right? Well, Martin Luther only wanted to get in on the action."

All twenty-eight heads focused on The Rod to see his reaction. He had a vein pulsating in his forehead. "Miranda." He sounded tired. His hands hung defeated at his side. He said softly, "There is no point discussing religion on only one level — the guttural." You could tell he thought he'd overstated things and tried to restore some equilibrium by saying, "We must learn to separate the flawed *institution* of the Church from God's holy *teachings*." However, it was too late. She'd snared him with his inflammatory use of the word *guttural*.

Miranda's voice was even and clear and she never hesitated. "Father Flanagan told us sex is beautiful and we have to prepare our souls for the conjugal meeting of one another. Our bodies are always holy tabernacles. After all, how else are new Catholics going to come into the world?" She paused for effect. "You don't think sex is guttural, do you?" There was a playfulness in her tone, a sort of mock shock.

Sex? For God's sake, what was she talking about?

"No, I don't." He was rasping now. He cleared his throat when he heard the unnatural sound of his voice.

"I didn't think so." She took the final bite of her icicle, which was now dripping into pools of red sticky liquid on her desk.

The girls who never listened, the ones who looked like Annette Funicello and carried around little suitcases because they went to hairdressing school for half a day, fell silent. They sat up and didn't fidget with their hair or do anything except closely survey The Rod's face. There was a long silence. He seemed unable to go on.

Miranda saw her advantage and grabbed it. When it comes to humiliation, Miranda was like a watchful retriever. No matter how many times you threw the bone away, she always brought it back, panting, and laid it at your feet. "M-a-y-b-e . . ." She dragged out the word while licking her icicle wrapper. "Martin Luther wanted to control his earthly passions, couldn't, then wham — flipped out. Maybe we only know it as a religious crisis. . . . You know the story has been cleaned up for the catechism. It *does* happen, doesn't it?"

"Yes," he said with his back turned to the class. He was looking out at the bubbling tar parking lot with the church on the far side.

"Maybe there was a young novice once, who, when she was running, let a little of her ankle show." She stuck out her Bass Weejun–shod foot to recreate the moment, "and he just lay awake at night dreaming of that ankle."

Father Rodwick had red blotches on his neck that started out the size of small islands, but grew into continents. He sank into his chair behind his desk. He put his head in his hands and rubbed his eyes as though he were tired.

Miranda's voice continued in that kind of husky whispering tone that I had never heard before. "I can't imagine what it would be like never to touch a woman. I mean, it would be fine if you were old like Father Flanagan." No one laughed. We were all sort of scared or at least incredulous. "But not so fine if you were young, say as young as Martin Luther."

He cut her off. "Catherine, please read aloud," he finally managed to whisper.

I had no idea why he was so upset. What crystallized for me at that moment was I actually *liked* him. I looked forward to his class and life seemed somehow larger. Whatever was going on, Miranda had carried it too far and all I wanted to do was help him out of whatever tight spot he felt himself to be in. However, I was at a loss for what to read. I picked up the *We Willing Workers* newsletter, the rag that we all laughed at. It was the only thing I had to read, so I read it. Not really knowing what was going on, or why The Rod was acting so strange, I had lost my nerve for reading it in my usual mocking tone, so I simply muttered in a monotone: "'May is the month for the blessed Virgin. How can we best serve her? A nice idea would be to have a May altar in her honour with a daily offering of flowers right in your own home.'"

As I was reading, Miranda leaned over and slipped a book on top of the newsletter. It was a paperback carefully covered in brown-lunch-bag paper entitled *Lady Chatterley's Lover*. She had a certain part circled and a note in the margin which said, "Read Now." As I read, I noticed that she had crossed out the game-keeper's name and inserted "The Rod.

> *The Rod took her in his arms again and drew her to him, and suddenly she became small in his arms, small and nestling. It was gone, the resistance was gone, and she began to melt in a marvellous peace. And as she melted small and wonderful in The Rod's arms, she became infi-*

nitely desirable to him, all his blood vessels seemed to scald with intense yet tender desire, for her, for her softness, for the penetrating beauty of her in The Rod's arms, passing into his blood. And softly, with that marvellous swoon-like caress of his hand in pure soft desire, softly he stroked the silky slope of her loins, down, down, between her soft warm buttocks, coming nearer and nearer to the very quick of her. And she felt him like a flame of desire, yet tender, and she felt herself melting in the flame. She let herself go. She felt The Rod's penis risen against her with silent amazing force and assertion and she let herself go to him. She yielded with a quiver that was like death, she went all open to The Rod. And oh, if The Rod were not tender to her now, how cruel, for she was all open to him and helpless!

She quivered again at the potent inexorable entry inside her, so strange and terrible. It might come with the thrust of a sword in her softly-opened body and that would be death. She clung in a sudden anguish of terror. But it came with a strange slow thrust of peace, she held nothing. She dared to let go everything, all herself, and be gone in the flood . . .

And it seemed she was like the sea, nothing but dark waves rising and heaving, heaving with a great swell, so that slowly her whole darkness was in motion, and she was ocean rolling its dark dumb mass. Oh, and far down inside her the deeps parted asunder, in long, far-travelling billows, and ever, at the quick of her, the depths parted and rolled asunder from the centre of soft plunging, as the plunger went deeper and deeper, touching lower, and she was deeper and deeper and deeper disclosed, the heavier the billows of her rolled away to some shore, uncovering her, and closer and closer plunged the palpable unknown, and further and further rolled the waves of herself away from herself, leaving her, till suddenly, in a soft, shuddering convulsion, the quick of all her plasm was touched, she knew herself touched, the consummation was upon her, and she was gone. She was gone, she was not, and she was born: a woman.

At the end of the passage, I was relieved, never looked up, and switched back to the newsletter and read, "'How to cut out a cardboard altar.'" As I was reading the strange passage Miranda had picked, what had shocked me most was how determined Miranda was in this plan. It was unlike her to go to so much trouble. I couldn't believe that The Rod hadn't stopped me. All he had to do was take the book away and punish us.

Father Flanagan's voice ripped through the hallway as he tore into the room. He stormed up the aisle with his cassock flying, and his Franciscan cord, tied in seven knots for seven mysteries, was flailing people as he proceeded. "The janitor came to my office to say you were reading filth. Exactly *what* is going on here?" God, he was really riled up. Fortunately I had given the book back to Miranda. His voice was thundering as I imagined the Archangel Michael's had been as he expelled Lucifer from heaven. "Father Rodwick, I repeat, what is going on?"

The Rod didn't answer, he simply looked at his desk blotter and wiped away imaginary eraser shreds. Jesus, I felt sorry for him. He tried. I don't know what the hell Miranda was doing or in what way I was part of it. He had attempted to discuss religious doubt and to teach us the things that the Jesuits cherished and he *did* treat us as more than "holy tabernacles." Still, we seemed determined to destroy him. When I gave it a second's thought I had no idea why. We were far worse to him than to Father Flanagan. Yet I owed The Rod something for making me feel normal instead of possessed.

I was slow in rising, but I did finally stand up. "Father Rodwick, thank you for letting me explain myself." Then I turned rather formally to Father Flanagan. "Father, what happened was we were reading the *W.W.W.* and suddenly Linda Low handed me a book, the likes of which I've never seen, and suggested I read it to the class. The cover was hidden so I assumed it was appropriate. Father Rodwick attempted to take the book, but I kept handing it around. Several people read from it. They'll probably want to identify themselves."

There was a long silence where everyone's eyes met mine with a stunned numbness, as though they were trying to get up after the ninth round. Feigning self-righteous indignation, I tried direct eye contact. "Come on, ladies, at least *I* had the decency to come forward."

Finally Miranda reluctantly raised her hand and said in her most chastened tone, "Father, I read last. Here's the book."

I gave a puzzled look to Miranda, the look that said "you had better have this under control." She shot back her haughty "don't sweat it" look. Father Flanagan examined the back cover to see Linda Low's name written in a perfect forgery of Linda's meticulous penmanship accompanied by her signature with matching curlicue flourishes on each of the L's. It was even written in the

same tasteless peacock-blue fountain-pen ink that Linda thought
so decorative. While I was stalling around grandstanding,
Miranda, the ultimate mimic, had written it in. Linda Low looked
as though her mind had permanently left her body. There was
only a hair-clipped empty shell before us.

"Linda," Father said gently. "Linda, is this true?"

She shook her head, then said, "Father, Father, you have *no*
idea what goes on here."

I interrupted, pretending that I couldn't stand it another
second. "Oh, give me a break, Guardian of Mary, come down off
the cross." Turning to Father Flanagan, I said, "This is nothing,
you should see her gym locker. It looks like a library for Mary
Magdalene *before* she asked for Christ's forgiveness."

He wasn't buying it. His eyes narrowed and he looked straight
at me. "You and Miranda are at the bottom of this."

I realized I had to give it my all and distract him from thinking of looking in her locker. "Father, *Father*," I said, upping the
ante in as shocked a tone as I could muster. "Do you want to see
my palms? Are *you* a doubting Thomas? Why should I lie? *Why
Linda Low*? Do you think I go off, buy books, put *Linda Low's*
name on them and read them aloud? I mean *really*, why would I
bother? Miranda and I have confessed, isn't that enough? The Lord
knows who the others are. Should we be punished for acknowl-
edging that we have succumbed to earthly temptation? I mean,
face it, you'll know the others in the confessional."

Father Flanagan looked dubious, but still in control; both The
Rod and Linda Low looked like they had been disembowelled and
undergone lobotomies. Father Flanagan looked around at the
path of psychological destruction and decided to call it a day.

"I want Catherine's, Miranda's, and Linda's mothers called, and I want them informed that their daughters deprived each student in this class of religious education, and if there is any more of this blasphemy you will each pay dearly. Out of respect for their mothers, don't mention the nature of this pornography or they'll think we're running the devil's workshop." At that, he turned on his heels, cassock spinning, and charged down the hall.

Outside, as we walked home, tugging on red licorice strings, Miranda spat the words which ricochet in my memory. "You really are a suck — I'm never coming to see you in the convent."

"I covered your ass, you stupid jerk, handing me that book. Christ, now our mothers are being called."

"So what? I have so much on my mother, she could never tell anyone about the call."

"What can you have on a *mother*? . . . Anyway, I don't have anything on mine."

"So just make sure that he calls on a day when Dolores is there cleaning. You must have something on Dolores."

"What?" I had no idea what she was talking about, nor did I care at this point. "Anyway, just forget it, I'll handle it." As if I could arrange to have a cleaning lady there when The Rod called. Why talk to someone who has resorted to mental telepathy?

"You're the biggest worrywart I've ever laid eyes on."

I just shook my head.

"Listen. First of all, he isn't going to call. What's he going to say? 'I let the girls read *Lady Chatterley's Lover*, and then we got caught and I thought I had better call you just to let you know.' I doubt it. Secondly, what if he does call? Linda Low is so boring, even her mother doesn't listen to her. My mother is in the twilight zone. My sister gave her a picture frame from Woolworth's for her birthday last year and she *still* has the picture of Tab Hunter in it that they put in it for display. I *think* I can handle her. Your parents aren't going to do anything about it because it's a book and any book is good in their minds. Besides, I think the guy who wrote it is famous 'cause it's a Penguin."

"Sure."

"You should have said that The Rod told you to read it. He was so dazed, Flanagan would have believed it."

"He could get in deep shit. What the hell happened to him, anyway, why was he so . . . so out of it?"

"*You're* the one who's out of it." She began imitating me in the voice of the bumbling idiot that I obviously resembled. "Passion is justified anger, blah, blah. Martin Luther felt about Christian doctrine, blah, blah, blah." She shook her head. "You are totally missing the point."

I stopped walking and simply looked at Miranda. I was completely confused.

Miranda stopped dead on the sidewalk and screamed, "He wants to do *it!*"

"What?" This conversation was out of sync, like an Elvis 45 played on 33.

"What Lady Chatterley did, nitwit." Miranda hit herself in the head. "Are you dense or what?"

I was feeling sort of weak. My body felt too heavy for my skeletal system. I felt I couldn't hold myself up. I didn't want her to say any more.

She saw me teetering, and gave it that last knockout blow. "He wants to be the gamekeeper, get it?"

"No, he's a priest. He studies philosophy. We're just kids. . . .
Even if he did want . . . *that* . . . he would pick a woman."

She exhaled in a world-weary way, as though she were sick of
explaining the obvious to an imbecile. "We get into the movies for
eighteen. I have breasts bigger than my mother's and a small
waist. *We* are what men want, not old saggy ladies with varicose
veins whose legs look like road maps. After twenty-five you start
looking hungry, pushing your breasts out of your bathing suit,
even if they're wrinkled. Men hate that desperate crap. *Now* is
when men want you, before babies and husbands leave your body
in a pile of bruised rubble."

"That's not true," I said, but I had a sinking feeling, and revul-
sion was beginning to grip my chest like a whalebone corset. I felt
prickly heat under my blouse. My mouth was dry. A part of me
knew that in matters of understanding the world, Miranda was
always at a distinct advantage.

She began staggering off the sidewalk with laughter as we
walked. Between doubled-over guffawing, she managed to say,
"You're a riot. You *actually* think that The Rod cares about your
rambling theories of transubstantiation?" Now she was laughing
so hard that she splayed herself on someone's lawn. As she was
getting up and dusting off her skirt she said, "He walks around
with a stick, or haven't you noticed?"

"No, he doesn't. What kind of stick?" I was picturing Saint
Patrick's staff, the one that scared the snakes out of Ireland. I was
at Miranda's mercy now and I knew it.

"The one under his cassock."

I had given up all semblance of knowing what she was talking about. Obviously my pretence hadn't worked anyway and I had made a complete fool of myself.

"*Cock, dick, penis, little Willie, plunger,* whatever word will register in your deranged little walnut brain. You *are* aware that before men do it, their thing gets bigger?"

"No, if that was true they would have to make pants differently." I tried to stick to the exterior.

Miranda opened her purse and read from *Lady Chatterley's Lover*:

> *"Oh, don't tease him," said Connie, crawling on her knees on the bed towards him and putting her arms round his white slender loins, and drawing him to her so that her hanging, swinging breasts touched the tip of the stirring, erect phallus, and caught the drop of moisture. She held the man fast.*
>
> *"Lie down!" he said. "Lie down! Let me come!" And afterwards, when they had been quite still the woman had to uncover the man again, to look at the mystery of the phallus. "And now he's tiny, and soft like a little bud of life!" she said, taking the soft small penis in her hand. . . .*

"Now do you get it, sacred heart? That's why he had to sit down at his desk, you moron."

"You're wrong," I said, breathless. I fell off the curb as we walked; the sidewalk suddenly seemed too narrow.

"Then why didn't he get up when Father Flanagan came in the room? After all, he is a Monsignor." Again Miranda had her finger on the pulse of the situation. "I would have had him crawling, but you were the only one who didn't get it and broke up the whole thing with your snore-fest philosophical drivel. Who cares? Not The Rod, I can assure you."

"He studied it for ten years. That's a decade!" I said, with a defensive lameness even I detected. I was arguing from form now. She was right. All the pieces fit. I realized it was best now to go on a quick offense so I said, "Screw off! I'm the one who had to spell out the Linda Low plot. You were happy to watch me swing for it."

"Bullshit, I came to your rescue," Miranda defended herself.

"Yeah, after I bailed you out."

Miranda turned at the corner of her street and started laughing again, and said over her shoulder, "Sure you don't need a compass to get home?"

As I walked home alone I realized that I was exhausted. I simply couldn't rehash the disgusting revelations of the day, so I read the ingredients on the back of my Owl Potato Chips bag. I was jarred by a fancy sports car which ground to a halt next to me. I kept walking because my mother had told me to do that. The car crept along next to me, trying to get my attention with its whining motor. I looked straight ahead and then I heard someone say, "Is this the road to Damascus?"

I knew that voice. I risked looking up and into the car window. It was The Rod. My heart began to gallop and I couldn't pull the reins. I was shocked at what he looked like. He wasn't in his cassock and his hair wasn't slicked back, it was streaked blond, and without the Brylcream it looked more free. He wore blue jeans and a short-sleeved blue broadcloth shirt which made his eyes look the colour of a mountain lake. He smiled a radiant warm smile. I was struck suddenly with the fact that Miranda and I had never discussed his looks. Anyone, anywhere, would have had to say he was handsome. He had perfectly chiselled features. Obviously he was hiding an equally amazingly muscular body under that cassock.

"I'm on my way to basketball. Can I give you a lift?"

"No thanks. I'm not going home."

"Oh." He said it with that tone that expected more information.

"My mother is at her study club on Fridays and my father is at the store, so I go to Howard Johnson's."

"All alone!"

"No, I meet the Apostles there for the Last Supper." He decided to ignore that remark, so I continued. "I do it every Friday. I actually enjoy it."

"The food there is awful."

"You obviously haven't had fried clams with double tartar."

"May I join you? I have an hour to kill."

What Miranda had said flooded my mind. I immediately decided she was crazy — after all, she had failed geometry and I got the highest regent's exam in the class. When I walked in front of the car to get in on the passenger side, I felt a burning naked feeling. Suddenly I hated what I was wearing. It was so schoolgirl ugly.

"It's amazingly hot," he said as I got in the car. "Sorry if the seat is sticky. Roll up the window and I'll put on the air conditioner." I had never been in an air-conditioned car before, or an air-conditioned home, for that matter. Maybe Miranda and I had acted crazy today because of the heat. I know people commit more crimes in the heat, they said so on the news. A tape recorder on the dashboard was playing music by some guy named Vivaldi or so it said on the tape cover, obviously Italian — probably someone from the Vatican.

The Rod looked so large in the car and so . . . manly. I could see his arms and legs and his neck for the first time. Suddenly I knew what Miranda meant when she spoke about "a little bit of ankle." The newly exposed parts looked so strong, the arms with muscles that moved when he shifted gears, which he seemed to do with a kind of violence. I wasn't used to the gearshift being right next to my leg and I was suddenly appalled that I hadn't shaved my legs. Why did I believe my mother, who said no one could see blond hair?

I felt nervous or something — a feeling I hadn't had before. How long does it take to eat clams? Not long, I hoped. He cruised into the H.J.'s parking lot and looked around at the cars nosing ahead, circling like vultures, looking for a parking spot.

"It's jammed. Look inside, standing room only," he said, idling in front. "People actually line up to eat this stuff?" He looked surprised. "Want to go for a bit of a ride?" he asked.

"Sure," I said in a devil-may-care tone that I certainly didn't feel.

"I'll take you to a restaurant that overlooks Niagara Falls. It's so hot we can eat on the patio and hear the roar of the Falls. It's close enough to the rapids that sometimes, depending on the wind, you feel the spray."

The Falls was miles away. I'm just a kid. Of course I couldn't go. "Sounds good," I said. As we drove on the thruway I began to relax. The die was cast now anyway. Joyful music filled the car. The loudspeakers were great and that Vivaldi guy was fairly catchy. Once I caught The Rod looking at me. I pulled up one of my kneesocks. This feeling was strange, a combination of nervous dread and happiness. What was particularly odd was that I was normally so chatty, but today I couldn't think of one thing to say. Suddenly everything I thought of saying seemed utterly trivial. My mind and my body were out of sync.

The restaurant was a throwback in time, like something from a set of one of those extravaganza movies. The Rainbow Inn was built on an overhang of rock at the edge of Niagara Falls, where supposedly the Indians had stopped, after several of their war canoes didn't make it over the Falls. When my mother drove me to my father's store, she had pointed out this exact spot, saying it was used as one of the locations for Marilyn Monroe's *Niagara*. The entrance was dark and there were flickering lanterns on the wall. There were stuffed animals in settings of their natural habitat, a beaver with a little whittled twig in his mouth next to a similarly chopped and stripped pile of wood. The main dining and dance room was huge. Windows on all sides dripped with mist. As the waiter guided us through to the patio, I saw a woman in an evening gown and white kid gloves with little pearl buttons. Odd, wearing an evening gown in Niagara Falls at 5:30 p.m. I guess it was no weirder than being out with a priest for dinner after reading *Lady Chatterley's Lover* in religious instruction class.

The patio was magical. Gorgeous tropical-looking flowers grew up the railing, because of the mist from the Falls, the waiter said. The patio was built on a promontory whose stone floor looked as if it had been worn away by generations of Indians, explorers, and now lovers and honeymooners. The wooden furniture was old and seemed almost part of the rock ledge. There were festoons of coloured lights among the flowers, and each table had a deep red candle flickering in the wind inside a hurricane globe. A rainbow hung above the Falls in the mist lit by the setting sun, casting a coloured light over the floor. We had to speak loudly. The Falls roared and the whirlpools made suctioning noises.

"What causes whirlpools, anyway?" I wondered aloud.

"I think it happens when opposing currents meet, two currents going in opposite directions at the same time," he said.

"This is an amazing place." I looked around. "The furniture looks as old as the rock."

"There is quite a story behind the place. This furniture was made by French-Canadian explorers. The Indians wouldn't let them go any further on the Niagara Gorge, and they were not as familiar with the Falls as the Indians. They wanted another route around the Falls. The Indians made them donate blankets and this furniture in exchange for information on another route across the Falls. The French Canadians had to wait for three months for the ice to form and during that time they made this furniture. They left it when the Indians took them across on the ice that builds up from the mist at the narrowest part of the river. It was a good deal all around. In summer this place is very cool because of the fine mist, but it is sheltered by the ice in winter, like an igloo. What's amazing about the furniture is that it has lasted all of these hundreds of years. Apparently the caning was done with buffalo gut, which gets tougher as it grows older. Look at the dowelling. The joints look like new."

I felt as though I'd never noticed the details of the physical world before, and he was adding colour to a black-and-white photo. Philosophy was only one of the things he made interesting.

"This is a very sacred spot for the Indians. Legend has it that the Indians offered the most beautiful virgin of their tribe to the gods each year, thanking them for another year of plenty."

"Offered how?" I asked.

"She actually stood on this jetty and jumped over the Falls. She was called 'the maid of the mist.' It was a sacrifice of one for the sake of the tribe's well-being in the next year. The legend also states that the mist we feel today is the tears of the sacrificed virgins crying for their loved ones."

I put my hand up to my face and felt the infinitesimal spray of salty tears. "It's hot," I said.

"Pin up your hair and let the mist hit your neck," he said in the nicest, most gentle way. He leaned over and held my hair while I pinned it.

The waiter approached. "We won't be serving dinner for about an hour. Would you care for any cocktails?"

An hour! I was starved. The Rod, who was so easily flipped out in class, was as sophisticated as someone from a Fred Astaire movie. He ordered two Manhattans, for the moment, and white wine to follow, saying he knew we were early. He knew that seven was *early* for dinner? Frankly I doubted it. The waiter said it was the hottest day since 1943 for this date and while leaving the drinks he said they were expecting a big crowd because it was ten degrees cooler here by the Falls. This was the first time in his working memory that the stone floor was hot after six. Even the cooling spray from the Falls couldn't keep up with the heat.

I took a sip of my drink, which was godawful. Is this what William Powell and Myrna Loy had so much fun drinking in the *Thin Man* movies? It tasted like Varsol and vinegar mixed together, but in a minute mine was gone and he'd only taken a sip. I was thirsty.

"My stomach is burning. Christ, I'm burning inside and out." As I said this, I ran my tongue over my swollen lips. I decided to take a walk on the wild side and confess: "I've never had *straight* alcohol before."

He smiled that incredible smile and said, "Well, this will be your first. Now you'll always remember me because you'll always remember your first glass of wine." If he thought the wine was what I would remember about tonight he was wrong. He lifted his glass and made a toast. "I'll be the first man to give you wine and you'll be the first woman to help me out of a situation that could have been disastrous for me." I didn't want to talk about that "situation." Anyway, it was true I had helped him out of it, but I'd also put him in it.

Drinking was interesting. I didn't feel the need to defend myself, plan the next attack, or get out any of my usual artillery. I stopped planning ahead. This must be what's known as *relaxing*, I thought. I have no idea how long we sat there. I would always remember it as one of those seconds or moments or hours that can't be improved upon.

The Rod broke into this reverie. "I want to talk about what's going to happen to you."

"When?" What was he talking about?

"When you grow up."

"You mean will I stay in the Church?" I had enough of being laughed at for one day and decided to play my cards closer to my chest. I would lay low and let him do the talking.

He leaned toward me; the candle cast a red dancing shadow on his face. "That, certainly, but what will become of you as a woman."

Woman. The word hung heavy; even the coloured lights, wine, and the rainbow couldn't lift it. Miranda was right. We weren't too young. Miranda was *always* right. I came smack up against it and it hurt. I wasn't a student on an outing with her teacher who was a priest, I was a woman out with a man. Why was I in another city with a priest, a man twice my age? God, everything was falling apart. Every single thing I thought of saying brought attention to the facts of the situation — to the *fact* that he was a man and I was a woman. That time when we shared ideas seemed so long ago and so wonderful, so uncomplicated, so innocent. The difference between us, the feelings I had, the sort of burning in my lungs, and the jumping around I felt in my legs were overwhelming me. I couldn't think of anything to say that didn't somehow refer to my feelings. Maybe it was the wine. I sure as hell hoped so. I looked up and thought he looked overwhelmingly handsome.

He leaned over as if he wanted to declare something, hesitated for a long moment, and finally said, "Actually I followed you in the car today, and waited for Miranda to leave. I wanted to talk to you about something."

I poured more wine all by myself; it was starting to taste better. Maybe I was thirsty. Besides, it went well with smoking.

He forged ahead, didn't seem to notice that I wasn't myself. "You're at a crucial time of your life. You're different from the other girls. You must know that." I *had* always felt different, but I figured that was my *problem.* He continued: "The choices aren't between Miranda and Linda Low. There is a whole other world out there where all your energy and questioning is normal." He was getting enthused now, in the way I saw him in class, and it didn't make me nervous. "I don't think of you as a doubting Thomas, a woman of little faith — rather, you are an empiricist. The questions you've asked about ideas and causes are the same questions Hume asked, for God's sake."

"Who's Hume?"

"A philosopher. Actually, a British empiricist."

"Oh."

"If you stay here you'll just spin your wheels and eventually sink into the muck."

"What muck?"

"Small-town life. This provincial Catholic school that's grooming Catholic mothers." He paused and leaned back in his chair and drew on his cigarette. "It's a beautiful calling, however, it's not the only one. You don't *have* to fit it." He looked as though he was searching for words and finally said, "If you don't fit the Linda Low model, you don't have to be Miranda." What did he have against Miranda? He resumed, "I want to call your mother."

"She'll have a busy line!" This struck me as funny and I laughed my head off. The wine had begun to take hold and I had more or less decided to let the evening unfold.

"I want to tell her to have you change schools. There's a school near Buffalo that is not a Catholic school, but I believe it is one that is far more suited to your needs. Small-town schools are not for everyone. In fact, if you're not cut from the same bolt as the others, your spirit can be broken, and I can see that you are teetering on the edge."

I hadn't said anything, but he must have been able to tell by my expression that this was not the welcome news he'd hoped it would be. My universe was well-ordered in Lewiston which was my whole world. I knew everyone in the town and they knew me. At the same time as I had these feelings of trepidation, I also *had* to acknowledge that the security of Lewiston had become confining, even stultifying. Actually, it had never been the same since Roy had left. It had become smaller.

Sensing my feelings, he forged ahead. I could tell by his voice that his confidence had been bolstered by the drinks. "You're smart, and you're surrounded by girls like Miranda who will marry, as her older sister and cousin did." He hesitated and added, "Under duress."

"Casting aspersions is a sin, as is your uncharitable behaviour," I said, smugly leaning on my catechism. It came in handy when I was threatened, and I wanted to keep the topic off the situation. Miranda was my friend and I felt that I should defend her. Sure she made me mad, but I didn't feel like letting everyone stomp all over her with army boots. There was no way she was as pathetic as her loser older sister and cousin. One shotgun wedding was bad enough, but two was, as my mother said, "upsetting for all concerned." Dolores said that bad blood ran in families and what did the Doyle women expect when they ran around with the likes of those brainless Rafferty boys who lived down by the river. She said, "Mrs. Doyle should have kept her eye on those girls. They've been boy-crazy since their first communions — the last time they'll ever rightfully wear white. Sleep with dogs, you get up with fleas."

"It's a fact," The Rod said.

"Can only *facts* be sins? What about fantasies, or intentions, or . . ."

He interrupted, and spoke in an exasperated tone. "Catherine, there's *nothing* wrong with the *We Willing Workers* for girls who

335

want to have children before they're twenty, and whose prime concern is making a Catholic home that is a foundation for successful family life. It's the most important thing in the world. It just isn't what *you* need. You have the makings of a logician."

"If that's the only difference, why didn't you bring Linda Low to dinner?" I couldn't believe I had said that.

"She wears curlers in her hair," he said in a matter-of-fact tone. We both started laughing. His unguarded nature made me feel a little silly. If he was honest, why couldn't I be?

"I'd miss Miranda — everyone who is like me."

"Miranda isn't like you." He looked away and drank a big gulp of wine. I'd finished mine. "Please, let me call your mother and suggest it. I won't if you don't want me to."

"Go ahead, but it doesn't mean I'm going."

"Great, enough said."

We drank a little more wine.

"You know that question about fact and fantasy and whether a sin is lodged in both?"

"Yeah, it was two minutes ago." We both laughed.

"Freud asked the same question."

"Who's Freud?"

"Not a philosopher, but a famous psychologist. Actually, the first psychiatrist."

"Maybe I'll meet him and this Hume character at my new school for empiricists," I said with as much sarcasm as I could muster. It wasn't much, because the wine made sarcasm seem sort of tawdry, bordering on boring.

"He's dead."

"Then he's probably at Hennepin Hall." We both laughed in an easy way, and I had a feeling for the first time in my life, since I'd left Roy and girlhood behind, that a male was sharing something with me. I loved my father, but he was serious and never said anything sarcastic. I felt I needed to be more pure in his presence. He was busy saving lives and he needed to have a good daughter because he was so good. Whenever I said anything like "Father Flanagan is a loser," he would say, "Now, Cathy, do not judge lest you be judged." Then he would put his arm around me to let me know that he still loved me, even if I was bad. The Rod was like my dad in that he was good, but he understood how I really *felt*, or maybe it would be more accurate to say *thought*, and he didn't seem bothered by it. In fact, it was a kind of bond for us.

"Father Flanagan isn't as stupid as you think. He's dumb like an old horse trader is dumb."

"I guess you know a lot of old horse traders — you taught religion at the Ponderosa?"

"I mean he knows plenty without letting on that he knows anything. The person in the deal thinks he fooled the old horse trader and only later when his horse stops dead in its tracks does he realize he's been hoodwinked. Horse traders know more than they let on. . . . Father Flanagan has horse sense and I'm the one who was taken."

"About what?"

"Life."

"Life?"

"Yes, life, what the hard parts are. He knew how complacent I was. He knew I thought I had everything down. Really all I had done was study. I wasn't ready to be a missionary by a long shot. I needed to deal with issues of *life* first."

"What do you mean by *life*? What issues?"

"Well . . . one example was teaching you girls. I was a miserable failure. Sure I knew philosophy, but that doesn't help to spread the word of God, strengthen, or restore the gift of faith. Often philosophy and faith are not mutually supportive. I don't think it has to be that way, but sometimes it is that way. For some people, philosophy fills the void of faith."

"What does this have to do with failing as our teacher?"

"Linda Low didn't need philosophy. She *had* faith. I used to look at her at morning mass and feel envy. Her face looked so serene and peaceful after communion. For her, the Eucharist really was the body and blood of our Lord. Eventually I withdrew. I began teaching one student — you. Father Flanagan always tried to help the majority, reach out to the needs of the people. You were a minority. He chose to silence you and Miranda and help the thirty other souls that were there. That's the successful missionary — helping the majority in any way he can." He ran his fingers through his hair, looking agitated.

"Look." I leaned over the table because I really wanted him to hear me, really listen. "First of all, the Linda Lows of this world have heard various versions of the Father Flanagans for years, it won't hurt them to hear something new. Surely God can't object to reasoned faith versus blind faith."

"That's not the point. Father Flanagan placed both you and Miranda in that class for a reason. He wanted to say to me, 'You're not ready to be a missionary.' I had to live through this to understand it."

"What about me? Linda Low already had faith — the year was made a lot better for me. I've read more this year than I've ever read,

I've thought more than I've ever thought. I know I'm not the major-ity, but I'm someone who's different because of you." I was embarrassed after I said that. I didn't want any feelings to leak out. I wanted to objectify things a little so I said, "Isn't it better to help one person a lot, even change their life, than to touch thirty a tiny bit?"

"Thank you, Cathy." That was the first time he hadn't called me Catherine. He reached over and touched my hand. Actually, he only touched the hairs on my hand, it was such a light touch. I looked down. There was a stain on the tablecloth.

"Honeymoon?"

Who the hell said that? I looked up. The black bandleader in a white tux was standing over our table, smiling.

"Yes," said The Rod.

"We were sayin' so." He nodded out the French doors at the rest of the band. "Only honeymooners like to have dinner so early." Both men laughed. "Your bride's like a china doll. She's from heaven, my man."

"Thank you, I think so too."

I was frozen in horror.

"What's your song?" he asked.

I looked up blankly, hoping that's what newlyweds did. When it became clear that my brain was completely gone, like one of those heart monitor machines that shows a straight line instead of spikes, The Rod interjected.

"Time after Time."

"You're on." When the bandleader left the table I felt my cheeks and they were very hot.

"I'd never have believed you were capable of blushing," said The Rod.

"We're even, because I never believed you were capable of lying. Lying's a sin, or haven't you heard?"

"Venial, compared to the rest of the evening," he replied cavalierly, standing up to dance. He held out his hand invitingly. I didn't want to dance. What if I didn't know how? I stood up and realized I would cause a bigger spectacle by refusing. Where he had learned to dance, I had no idea. What did they do in Jesuit seminary, dance with each other?

When I walked through those French doors, the chandelier was going around in a circle, and the Falls were now only a dull roar. The band was the Duke Ellington type that my father played on his 78s by the pool. The musicians all wore white tuxedos, were black, and had straightened shiny hair. The dance floor was huge, painted pink, flanked by substantial Greek columns with large pots of ivy growing up around their bases.

I did know how to dance. I'd forgotten all those years I went to ballroom dance classes. I suddenly realized that people danced because they wanted to be near each other. It had nothing to do with the dance steps. The Rod's hand felt so strong on my back and I always knew which way he was going to move, which seemed miraculous to me. I danced with my back as stiff as I could. What if my breasts touched him? What did other girls, or women or whatever, do about that problem? He must have known I was nervous because he rubbed my back a little with his hand. At first I found it irritating, but then I liked it. I felt my muscles relax, as if my body should fit into his, like pieces of a jigsaw puzzle, and my neck fell on his shoulder. He hadn't seemed so tall at school. One song drifted into another. They were playing "My Funny Valentine" and then "Chances Are." I felt his breathing in my ear, coming in short stabs. Suddenly all of the song lyrics I had heard and all of the talk about passion became clear to me. Suddenly I got it. *This* was enlightenment on the road to Damascus. He started to dance differently, with his legs in a funny position so we were sort of rubbing against one another. My body just seemed to follow his, effortlessly.

The music stopped, but we didn't. Faster music started and my knees felt weak. I clung to him, partly because I was drunk and partly because I didn't want this to be over. I knew I would never have this again when it ended. I felt us being ripped apart.

"Cathy, we have to sit down," he whispered hoarsely.

Sit down. *Sit down.* I couldn't possibly sit down and talk about leaps of faith again. I was too far over the Falls for that. I had already been sacrificed.

I couldn't breathe. The chandelier was spinning. I had to get away. I ran past the band so fast they were only zebra stripes in my peripheral vision. Air, I needed air. I didn't know what drunk felt like and I wasn't sure what lust or passion felt like, but I *did* know that a lot of new sensations were hitting me at once. My body was a cauldron in which new chemicals were added to the brew and it had bubbled over. I forced open the French doors and flung myself out on an old wrought-iron balcony, filling my collapsed lungs with the cool mist. I looked down hundreds of feet, and saw Satan's descent into hell filled with rising mist.

Through the thicket I glimpsed a rickety staircase leading down the gorge that obviously hadn't been used in years. It was overgrown with plants; stubborn roots had splayed the timber steps and grown through the rotted wood. I didn't care. I descended into the mist and kept going. Seagulls flew up and down, like helicopters in a war zone. Near the bottom of the gorge the stairway ended and I had to sidestep my way. As I descended and got closer to the rapids, the mist became heavier and turned into drizzle. Now I was so low the drizzle turned into pelting rain which lashed my already raw face. There were all kinds of angry spiky plants growing, vegetation that can only grow in constant rain. I began sliding and realized I was too drunk to stop myself. I was staggering. The Falls roared and the whirlpools made sucking noises, as though everything were being pulled under. Mist covered my eyes, and everything was melting and blurred. When I got near the edge, the gush of the Falls was deafening and I could see that the water in the river was travelling at a dizzying rate.

I leaned against a tree and held on, and even though I'd stopped moving I still felt pulled, mesmerized by the twirling water. I felt magnetically drawn toward the vortex of the spinning whirlpools. I remembered once, years ago, Miranda threw a pop can in a whirlpool and it spun around and was sucked into the centre in less than a second, looking like a flash of silver. I was too drunk to make it back up the hill. The water in my face was at least cooling and must have been sobering.

I felt a hand on my shoulder. It was The Rod. He smiled and pointed to an indentation in the rocks about fifty feet up. He took my arm and began hauling me up the gorge; his shoes had better grip and he made it up to a crevice in the gorge. I knocked a birds' nest off the ledge and crawled up. He pushed me the last foot, and when we were both safe, he turned his face into the wall of rock, lit two cigarettes, and handed me one. I leaned back against the rock and smoked. We couldn't talk because of the deafening torrent. I had calmed down by the end of my cigarette, and looked up at him. He looked at me, and I couldn't help smiling at the absurdity of us, too close to the Falls, damp, crouching on a bird roost, having a cigarette. He smiled back the warmest and most accepting smile that I ever remember receiving. That was the best cigarette I ever had or ever would have. We huddled on that birds' perch for a long time until evicted seagulls began showing up in legions to reclaim their turf from the squatters. We watched the sunset from our roost and saw the rainbow break into a prism above us. Each foam peak took on a different glint of warm orange sunlight, and the mist above us fell in the brilliant colours of fireworks.

Finally, after sunset, sobered by the drizzle and the air, I pointed to my stomach and then to my mouth indicating I was hungry. Actually, when I thought about not having eaten since breakfast, I was ravenous. He pantomimed agreement. We made it up far more easily than we had slid down. When we sat down to dinner we were sobered up but still damp; however, with the heat it actually felt refreshing. My soggy knee socks gave off a wet woolly homey smell. He retained the essence of English Leather. I'd aged since cocktails.

—

We drove home in contented silence. I didn't want to talk about anything that had happened because then it would be just events: cocktails, dancing, sunset, dinner. *Big deal.*

Finally, as we exited the thruway he said, "You were a little too close to the Falls."

"Yeah."

"I'm sorry I let you drink so much, I guess I wasn't paying

attention. I'm a little unused to girls of your age — or any age, I guess."

"Miraculous sunset, huh? Now *that* could make anyone believe in . . . something," I said.

"Sure does," he agreed.

—

When I saw Miranda at school the next day I wanted to tell her, but I knew I couldn't. Anyway, what was I going to say? I was in another city with The Rod, got drunk, and almost fell into Niagara Falls. No one is quite *that* stupid. I knew I couldn't tell anyone about it. Still, I couldn't help mentioning his name.

As we walked along, kilts swinging, Capezios hitting the sidewalk in unison, I heard myself saying, "I saw The Rod on his way to basketball last night, not half-bad out of his cassock." I kept walking, clutching my notebook across my chest.

"He's a jerk," she said in a world-weary tone.

"No." I was sounding too strident, so I cooled my voice a bit. "Ya know, I don't really think so." I *never* went against Miranda in matters of character and I knew she wouldn't take kindly to it.

"Listen, Virgin Mother, if you must know, I've seen him out of his cassock as well *and* out of his basketball uniform — if you know what I mean . . . if you get the drift."

I didn't and we kept walking.

"Mary Magdalene, I better tell you the truth about this messiah before you start washin' his feet." She shook her head impatiently.

"I'm sick of you thinking you know the truth." I was, arguing from form again because, as usual, she seemed to know the truth. I was scared now, really scared, and I didn't want to hear it.

Her Capezioed feet stopped ominously. "I've done it, the big *it*, with him, night after night at the Sunset Motel on Niagara Falls Boulevard."

"That's a lie." I decided to keep it simple. I kept walking, assured when each shaky foot struck the sidewalk. I repeated tap-dancing steps I'd learned. Shuffle-ball-change. Then I started over. Shuffle-kick-ball-change. Shuffle-hop-ball-change.

She caught up, interrupting my rhythm, and said disgustedly, "I'm sick of both of you; neither of you knows your ass from Saran Wrap."

"Liar." I continued my dance steps, saying all the different patterns to myself. I heard my taps ricocheting off the pavement.

"Does our little scientist want proof?" she said, in that singsong voice which always spells retribution.

"Yes!" I'd thrown down the gauntlet. It was too late. She was going to rub my nose in it. Okay, go ahead. Make it hurt as much as you can.

"You are so naïve it's unbelievable. Do you have *any* idea what's been going on? Are you a musketeer or what? The entire class knows — *everyone* knows except you."

"That you have done something with Father Rodwick is your first lie, and your second is that everyone but me knows about it."

Miranda seemed nonplussed. "Fine. I'll bring proof for you tomorrow in the lavatory at three."

"You think everyone knows about this? You actually think anyone believes you? This man is a priest!"

"Cathy, even Linda Low gets it — not all the details, of course, but she gets the *drift*. Anne Marie Vesture, who decorates the altar when we have geometry, is in on this one. You are the only one who hasn't followed this blow by blow. Haven't you noticed everyone is quiet when you enter the room? Haven't you heard snickering when you and The Rod get into mental masturbation?"

Mental *masturbation*? I felt sick. My mouth felt like I had eaten aluminum foil. I thought they laughed because I was genuinely funny. Oh God . . . this was reminding me of my father's line "Make sure they're laughing with you and not at you."

"No, Miranda, I haven't noticed those things because you've made them up."

Fortunately our paths diverged at this point and I headed the rest of the way home alone. As I walked along I still harboured some hope that Miranda was just talking. After all, she was innately quite lazy. When I actually thought of it, what could she do to prove anything? This whole thing was a figment of our over-active imaginations. Rationally, what had transpired was a handsome man, who happened to be a priest, walked into our lives to teach us the passion of our Lord and we both mistook it for the earthly variety. We were a bunch of silly schoolgirls "getting hysterical." That's what my father said when we thought there was a ghost in the recreation room at my slumber party. He sent us all straight back to bed and told us to use our heads for more than a hat rack. The ghost was honestly gone after that.

Maybe by confronting this whole thing head-on, I could make it go away. She didn't expect me to show up. What could she have done — taken a picture? I doubted it. Who would develop it? Bring a receipt from the hotel? Anyone could produce one of those. A signed confession from him? Unlikely. Witnesses? Who? Linda Low? In the past I'd been the only one stupid enough to get in on her shenanigans and I wasn't there.

Next, why would a man who had devoted years to being a

priest, taken vows of celibacy, have done it with a teenage girl? He would be taking the last 10 years of his life and throwing them away. He would burn in hell for eternity, which made life look like a drop in a bucket. Everyone in this town knew him. Who was going to let him into a motel?

If you reason out things logically, they are less scary. Just stare down the dragon — face Goliath. He never even *liked* Miranda. She never cared about one thing he cared about. Why would he have risked his life, career, and eternity for her?

—

The next day I climbed the stairs toward the lavatory. Listening to my echoing footsteps, I knew that I was walking down death row to the execution of my innocence.

Miranda was standing at the sink teasing and spraying her hair while her cigarette burned away, leaving a brown nicotine stain in its wake. When she saw me she took a long drag and her ashes sizzled in the sink. "Well, now that the prodigal postulate has arrived, we may proceed."

I really felt sick to my stomach — the same nausea as when all the car windows were closed and my father smoked cigars. Maybe it was the closeness, the smoke, the loose powder hanging in the air webbed in hairspray, and the cloying perfume scent. Feeling faint, I grabbed a handle of a stall door. She didn't say anything for a long time so I finally said, "Get to the point. I don't have a whole lot of time for slander."

"Fine," she said calmly, anointing her plunging neckline with Shalamar. "I've done it, the big *it*, night after night with The Rod in the Sunset Motel. Done it till I could hardly walk," she said, directly into the mirror, while applying white lipstick.

"What about last Friday night?"

"Yup."

I pounced. "You're such a *liar*. *I* was with him Friday night dining and dancing in another city." I'd caught her. The relief I felt flooded into every one of my cells, letting me know exactly how important this had been to me as I sank down on the edge of one of the basins.

"I know. His pants were filthy. What were you doing — fighting over Martin Luther?"

"You're a liar. Why would a priest risk ten years of education, a future in the church, and all of eternity on *you*, someone he doesn't even like." I struck my cleats against the painted cement floor, stomping toward the door. I swung around. "I want *proof*. Don't bother giving me receipts from the Sunset Motel. I'm sure your mother has plenty of them."

"Now, let's see, how could I prove that a priest had his clothes off? Let's start with exhibit A." Miranda reached into her bag and, while rifling through it, said in that singsong mocking voice that was bone-chilling and made the hair on my neck stand on end, "Now, what is the first layer of clothing a Jesuit puts on so that he feels the roughness of the hair shirt of good ol' yesteryear? After all, before he's entirely dressed, why not offer up your sufferings for the sins of mankind?"

I thought of the priest's scapular, but I refused to believe that she had Father Rodwick's. If she had it then he had, indeed, taken his clothes off in her presence, which was too preposterous to even imagine, let alone contemplate as a reality.

Recognizing my shock, Miranda pushed ahead with her advantage. "Oh dear, does our philosophical genius need *another* hint? Okay. What has a rough cloth on one side and a holy picture on the other?"

There was no other way she could have got the scapular. It's worn under the priests' clothing. "Miranda, you're embarrassing yourself with this pathetic fantasy. If you have it, show it right now or forever hold your peace."

She said, "Oh, I thought you'd never ask." She held up his worn scapular to the barred light of the lavatory. It said, "The Society of Jesus, 1957." It even smelled like Father Rodwick's English Leather. "Poor dear looked for it for over an hour before he decided he must have left it at the rectory." The suspended scapular swung back and forth like a pendulum casting a shadow on the cement floor and hair-woven drain.

I looked down. I'd seen enough for one day. "Let's go," I said, feeling as if my brain, heart, or soul, or whatever it was that felt things, had been sprayed with Novocaine — an anaesthesia that took years to wear off. We filed out of the lavatory silently and slunk to our religious instruction class. As I nosed down the hallway, I wondered what was ahead. Things had gone too far and everyone had known it long before me.

The room was filled — except for two empty chairs — with twenty-eight expectant teenage faces. The others all knew it was the last throes of battle and it was time to see who was left standing. The foreboding silence was deafening. As they heard the jangle of the rosary beads announcing the arrival of the jejune Jesuit, they listened for his jaunty step along the hall and the hum of his Gregorian chant. How could he come back? No one flinched a muscle, but focused on the crucifix in the front of the room under the clock.

The lively step was the confident stride of the victor, bouncing to the front of the class. There before us stood Father Flanagan. Not one of the girls asked where Father Rodwick was. He silently passed out the *We Willing Workers* newsletter and said, as blank as a drink of water, assured of his position, "Catherine McClure, please grace us with your oratory, beginning on page one."

"How to Start a Guardians of Mary branch club in your community. . . ." I droned on to the end.